MACROECONOMICS
AND
MONETARY THEORY

Harry G. Johnson

Professor of Economics
The London School of Economics and Political Science and
The University of Chicago

ALDINE PUBLISHING COMPANY/Chicago

About the Author

Harry G. Johnson is Professor of Economics at the London School of Economics and the University of Chicago. Educated at the University of Toronto and at Cambridge, Harvard, and Manchester Universities, he is a Fellow of the American Academy of Arts and Sciences and a Member of the Executive Committee of the American Economic Association. He has been editor of *The Manchester School* and the *Journal of Political Economy* and has served on the research staff of the Royal Commission on Banking and Finance, as a Consultant to the Board of Governors of the Federal Reserve System and as a Member of the Review Committee on Balance of Payments Statistics.

LECTURES IN ECONOMICS

1 *Macroeconomics and Monetary Theory*   by Harry G. Johnson
2 *Introductory Econometrics*   by Kenneth F. Wallis

Copyright © 1972 by Harry G. Johnson

First published in Great Britain, 1972

First U.S. edition published 1972 by
Aldine Publishing Company
529 South Wabash Avenue
Chicago, Illinois 60605

ISBN 0-202-06053-5 cloth
ISBN 0-202-06054-3 paper
Library of Congress Catalog Number 72-87564

Second printing, 1974

Printed in the United States of America

CONTENTS

PART V SOME MAJOR POLICY ISSUES

APPENDIX

PREFACE

The lecture notes presented in this book constitute the substance of a graduate course I have been giving, at a length gradually increasing from ten to about forty lectures, since 1964-65 at the London School of Economics. The notes were transcribed lecture by lecture in the 1969-70 session by a team of scribes organized by Hamish Gray and consisting of Bruce Brittain, Donna Hamway, Parker Hudson, Ninos Hadjigeorgiou, Ron Schaffer and David Stanton. They were then checked by myself for accuracy before distribution to students though I did not attempt to reinsert the finer details of analysis that the scribes missed. I am grateful to David Laidler for some later comments and I have since re-read them though rather hastily, and added to them where I thought necessary for clarity. They remain lecture notes, however.

In present circumstances there seem to be two cogent reasons for the publication of lecture notes. The first is that one's professional responsibilities and interests tend to be preoccupied by keeping up with the subject and attempting to contribute to its advance, leaving little if any time for the writing of textbooks. Yet textbooks are the medium through which advances of knowledge are diffused from the major research centres to students and their teachers in other university institutions concerned primarily with teaching; and good textbooks are essential to the establishment and maintenance of intellectual democracy and equality of educational opportunity in the far-flung contemporary university system, in which only a small minority of students can study at the major centres of research. The publication of lecture notes is a compromise solution to the dilemma.

The second, and perhaps more positive, reason is that the amount of material in the form of articles, textbooks, and specialized monographs available for the student to read is far greater than he can possibly manage – and frequently either more prolix or more detailed and technical than is appropriate to his requirements. Lecture notes provide a compact survey of the important problems, analytical techniques, and results to be found in the literature, at a level of exposition adjusted to the particular level of qualification of the student. A homogeneous level of exposition is of course the hall-mark of the textbook; but compactness is usually not, though it may save the student a great deal of reading time. Further, lecture notes enable both students and their teachers to grasp fairly quickly how a field of knowledge is envisaged by the lecturer, what subjects are considered important and what not, in contrast to the text-book, which attempts to be a comprehensive representation of the literature as it stands.

The approach of the lectures to the field is explained in the first lecture, and need not be discussed here. There is, however, one general comment that should be made. The structure of the series is in a sense schizophrenic, dealing as it does first with the broad outlines of Keynesian economics and then with monetary theory viewed against the background of the neo-classical quantity-theory tradition, with Keynes appearing first as the founder of Keynesianism and later as the founder of the capital-theoretic contemporary approach to monetary theory. This schizophrenia is the result of the fact, which Axel Leijonhufvud's monumental book *On Keynesian Economics and the Economics of Keynes* has shown, that Keynesian economics as it has been developed by the followers of

Keynes, especially by the Harvard group led by Alvin Hansen and by the econometricians and forecasters everywhere, is something quite different from the thinking of Keynes himself, which was deeply rooted in the preceding quantity theory tradition. As time passes, it should become possible to develop a more unified and homogeneous synthetic approach to the field, in which Keynes will appear as the great intellectual bridge between the neo-classical and the contemporary theories of money and macro-economics.

London   HARRY G. JOHNSON
March 17, 1971.

PART I

MACROECONOMICS

CHAPTER 1

INTRODUCTION: MACROECONOMICS AND MONETARY THEORY

Macroeconomics is an outgrowth from the main stream of classical monetary theory following Keynes. Keynes changed the emphasis from determination of the level of money prices to determination of the level of output and employment. He also changed the key relationship from demand and supply of money as determining the price level to the relationship between consumption expenditure and income, in conjunction with private investment expenditure, as determining the level of output and therefore employment demanded. The income multiplier replaced the velocity of circulation as the key concept of monetary theory.

The tendency of the past twenty-five years has been to reintegrate Keynesian and classical monetary theory into one general system of analysis. Moreover, as inflation has succeeded mass unemployment as a major policy problem, interest in classical monetary theory has revived, while Keynesians have increasingly emphasized the monetary aspects of Keynesian theory.

The terms macroeconomics and monetary theory involve quite different lines of differentiation of the subject-matter from the rest of economics. Classical theory distinguished between 'real' theory — the theory of the determination of the values of factors and commodities in terms of one another — from "monetary" theory — the theory of the determination of the price level or the purchasing power of money. This separation is 'the classical dichotomy'; and its legitimacy has been a key question in monetary theory since Keynes's *General Theory*.

By contrast, Keynesian economics distinguishes between 'macroeconomics' and 'microeconomics'. Microeconomics is concerned with the demand for and supply of individual commodities and factors and the determination of their relative prices and quantities. Macroeconomics is the theory of the determination of economic aggregates and averages — the amount and value of total output, employment, consumption and investment; the price level, the wage level, the interest rate, and the growth rate of the economy.

Because aggregate relationships are sums or averages of microeconomic relationships, it is desirable, though not strictly necessary, that macroeconomic relationships be plausible or logical in terms of microeconomic theory. Early Keynesian theories of inflation assumed 'money illusion' — behaviour based on the assumption of stability in the value of money when that value was being reduced by inflation — which is inconsistent with microeconomic rationality. Such inconsistency is not theoretically satisfactory; and the concern to provide a rational basis in microeconomic theory for macroeconomic relationships has affected every aspect of Keynesian macroeconomic analysis, and made it increasingly difficult to draw a clear distinction between macroeconomics and microeconomics.

The proper contemporary distinction is not between two separate branches of economic theory, but between two areas of application or contexts of the theory of rational maximizing behaviour. In the one (the microeconomic) context, it is assumed either that the overall workings of the economic system can be disregarded, or that the macroeconomic relationships are in full general equilibrium. In the other (the macroeconomic) context, it is assumed that the maximizing decisions of individual economic units (firms and households) will not necessarily add up to a macroeconomic equilibrium, but will produce a disequilibrium situation that will in the course of time produce changes in the individual decisions. One should note, however, that for analytical simplicity standard macroeconomic analysis is generally set up so that such a disequilibrium situation is described as a situation of short-run equilibrium.

These alternative definitions of the subject-matter suggest two alternative approaches to an organized exposition of it:

(i) to follow the traditional lines of monetary theory and treat macroeconomics as a branch of it built on special but practically useful assumptions;

(ii) to start with macroeconomic theory as developed from Keynes, and treat the neo-classical monetary theory elements that have been introduced subsequently as revisions, qualifications, etc. (The main developments in macroeconomic theory itself have been the Harrod-Domar equation and the Phillips-curve trade-off between unemployment and inflation.)

The first approach is logically more satisfactory, since it permits concentration on basic theoretical issues. The second, however, is more appropriate to the present position of dominance in economic teaching and policy thinking of Keynesian macroeconomic models, and to the preparation that most graduate students will have had. Most of the course will, however, be concerned with monetary theory, on the twin grounds that graduate students should be familiar with the main outlines of macroeconomic models, and that most of the interesting developments since Keynes have been in monetary theory rather than in macroeconomics.

In monetary theory, the basic assumption is that *the demand for and supply of money exercise a significant influence on the economy.* This raises three perennial issues in monetary theory.

(1) *Is money important or are its effects swamped by other factors?* There has always been a school of thought which denies any influence to money. This goes back to the classical controversy between the 'banking' and 'currency' schools. The banking school claimed that the money supply would change in response to demand, so that monetary policy could not influence the economy. In this crude form the contention is obviously wrong, but one variant of it, the so-called 'real bills' doctrine, has remained a powerful element in thought on central banking policy. This doctrine asserts that money will take care of itself and cause no problems if loans are made only for productive purposes, and not for speculation. In modern times, this doctrine is reflected in Federal Reserve concern about 'the quality of credit', and in British efforts to discriminate between 'desirable' and 'undesirable' types of bank lending.

The Keynesian revolution raised the same question in a more sophisticated form: more accurately, Keynesian theory raised it in one form and post-Keynesian theory has raised it in another. Keynes's emphasis on the interest rate as the variable through which monetary policy influences aggregate demand and activity raised the two possibilities (i) that consumption and investment might be completely inelastic with respect to the interest rate, so that changes in the interest rate could not influence aggregate demand, and (ii) that the demand for money might be perfectly interest-elastic, so that monetary policy could not influence interest rates. Post-Keynesian interest theory has introduced a variety of monetary assets in place of Keynes's simple distinction between cash and bonds, and suggested that if substitutability between money and near-money assets is high, monetary policy may have no real influence. This view is reflected in the Radcliffe Committee's emphasis on 'liquidity' and the Federal Reserve's emphasis on 'credit conditions', rather than the money supply, as the variable the central bank seeks to control.

Whatever form it takes, the contention that money does not exercise a significant influence on the economy is inconsistent with both the empirical evidence and the behaviour of economic policy-makers.

(2) *Does money influence real variables (the interest rate, output, employment) on the level of prices?*

Classical theory concentrated on the influence of money on prices; Keynesian theory emphasizes the influence on real variables. Subsequent analysis has concluded that this is a question of the relevant time-dimension. Classical theory assumed sufficient flexibility of wages and prices to maintain full employment, in which case money influences prices. Keynesian theory assumed rigidity of wages, in which case money influences quantities. The Keynesian theory is appropriate to the short run; but the question is whether the longer-run analysis of the influence of money on prices can safely be neglected. The inflationary experience of both the United States and the United Kingdom suggests that such neglect may be dangerous.

(3) *Does the influence of money on the economy operate through a desired relation between income and interest rates on the one hand and people's cash balances on the other, adjustments being made through changes in the rate of spending, or does it operate through the influence of money demand and supply on interest rates, adjustment being made through changes in investment and saving?* This issue can be summarized in a distinction between 'cash-balance mechanics' and 'interest-rate mechanics' of the adjustment to monetary disturbances.

Consideration of this issue leads into a basic methodological conflict between those who believe the function of theory is to construct general equilibrium models of the economy, and the "positive economists" (led by Milton Friedman) who believe that the essence of theory is to find simple relationships between key variables. According to the 'positive' school, the essence of the quantity theory is the velocity relationship that relates money income to the quantity of money, while the essence of the Keynesian theory is the multiplier relationship between investment and total income; and the issue is whether one or the other relationship has the greater predictive power.

To illustrate, consider the identity $E=Y=PX$, where E is expenditure, Y is income, X is output, and P is its price level. According to the quantity theory, $E=MV$, the quantity of money multiplied by the velocity of circulation. V is asserted to be a stable function of a few variables, e.g. $V = V(X,i)$ where i is the interest rate. In the simplest version, X and i are assumed to be determined by real forces, at the full employment level, and hence P is determined by M via V; in a more complex version, the division of Y between P and X is left open. In the Keynesian theory, wages are assumed inflexible in the relevant period; hence it is legitimate to deflate money variables by the money wage rate to transform the analysis into real terms. Hence $Y_W = P_W X$, where P_W is determined by the rising marginal labour cost of production. $E_W = C_W + I_W$; the sum of consumption and investment expenditure. The basic postulate of the theory is that $C_W = f(Y_W)$, and hence, through the multiplier relationship, $Y_W = E_W = m(I_W)$, where m is the multiplier relationship and can be taken as constant for small changes in I_W. The issue is whether V or m is the more stable relationship and hence the more powerful predictor. We will return to this question much later on in the course (Chapter XVII below).

CHAPTER 2

THE KEYNESIAN INCOME-EXPENDITURE MODEL

The full Keynesian model divides the economy into four aggregate markets: goods, labour, money, and bonds. Two markets are for stocks (money and bonds) and two for flows (goods and labour). This is a short-run equilibrium model: technology and the capital stock are assumed given.

The analysis is usually simplified by concentrating on one or two of these markets. One market can always be eliminated in a general equilibrium system via Walras' law. This law uses the budget constraint to establish that one of the markets must be in equilibrium if all the others are. The bond market is usually eliminated in Keynesian analysis. One can simplify still further and concentrate solely on the goods market. Two assumptions are made: the labour market clears automatically and the money and bond markets are kept in equilibrium by monetary policy which holds the interest rate constant. Thus we can concentrate on the goods market as the determinant of equilibrium income. Diagrammatically:

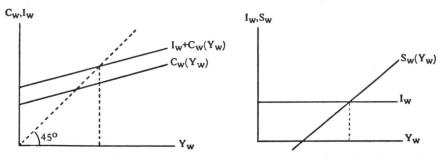

Money is left completely out of this simple model, which assumes a constant interest rate.

A more complex Keynesian model still ignores the effects of changes in output on income distribution by assuming the consumption function includes the appropriate income weights, but introduces money. The model is for a closed economy and initially ignores prices, costs, and labour. The money market is not eliminated so the interest rate is another variable determined jointly with the level of output. ('Keynesian' models proliferated after the General Theory and do not necessarily describe what Keynes meant.)

We shall utilize four behavioural relationships to determine the level of output and the rate of interest. We continue the 'Keynesian' practice of assuming wage rigidity by measuring everything in terms of wage units, i.e. dividing all money magnitudes by the money wage rate. This procedure gives money variables with labour units as the unit of account. But deflating money magnitudes by the wage rate does not give real quantities. The reason is that the relation between prices of commodities and the wage rate itself may change as output changes.

Ignore the labour market and eliminate the bonds market by Walras' law. This leaves only the money and goods markets. In the goods market, output is assumed to be in elastic supply (underemployment). Demand for output is separated into consumption and investment. Since consumption is determined largely by the level of income, the condition for equilibrium in the goods market can be defined either as total demand equals total output or the difference between total output and demand for consumer goods equals the demand for investment goods, i.e. savings equals investment.

In the simplest form we assume savings is a simple function of income. One can readily allow for the interest rate but the relationship is not straight-forward since a higher interest rate induces more savings at a given level of utility, but also means more future income for a given amount of savings. One might save less but be as well off in terms of future income. Leijonhufvud however points out that a fall in the interest rate raises the present value of a given stock of wealth and so stimulates consumption. For equivalent reasons, an increase in the interest rate will increase savings. This he claims is a neglected aspect of *The General Theory*.

Graph the savings function on the assumption that savings is determined by the level of income. Each vertical line shows a different (constant) amount of savings at each level of income. We can allow for the possibility that savings is a function of both income and the interest rate. If savings increase with the interest rate, the curves will bend to the left implying the same amount of savings is maintained at a lower level of income. Conversely, curves bending to the right imply that an increase in the interest rate lowers savings at a given level of income, so that income must rise to offset a rise in the interest rate. Hence, each curve represents a fixed amount of savings and shows the combinations of interest rate and income at which that amount of savings would be maintained.

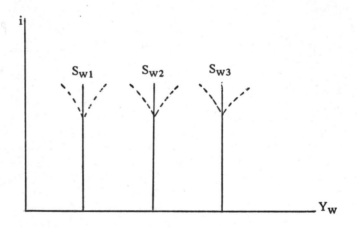

Now consider the investment function. We can start with given levels of income and postulate that there is a relationship between the level of investment and the interest rate such that, as the interest rate falls, more investment is undertaken (real investment). Typically we assume that the propensity to invest is independent of the level of income, although this is not necessarily the case. (One must distinguish the relationship between the level of investment and the level of income from the accelerator relationship, which relates the level of investment to *changes* in income levels. We are here concerned with the static relationship.)

The simplest relationship makes investment a function of the interest rate. A series of horizontal lines represent the amounts of investment undertaken at different interest rates. Assuming income influences investment these curves would slope upwards: the higher the interest rate, the higher the level of income needed to maintain the same level of investment. We can then write $I_W = I_W(i, Y_W)$. However, we will ignore the influence of income.

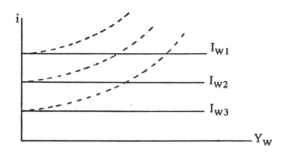

These graphs give the relationship for equilibrium in the goods market. If we superimpose diagrams, the intersections of the contours, (S_{W1} and I_{W1}, S_{W2} and I_{W2}, S_{W3} and I_{W3}) trace out a relationship between the interest rate and level of income which equates savings and investment. These combinations represent equilibrium in the goods market — the IS curve. (This curve does not tell us what the level of output or the interest rate will be. It only says that whatever equilibrium there is must lie on it. The IS curve is further discussed on p.15 below.)

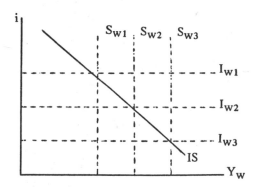

We now turn to the money market. Following Keynes the demand for money can be visualised as consisting of two parts: one for market transactions, the other for money as an asset related to the interest rate. The second component is the 'liquidity preference' demand for many, or as more recent writers put it, the 'asset demand' (i.e. demand for money as a form of wealth). It can be shown on a diagram where M_{W1} represents transactions demand for money and M_{W2} represents asset demand. We then have a series of vertical lines corresponding to different levels of income and therefore the demand for transaction balances. The simplest Keynesian version assumes that transactions demand is insensitive to changes in the interest rate. M_{w2} is a downward sloping curve: the lower the interest rate, the smaller the opportunity cost of holding money.

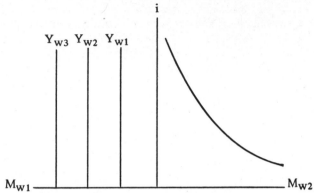

More generally, we could argue that there is no need to separate out the two demands. All we need is the notion that the demand for money increases as income rises and as the interest rate falls. Another diagram shows the combinations of interest rate and quantity of money which people would be satisfied to hold at different levels of income. Assuming the quantity of money is given (M_{w0}) we can trace out a relationship between the interest rate and levels of income which is consistent with equilibrium in the money market. This gives us an LM curve.

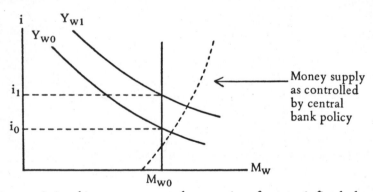

However, it is arbitrary to assume the quantity of money is fixed, the main reason being that the Central Bank does not directly control the quantity of money, but rather controls the cash base of the monetary system. The actual quantity of money is determined by private decisions of individuals and commercial banks with respect to the division of public holdings of money between currency and holdings of bank deposits and the cash reserve ratio maintained by commercial banks. Banks typically carry excess reserves and the opportunity cost of holding these reserves is the benefit they would get from holding extra earning assets. Excess cash holdings will vary inversely with the interest rate. We might postulate that the public's decision to hold currency as compared with bank deposits would also be governed in part by the general level of interest rates. Both considerations suggest some elasticity of the money supply (the higher the interest rate, the greater the quantity of money supplied). But this recognition does not alter our previous conclusion that there exists a relationship between the level of income and the rate of interest required to preserve equilibrium in the money market. This relationship will, as before, be given by the LM curve. Flexibility of the money supply simply makes the LM curve more elastic. (Though we have suppressed the bond market there must, by Walras' law, be equilibrium there too.)

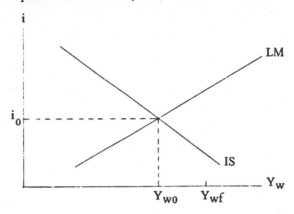

We then have two curves: IS shows possible equilibria in the goods market and LM possible equilibria in the money market. The intersection of the two curves gives full equilibrium in the system and determines simultaneously the rate of interest and the level of output. But this analysis is valid only so long as there is unemployed labour ($Y_{wo} < Y_{wf}$).

Real output, the price level and the labour market

Total income in wage unit is defined as physical quantities of output times the price level ($Y_w = P_w X$). We have yet to determine the price level (measured in labour units) and X. (An alternative presentation is given in Chapter 8 where we do not deflate money magnitudes by the money wage rate). Under competitive conditions, the price of output is determined by the (rising) marginal cost of labour. The price of labour in terms of goods equals its marginal product. Assuming a fixed capital stock, an increase in output must be accompanied by a more than proportional increase in the amount of labour employed. The real marginal product of labour ($=W_w/P_w$) falls so that its marginal cost per unit of output increases. Hence prices must increase as output increases, which can be represented by a supply curve (S) of price against output. The position on this curve is given by the Y_w already found from IS/LM analysis. Each Y_w determines a rectangular hyperbola showing a given money value of output as consistent with any number of combinations of price level and quantity of output produced. The interesection of this curve with the supply curve gives the physical quantity of output and the price level ($Y_{wo} = P_{wo}X_0$, $Y_{w1} = P_{w1}X_1$ etc.) The inverse of the price level (measured in wage units) is the real wage rate.

In summary, $\dfrac{1}{P_w} = \dfrac{1}{P/W} = \dfrac{W}{P} = MPP_L$.

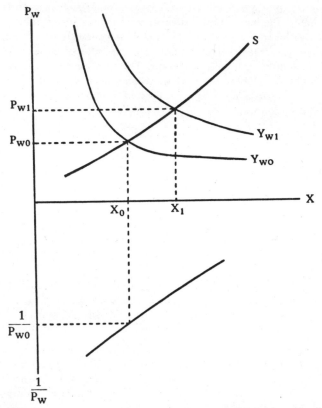

The amount of labour supplied is an increasing function of the *real* wage rate. (The supply price of labour is measured in wage units, and hence does not shift with proportional changes in money prices and wages.) The relation between the real wage rate and the supply and demand for labour can be shown on the following diagram.

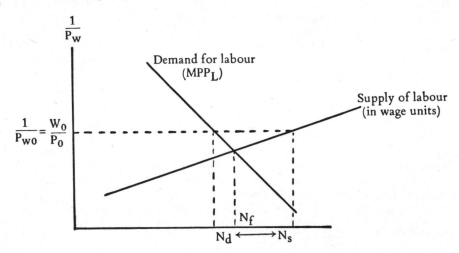

The level of employment is fixed by the equilibrium value of Y_w. This in turn determines a real wage at which less labour is employed than would be willing to work for the given money wage (W_o), This difference Keynes called involuntary unemployment; it can be measured by $N_s - N_d$ though a more satisfactory measure might be $(N_f - N_d)$, where N_f is the classical equilibrium position.

The Neo-Classical reply is that if, at the going wage rate, the supply of labour exceeds demand, then either the wage rate will fall or else existing unemployment is the result of individual choice to withhold labour from the market. The counter-argument is that in a money economy labour bargains for money not real wages. The real wage rate and the level of employment are determined by aggregate demand. Assuming rationality (i.e. behaviour is determined by real, not money quantities) then, if labour competition bids down the money wage rate, prices will also fall (through the equation of price with marginal cost). There will be no change in the goods market since real income, and so consumption, is unchanged and, if investors are rational, their behaviour will not change unless the interest rate changes. No alteration in the money wage produces a change on the demand side of the money market, since the demand for money is defined in real terms. This suggests that a money wage change must operate by altering the real quantity of money. Assuming the nominal quantity of money is fixed, a fall in the money wage rate is equivalent to an increase in the real money supply via a fall in prices. The effect of a fall in money wages is therefore to shift the LM curve to the right. This implies a higher level of real output, with the process continuing until full employment is achieved.

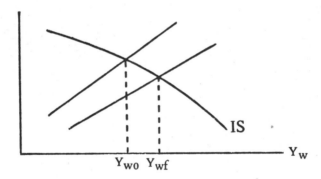

$$Y_{wo} \quad Y_{wf}$$

Under what conditions will the system fail to work? Although theoretical analysis gives us the general shapes of the IS and LM curves, it does not ensure that a money wage fall will result in a full employment level of output. Given a full employment level of income (Y_{wf}) there are two cases in which a money wage fall may not achieve full employment: (1) if the IS curve cuts the income axis at a point short of full employment (i.e. there is not enough interest elasticity for investment and savings to reach the aggregate demand corresponding to full employment) or (2) a liquidity trap situation in which, at the minimum rate of interest, savings and investment fall short of the full employment level. In one statement: full employment will not be achieved by monetary expansion (wage cuts) if savings from a full employment income exceed investment at the lowest rate of interest the money market allows.

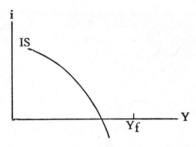

This contention gave rise to one of the major disputes over the Keynesian analysis. Does Keynesian under-employment equilibrium depend on the assumption of rigid wages, which Keynes introduced into the theory by measuring all magnitudes in wage units. If it does, then Keynes merely switched assumptions from the flexible wages of classical theory to rigid wages. If, on the other hand, under-employment is compatible with flexible wages, then there is a definite departure from classical theory.

From hereon we discontinue the practice of deflating in wage units. A presentation of the Keynesian model in which money variables are not deflated by wage units is discussed in Chapter 8 and in more detail by Marcus Miller in the Appendix at the end of the book.

The Pigou effect

The foregoing argument is consistent with Keynes's view of the factors determining consumption. Against it may be brought an argument originated by Pigou which incorporates the assumption that consumption depends on wealth as well as income. Included in wealth is the quantity of money people hold. As money wages fall, the quantity of money in real terms, and so wealth, rises and with it consumption. Hence under-employment cannot occur.

The Pigou argument assumes that money is of a special nature: it is regarded by the community as a net asset or net wealth. This involves a distinction between outside and inside money. Outside money represents wealth to which there corresponds no debt: for example, a system in which money consists of gold coins in a country having no gold mines, or of paper currency printed by the government. Inside money is typified by bank deposits created by a private banking system: for every dollar of assets there corresponds a dollar's worth of debt. Inside money, then, does not allow a net wealth (Pigou) effect: a price rise makes the person holding a dollar poorer while making a person owing a dollar richer in real terms. Hence, the money price level has no effect on the real wealth of the community as a whole. Pigou's argument therefore assumes outside money so that wealth changes can shift the IS curve.

Loanable funds versus liquidity preference

Another controversy in Keynesian theory is the loanable funds versus liquidity preference debate. The dispute was whether the rate of interest was determined by the demand and supply of money (Keynes) or by the demand and supply of bonds (Robertson). The question can be approached by noting that we have a general equilibrium system with one redundant equation. The intersection of the IS and LM curves describes a general equilibrium and so implies equilibrium in the bonds market. But one could equally well drop the money market and use a bond-market equilibrium relation between i and Y with the IS curve to determine equilibrium. There is thus no difference between the two theories for the determination of equilibrium.

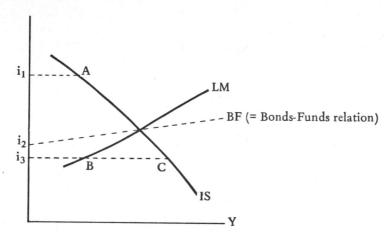

The point is illustrated in the diagram. BF is the redundant relation between i and Y for bond market equilibrium. It must pass through the intersection of the IS and LM curves, and lie between them as shown. The reason for the latter is as follows: point A on IS represents equilibrium in the goods market with the interest rate i_1 higher than the equilibrium rate i_2 for that level of output. At this point there is excess supply of money to which must correspond an excess demand for bonds. Point B represents equilibrium in the money market, with an excess demand for goods, by comparison with C, which represents goods-market equilibrium. To the excess demand for goods must correspond an excess supply of bonds. The BF curve with bond market equilibrium and excess demand for goods matched by excess supply of money and vice versa, must pass between A and B.

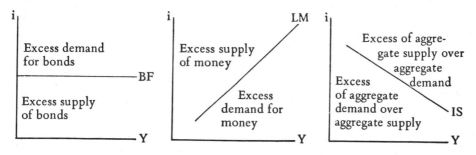

The conclusion is that in static equilibrium it makes no difference which market is dropped. We could follow the liquidity preference practice of dropping the bond market (the BF curve) or the loanable funds practice of dropping the money market (the LM curve).

The controversy has more recently focused on the dynamic aspects of equilibrium, or specifically, the movement of the interest rate. The liquidity preference approach holds that the interest rate adjusts in the direction required for equilibrium in the money market, while the loanable funds approach holds that it adjusts in the direction required for equilibrium in the bonds market. The two approaches give different dynamic predictions in the two areas of the following diagram between the LM and BF curves. While it is not conclusive, the loanable funds theory, on the face of it, seems more plausible since the liquidity preference approach produces the result that interest rates rise despite an excess demand for bonds, and vice versa (see arrows). The liquidity preference retort is that the problem of dynamic adjustment is not so straight-forward. More specifically, it is not implausible that prices in one market might rise even though there is excess supply in that market if excess demand in another market is strong enough.

Movements in the interest rate as predicted by the two dynamic theories can be shown diagrammatically:

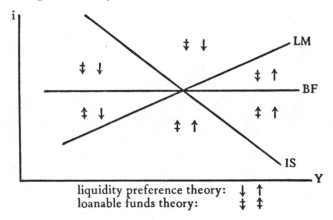

CHAPTER 3

APPLICATIONS OF KEYNESIAN MODEL TO ECONOMIC POLICY

The Keynesian model has thus far been developed on the assumption that no government exists. The model, however, suggests ways in which government policy might influence the economy in attempting to achieve full employment. Fiscal policy was at first considered to be the main instrument with which to achieve this objective. In the post-war period the concentration on fiscal policy came to be considered too narrow, and the analysis developed into a theory of economic policy, including both fiscal and monetary instruments.

The downward slope of the IS curve has been questioned on two grounds. First, an upward sloping IS curve might result from the interrelation between the level of production and the rate of return on real capital. In our previous production model we assumed a fixed capital stock. But the amount of labour must be varied to vary output. Therefore, as output increases, the marginal product of labour falls and the marginal product of capital rises. If the interest rate is related to the marginal rate of return on capital, then we have a positive relationship between the interest rate and the level of output since the return on capital rises as output is expanded. The second argument assumes we can divide the economy into two sectors, one producing capital goods, the other consumer goods. If we further assume the capital goods sector is more capital intensive, then, as investment rises, there should be a rise in the rate of return on capital as the demand for capital goods increases. However we shall assume a downward sloping IS curve, reflecting the assumption that a lower rate of interest is required to induce a higher level of investment.

The Keynesian model suggests that economic policy makers can influence the level of employment through the use of fiscal and monetary instruments involving shifts of the IS and LM curves respectively. Introducing the government explicitly, we must redefine our conditions for equilibrium in the goods market to account for government expenditures and taxes. The new notation is I+G, S+T.

The government uses monetary policy to change the money supply either through open market operations (with no change in wealth i.e. inside money) or through printing money. (Patinkin argues that a deficit financed by printing money is considered a change in wealth as people see it.) Fiscal policy, on the other hand is used to change the level of aggregate demand. This is done by altering either taxes or government expenditures. To keep fiscal and monetary policy separate we implicitly assume the government must finance any deficit by borrowing (issuing bonds): i.e. the money supply is held constant.

If the government were to simultaneously increase its expenditures and taxes by the same amount, the analysis would involve the balanced budget theorem. The net effect is an increase in income equal to the increase in government expenditures (also equal to the increase in taxes). The leakage from taxes and injection from spending do not cancel out because the increase in taxes is partly offset by a reduction in private savings. The balanced budget multiplier is unity because private saving as a function of income after tax must equal private investment, which remains unchanged if we ignore repercussions on interest rates; this requires constant after-tax income, to which government expenditure is added to get total national income.

In this analysis we avoid two complications: (i) that government expenditure is likely to affect private consumption expenditure; and (ii) that when the government runs a deficit, rational individuals will collectively recognize that they will have a higher tax burden in the future and will therefore discount the increased government expenditures or reduction in their own taxes.

The government might wish to maintain a balanced budget and to hold government activity at some level determined by social considerations. In this case the I+G, S+T curve would be fixed, and the government must use monetary policy to control employment, or the government might wish to maintain some level of interest rates. In this case fiscal policy is the instrument with which it must control employment. In both cases it is assumed possible to achieve full-employment by the instrument left to the government.

However, there are cases in which it may not be possible to achieve full-employment using only one instrument. Cases in which fiscal policy is necessary are shown in the following diagrams. In the first the IS curve is interest inelastic, and only fiscal policy can influence employment. In the second the LM curve is perfectly elastic in the neighbourhood of full-employment (i.e. the liquidity trap) and fiscal policy is again necessary.

In the case where the LM curve is zero interest elastic monetary policy is the only effective instrument. This is shown in the third diagram. Keynes's theory of demand for money implied that the LM curve was not vertical but sloped, reflecting the interest elasticity of the liquidity preference demand for money.

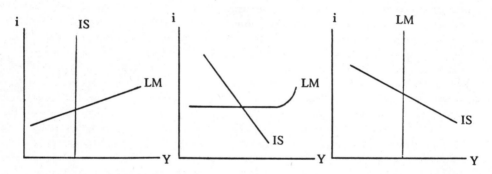

Economic policy in an open economy

We shall now open the model to foreign trade. We ignore international capital movements and the longer range implications of balance of payment surpluses and deficits on the domestic money supply. We further assume the country is on a fixed exchange rate.

In this open model there are three injections of demand (private investment, government expenditure and exports) and three leakages (private savings, taxes and imports). In place of the IS curve, we now have the condition $I + G + X = S + T + M$.

The demand for imports can be viewed as a function of two variables, the level of income ($\frac{dM}{dY} > 0$) and the exchange rate (in combination with the country's price level which we can assume constant for the moment).

Given the exchange rate, the balance of trade (excess of exports over imports) can be thought of as a function of the level of output or income. We can measure the balance of trade (B) as in the diagram; anything below the abscissa is a trade deficit, anything above a trade surplus. At the level of income where the balance of trade function crosses the absciss, exports equal imports.

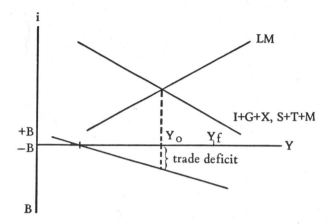

In an open economy, the government has an additional objective — to balance the balance of trade. Monetary and fiscal policy work in the same direction and so are unlikely to achieve both full employment and a balanced trade balance. (Compare points Y_0 and Y_f in the diagram.) Some other instrument is therefore needed.

One possibility is to vary the exchange rate (domestic prices and wages assumed rigid). The purpose of a devaluation is to shift foreign demand towards exports, while shifting domestic demand away from imports. If the values of imports and exports are considered in terms of domestic currency, then devaluation clearly increases the value of exports in domestic currency. But on the imports side, it is not so simple, since devaluation raises the domestic price of imports. Hence the effect of devaluation on the value of imports depends strictly on the elasticity of demand for imports.

The Marshall-Lerner criterion has been developed to determine whether or not the increase in export values following devaluation will outweigh any increase in the domestic value of imports. Define the trade balance as exports minus the product of imports and the domestic price of imports ($B = X - pM$, i.e. in terms of domestic currency). Domestic currency prices of exports are fixed, so the price of exports can be set equal to unity. This leaves the price of imports. Differentiate B with respect to p.

$$\frac{\partial B}{\partial p} = \frac{\partial X}{\partial p} - M - p\,\frac{\partial M}{\partial p} = M\left(\frac{X}{pM}\,\eta_x + \eta_M - 1\right)$$

If this expression is positive, then devaluation initially improves your trade balance and conversely. But the impact effect of devaluation will also tend to change income. These expansionary effects must be taken into account in policy making so the next stage of the argument asserts that an exchange rate change shifts the I + G + X, S + T + M curve as well as B. If the devaluation shifts demand from imports to domestic goods, it will have an expansionary effect on income and the trade balance will not improve as much as would have been predicted from the shift in the B function alone.

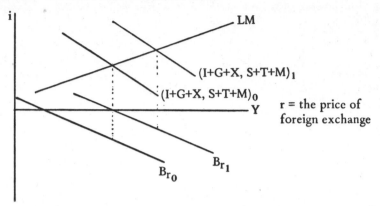

r = the price of foreign exchange

The above analysis assumes some unemployment and the fulfillment of the Marshall-Lerner condition: there must be sufficient capacity in the domestic economy to meet the extra demand for home goods generated by the devaluation. The crucial lesson for policy-making is that monetary and/or fiscal policy must be used with devaluation if there is no unemployment in the economy.

Devaluation has both an *impact effect,* depending on the Marshall-Lerner stability conditions, and a *multiplier effect* depending on the equilibrium level of demand, which determines the outcome for the balance of payments. The theories of devaluation and of stability conditions must be distinguished: stability of equilibrium is a different problem from the effects of charging pegged exchange rates.

To recap, once the economy is open, policy problems become more complex. There are two policy instruments at our disposal, fiscal and monetary, which affect output through their influence on total demand, and affect the trade balance through their influence on imports and by pulling back goods which would normally be exported. We have two objectives: full employment and a balanced balance of payments. (The balanced balance of payments can be considered a constraint on the first objective.) The two instruments, however, act in the same way to achieve the full employment objective, and in so doing worsen the balance of trade position.

The exchange rate is introduced as the needed instrument which operates via the division of total demand (domestic and foreign) between foreign and domestic goods. However, any instrument operating on this division of expenditure also influences the level of income, i.e. will shift not only the B, but also the IS curve. The shift in demand from foreign to domestic goods causes the IS curve to shift. The government then has two instruments — fiscal/monetary policy and the exchange rate — and must use these instruments in some combination to secure both objectives. The analysis continues to assume domestic price and wage rigidity (though domestic price changes could offset the effects of devaluation or other policies).

These policy instruments may be used to achieve pre-determined targets. For example, the government might set a desired level of income and balance of payments, then alter government expenditure and the exchange rate to achieve them. If r equals the price of foreign currency, and G, government expenditure, we can write

$$Y = f(G,r) \qquad f_G > 0, f_r > 0$$

$$B = g(G,r) \qquad g_G < 0, g_r > 0$$

The changes required to fulfill the targets are dY and dB. Solving for dG and dr

$$dY = f_G dG + f_r dr$$

$$dB = g_G dG + g_r dr$$

$$dG = \frac{g_r}{\Delta} dY - \frac{f_r}{\Delta} dB$$

$$dr = -\frac{g_G}{\Delta} dY + \frac{f_G}{\Delta} dB$$

$$\Delta = f_G g_r - f_r g_G$$

Notice that to change only one target variable both policy variables must be used.

Implications of analysis for economic policy

A single policy instrument (e.g. fiscal policy, monetary policy or the exchange rate) can be used in one of two situations. In non-dilemma cases both targets are improved. In dilemma cases one target can be improved only at the expense of another objective. Examples of non-dilemma cases for fiscal/monetary policy are inflation combined with a deficit, in which the correct policy is to deflate, and unemployment combined with a surplus, in which the correct policy is to inflate. Dilemma cases for fiscal/monetary policy are the combination of inflation and surplus or of unemployment and deficit. Non-dilemma cases for exchange rate policy are inflation and a surplus, or deflation and a deficit; dilemma cases are inflation and a deficit, or deflation and a surplus. Note that dilemma cases for one instrument are non-dilemma cases for the other; this is what makes it possible to solve any problem by using a combination of instruments.

Consider the case of devaluation for a country at or near full-employment. Since devaluation will increase aggregate demand, it must be accompanied by a deflationary policy in which the government undertakes to reduce demand. If it is not, and the capacity needed to produce the extra output is not available, excess pressure of demand is likely to force domestic prices and wages up with no improvement in the balance of trade target. This moves us to a different set of theoretical considerations. The question is essentially whether there is anything in the process of inflation triggered by devaluation, which will itself counter inflation. Two formulations of this issue are the absorption approach and the elasticity approach.

The absorption approach asks whether there is anything in the process of inflation which reduces aggregate demand and thus allows for an improved balance of trade. Two analyses have been employed. The Keynesian analysis asks what happens to real investment and consumption as prices rise. The monetary analysis suggests that an automatic deflationary tendency operates through rising prices to reduce the real value of the money supply. The first of these approaches involves a leftward shift in the IS curve. The second argues that inflation shifts the LM curve, i.e. there is a real balance effect.

The elasticity approach ignores the problem of absorption, and must assume either that there is unemployment, or that appropriate fiscal/monetary measures are taken. (The mechanism of international adjustment is further discussed in Chapter 21 below.)

Although exchange rate changes are the typical method of affecting the division of expenditure between domestic and foreign goods, there are others. Examples are export subsidies and import controls, both of which have the side effect of increasing demand for domestic output. Unfortunately, these methods are no less painful than devaluation, and are, in fact, likely to raise the same problems of inflationary effects. (An exception is a temporary import restriction which may lead people temporarily to disinvest in stocks or reduce consumption.)

A considerable number of fallacious arguments exist for improving the balance of trade. One of these is that a deficit can be overcome by increasing productivity. This argument of course fails to take into account the output equals income identity: higher productivity means higher income for someone. A second line of argument is that major items of overseas expenditure should be cut. This assumes that by stopping spending in one direction you can prevent the money from being spent elsewhere; if you can, what you are really doing is deflating demand, and the effects will be the same as for any other deflation.

Inclusion of the capital account

The preceding analysis assumed countries are both free and willing to change exchange rates and impose restrictions. These assumptions are not very realistic as has been shown by the unwillingness of countries to change their exchange rates. Since the late 1950's, the rapid growth of an integrated world capital market and the convertibility of major currencies enable us to rescue our analysis. The analysis will now assume fixed exchange rates and include capital movements.

We assume the country in question is small in relation to the rest of the world so that changes in its interest rate do not lead to reactions elsewhere. The flow of capital into a country is a function of its interest rate relative to interest rates elsewhere.

The north west quadrant of the diagram is used only to transfer the interest rate (i) from the vertical to the horizontal axis. This is done using 45° lines so that the interest rate measured on one axis will equal that measured on the other. In the south west quadrant we introduce the capital inflow curve, $K(i)$.

The case represented is of full employment (Y_f), a trade deficit (B_0) and a capital inflow (K_0). K_0 minus B_0 measures the overall surplus. The problem is then to find a combination of policies which will reduce the interest rate to a level at which the capital account inflow equals the trade deficit without deviating from full employment. In this situation monetary and fiscal policies perform different roles: attempts to reduce the interest rate by increasing the money supply will increase effective demand above the full-employment level, i.e. inflationary pressure. This could be counteracted either by reducing government expenditures or by increasing taxes. In this way the target can be achieved without changing the level of output and employment. More generally, in situations where the exchange rate (r) is not a policy instrument, some combination of fiscal and monetary policy can be found which will achieve the targets. In the literature this is known as the theory of fiscal-monetary policy mix.

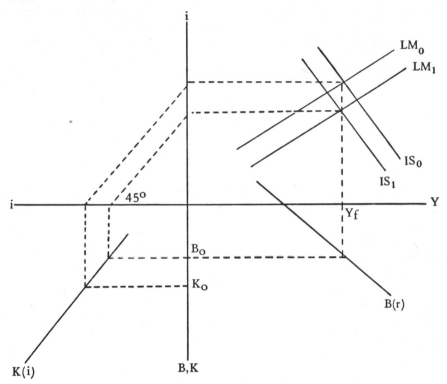

International reactions

In a two economy world new problems arise. If we consider the case of a larger country whose actions are likely to result in retaliation, then this country cannot achieve its policy objectives unless others let it. One aspect of this inter-dependence is the redundancy problem. Assume that two countries have two policy instruments, fiscal and monetary, to achieve two objectives, full-employment and a balanced balance of payments. If the balance of payments is balanced in one of the countries, it must be balanced in the other. Hence, there is one less objective than there are instruments, and one of the countries will not have to use a mixed policy. One instrument is redundant, but only one country can have this degree of freedom. In the real world, the basic dispute has been between the Americans and Europeans, the former arguing for low interest rates and the latter, particularly the Germans, arguing for freedom of fiscal policy.

The use of fiscal-monetary mix to achieve a balanced balance of payments is only a holding operation. In the long-run there must be an adjustment of real factors. Also, it raises welfare problems. For example, over a recent period the US managed to balance its payments through a huge inflow of capital. This transfer of capital from poor to rich would not seem to maximize world welfare.

A further point is that, if capital movements must be made equal to the current account balance, it might be better to achieve this by direct controls rather than by changes in the fiscal-monetary mix, since the latter may distort private saving and investment.

The degree of mobility of capital directly influences the effectiveness of policy instruments. The more elastic capital movements are with respect to changes in the interest rate, the more effective fiscal and monetary policies are in changing the balance of payments. However, the mobility of capital can itself be thought of as increasing the elasticity of the LM curve: capital movements bring in reserves which the central bank converts into domestic money. Therefore, in an economy of fixed exchange rates and mobile capital, fiscal policy has a major effect on the level of output and employment while monetary policy influences the interest rate and thereby the balance of payments.

The assignment problem

The assignment problem concerns assigning the correct target objective to each of the two agencies, the Central Bank and the Treasury. The theory is that problems are not simultaneously solved, but rather that targets are solved for independently. Since each agency controls one policy instrument, that agency should receive the target over which it has the most influence. In the UK and most other countries the assignment is correct since the Treasury is assigned the full-employement target and the Bank is assigned the balance of payments.

CHAPTER 4

THE CONSUMPTION FUNCTION*

We shall now consider specific elements of the Keynesian macroeconomic model but in Part I deal only with the real side of the economy, i.e. the saving function and the propensity to consume, and the investment function. The Keynesian approach to macroeconomics emphasises these relationships as determinants of consumption and investment rather than the monetary sector.

We start with the theory of the propensity to consume and the consumption function, proceeding from the income identity $Y = C+I$ or, if we want to be more realistic, $Y = C+I+G$ i.e. income equals expenditures.

What turns the Keynesian approach from an identity into a (falsifiable) theory with predictive power is the proposition that $C=f(Y)$, or alternatively $Y=m(I)$. This is the simplest form of what is known as the income multiplier $\left(\dfrac{dY}{dI} = \dfrac{1}{1-C'(Y)} = \dfrac{1}{S'(Y)} \right)$. It is a very powerful relationship for it allows us to predict what will happen to total income from what happens to one part of it. Before Keynes nobody had succeeded in relating consumption to the whole system although much effort had been spent on analysing consumption behviour and its possible role in causing depressions. By showing how consumption might be determined Keynes simultaneously provided an alternative to the classical quantity theory velocity relationship, relating the quantity of money to the price level, and provided respectability to 'under-consumptionist' theories of depression.

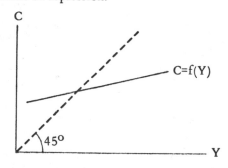

The aggregate propensity to consume as Keynes presented it rests however on a very weak theoretical assumption, the so-called 'fundamental psychological law': when income rises, consumption expenditure rises, but not by as much. (This proposition related to the slope of the consumption function and not the intercept term). Further assumptions that were generally made by Keynesians, though not necessary for the theory, were that at some low level of income consumption would exceed income, and that the marginal propensity to consume decreases as income rises. This basis for the consumption function was accepted for quite a long period — economic theory has relied from time to time on this sort of psychological rule — and it proved very appealing to

---

* This and the following lecture incorporate "Notes on Capital Theory applied to Consumption Function Theory" distributed by Professor Johnson.

econometricians at a time when national income accounting was providing the statistical material required to measure its components. Finally, the Keynesian theory made the propensity to consume a very important relationship from a policy point of view, and hence worth working on.

The early studies found that this simple relationship fitted cross section and time series data fairly well. But as data became available which extended over several cycles, it appeared that the relationship no longer held. The easiest way to show that it cannot be true over the long run is to start with the present and project the function backwards into the past. You then have the prediction that in the 19th century people must have been living extravagantly beyond their incomes. This however does not fit the facts, which refutes the assumed law. Another way of doing the test is to project the relationship forward. We would then find that the proportional gap between income and consumption expenditure should increase with the level of income, and the savings ratio rise secularly; this is inconsistent with the evidence, but what really did the damage to the simple Keynesian model was the predictions based on it of what would happen in the post war II period. The prediction for the United States was, given the very large rise in income during the war, that there would be a tremendous gap between the full employment level of income and consumption. In conjunction with forecasts of the level of investment many economists predicted that there would be 8 million unemployed. Many countries therefore based their policies on an expected slump. This led among other things to the continuation of war-time 'cheap money' policies. But the fears did not materialise and the reason was not that realised investment was much higher than predicted, but that consumption turned out to be very much higher.

Another more scholarly concern about the simple theory of the consumption function was the result of the development of long-run data by Kuznets which showed that over the long-run consumption was proportional to income (i.e. the proportion of income saved seemed to be fairly constant).

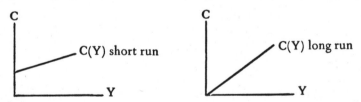

This evidence raised the possibility that the short run consumption function might be different from the one observed in the long run. Some reconciliation of these two theories was necessary. In the early post-war period, economists working on this problem attempted to extend the concept of the consumption function in various ways; in part, this was due to the appearance of more data — to include more elements in a theory one needs more facts. (Many developments of Keynesian theory had to wait for data.)

One obvious assumption was that peoples' consumption is influenced by their wealth as well as by their current income. In the short run wealth is fairly constant, but over a long period, it will rise and so make long-run consumption from a given level of income higher than in the short-run. In the long run, income and wealth grow more or less together so that consumption comes out as a fairly constant proportion of income. But over short runs, there are variations in income relative to wealth which induces different consumption behaviour. One particular way of formulating this, is the assertion that consumption is a function partly of income and partly of wealth (with different coefficients on each variable).

Another hypothesis reflects a sociological approach. Consumption is a function, not of absolute income, but of income relative to that of other people or to past experience. If income rises people will save a higher proportion of the new level than before. But with time, they count upon the higher income so the proportion consumed rises. This kind of hypothesis was used by Duesenberry and Modigliani. Duesenberry's relative income hypothesis has been suggested as an explanation of balance of payments problems in under-developed countries. They try to live up to consumption patterns in the developed world but do not have the resources to maintain the desired standards.

A third hypothesis proposed by Lawrence Klein concentrated on the fact that as a result of the method used to finance the war, consumers accumulated large liquid asset holdings (cash balances and government bonds). This argument however, which says that consumers were more liquid than they wanted to be and so spent the excess liquidity, raises a number of objections. It posited a disequilibrium between income and liquid assets whereas one would normally expect this relationship to be in equilibrium. Moreover, given a strong propensity to save, one might equally expect more liquid assets to lead to more saving rather than more consumption. In any case, the liquidity explanation faded into the wealth explanation.

All these theories try to explain the inconsistency between the short-run and long-run consumption function by fairly simple extensions of the variables that Keynes worked with. Subsequent work has tried to examine the basic theory of consumption and saving more deeply, rather than take an ad hoc approach to specific historical episodes by introducing new variables.

One of the major criticisms raised against Keynes was concerned with the problem of aggregating individual consumption functions. Many people raised the methodological question of why one should assume that every individual has a definite stable behaviour pattern that can be added to that of other individuals to yield a stable relationship for the community. The problem is that income is redistributed from period to period so that different groups of people have different weights in the total. This kind of concern is mostly reflected in the early work of Klein.

The two major contemporary hypotheses about the consumption function — the Friedman permanent income and Modigliani—Brumberg—Ando life-cycle-saving hypotheses — are both founded on capital theory. Both of these attempt to penetrate the surface of current income and relate consumption behaviour to more fundamental concepts. (A third explanation attempts to relate saving behaviour to a desired 'wealth-to-income' ratio, but it is not substantively different from the first two and we will not be concerned with it.) We deal first with what these theories have in common.

Irving Fisher and the definition of income

The crucial concepts derive from the neo-classical theory of capital accumulation and particularly from the pioneering work on income and wealth by Irving Fisher, and to some extent from Pigou. The problem comes when we try to define income and understand Fisher's view of it. Income properly defined is simply the stream of consumption goods enjoyed over time. It is not total output. Production of investment goods, saving and so forth, is simply a way of redistributing a stream of services over time to yield a preferred distribution of consumption. Saving and investment are therefore not alternatives to consumption. This vision is to be contrasted with the general picture given by Keynes, in which the individual simply chooses between using his income in two ways — consumption or saving — with very little attempt to explain why he chooses to save. The Fisher approach may also be contrasted with the parallel and traditional view laid down by Hicks in *Value and Capital,* in which you have N goods to choose from, and one of these is called saving. Are saving and investment just something on which people spend money, an alternative to consumption, or are they maximising adjustments given an income stream?

The answer to this has important implications for the theory of consumption because it means that one must distinguish between current income receipts (resources becoming available) and their function as a constraint on what the individual can do to maximise his utility. Underlying current income (the basis of the Keynesian approach to consumption) is a more fundamental notion involving the concept of a stream of such receipts over time which constitutes the individual's 'wealth' and the fundamental constraint on his maximizing behaviour. Wealth can be defined as the present value of all expected income receipts, $\sum_{t=0}^{n} \frac{Y_t}{(1+i)^t}$ where i is the interest rate and Y_t income receipts at time t.) Wealth can be converted into an approximation to Friedman's permanent income, $\frac{W}{i} = Y_p$, and for both Friedman and Fisher it is wealth that is the basic determinant of consumption. It enables an individual to choose an optimum pattern of consumption over time.

A distinction must be made between purchases of goods and consumption. You can buy commodities and store them. Similarly, you can buy commodities that yield services over a longish period: you consume the services of your car or fridge over time though you buy them at one moment. One therefore has to think of the consumer as consuming a stream of services over time from goods he purchases and rearranging his resources to optimise these streams. Since national income accounting works on the basis that purchase is equivalent to consumption, we make a crude distinction between consumers' durable and other goods, and think of the purchase of durable goods as being analogous to producers' investment. Contemporary theorists are attempting estimates of consumption within the Fisherine framework.

The Permanent Income hypothesis (Friedman)

Friedman's permanent income hypothesis may be introduced with the aid of the Fisher diagram using a two period analysis (though a two period diagram does not really capture the notion of *permanent* income). Wealth in the present (W_1) equals $R_1 + \frac{R_2}{1+i}$ and wealth in period 2 (W_2) equals $R_2 + R_1(1+i)$ where R_1 are receipts in period 1, R_2 are receipts in period 2, C_1 is consumption in period 1 and C_2 is consumption in period 2. The slope of the budget (wealth) line is given by $\frac{W_i}{W_2} = \frac{1}{1+i}$. It reflects the interest rate and so the possible rate of transformation of present into future wealth. A 45° slope of the budget line implies that you can put aside resources now and receive back the same amount in the future. This is the case for instance if there is no market for loans, or a market in which the individual could store resources at zero cost and zero rate of return. But in the normal situation, one can have more resources in the future than in the present, and the terms on which it is possible to exchange present for future resources can be represented by a line which is less steep than the 45° line (i.e. one can sacrifice present consumption to get a greater amount in the future).

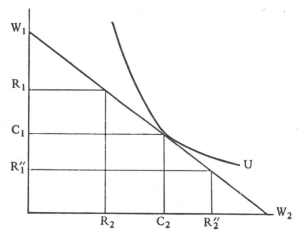

Given this market, the individual has a budget line which can be brought in relation to a set of indifference curves (e.g. U in diagram) representing his preferences between present and future consumption. Notice that the budget line will be the same for an infinite variety of combinations of receipts in this and the next period. In other words, we have exactly the same opportunities with R_1 R_2 as with R_1'' R_2'' given the rate of interest. This suggests that the basic determinant of behaviour is not the amount of receipts he gets in the two periods but the present value of them at the start. The individual can consume everything he gets at the beginning of the period (R_1 plus the amount he can borrow at the interest rate i) or hold everything and consume it at the end of the second period. The amounts of R_1 and R_2 are not basic to his behaviour, the crucial determinant is the budget constraint $R_1 + \frac{R_2}{1+i}$ (the second term representing the present value of R_2). This expression gives us his wealth, i.e. the present value of his income receipts. Consumption behaviour will then be determined by this wealth (and the rate of interest) and the set of indifference curves representing preferences between present and future consumption.

The important point is that his optimum consumption choice $C_1 C_2$ will be independent of the time-distribution of his cash receipts $R_1 R_2$, provided that their amounts are such as to give him the same initial wealth position W_1. The consumption choice will be determined by his tastes, and by his wealth and the rate of interest, since the rate of interest fixes the slope of the wealth constraint $W_1 W_2$. Hence we should not expect to find a stable behaviour relation between current consumption C_1 and current cash receipts R_1, because any number of values of R_1 is consistent with a given W_1. For example, if receipts are $R_1 R_2$ the individual is saving in period 1 and dis-saving in period 2. If receipts are $R_1'' R_2''$ the reverse is true.

Friedman moves from this two period case where the consumer uses up all his resources to a position where the consumer, while not planning his lifetime's expenditure, is considered at a particular moment of time to be taking account of a sequence of periods. The individual may receive an infinite number of patterns of cash receipts during these periods consistent with a given level of wealth. We may then draw the same diagram again bearing in mind that we no longer have an individual with just two periods to consider but one confronted with an infinite number of periods, each of which is small.

The difficulty is to get from wealth to an appropriate concept of income. One approach — not that chosen by Friedman — would be to define 'permanent income' as that level of consumption that could be maintained over time. Returning to the two period illustration, draw a 45° line through the origin, intersecting the wealth constraint $W_1 W_2$ to give 'permanent income' (R_p) on the two axes. Consumption in each period could then be considered a function of 'permanent income' and the rate of interest. Indifference curves are assumed symmetrical around the 45° line i.e. individuals will consume all their income if the interest rate is zero. It is only when the interest rate is positive that we get a consumption function below the 45° line ($C_1 C_2$). This point is not developed by Friedman but it is by Modigliani and Brumberg. (The economy can only grow if the interest rate is positive. Pigou asserted individuals suffered from myopia which led them to stop saving before the interest rate fell to zero. But we do not require irrationality. Ramsey said a society might stop growing (i) because of satiety with consumption or (ii) because technological possibilities became exhausted.)

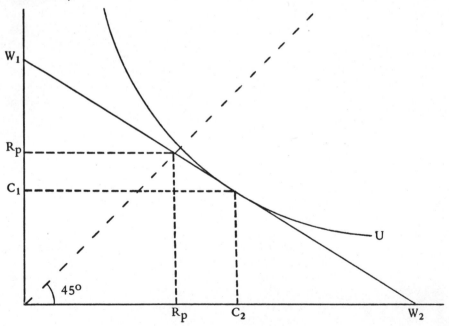

There would be a different function in the two periods, unless it so happened that the individual chose to divide his consumption equally between them. If we assume that his utility function is homogeneous, there will be only one interest rate at which he would do this, which would be the interest rate implicit in the slope of his indifference curve where it cuts the 45° line.

The difficulty is implicit in the Fisher diagram, which imposes a finite life on the individual. To make sense of the permanent income hypothesis, we must posit a more permanent individual.

The Leontief Diagram and Permanent Income

The individual is in receipt of a permanent income Y_p which is *not* Friedman's empirical Y_p. (Friedman's permanent income is based on expected future cash receipts or on a weighted distributed lag of previous income). This permanent income could be produced in perpetuity with the existing capital stock (including human capital): it is a technological possibility (whereas Friedman's is an expected income stream).

Y_p can be all consumed or part can be saved and thereby converted into capital which will increase permanent income by the interest earned on savings. This is shown in the following diagram. On the ordinate we have Y_p = permanent income, C_p = permanent consumption, and on the abscissa Y_c = current income and C_c = current consumption.

If the individual decides not to consume all his current income, current consumption is less than current income by the amount $Y_{c1}-C_1$. This saving can be converted into capital and will increase permanent income by $Y_{p2}-Y_{p1}$. The higher the rate of interest (i.e. the steeper the slope of the budget line) the larger the increase in permanent income from any increment in savings.

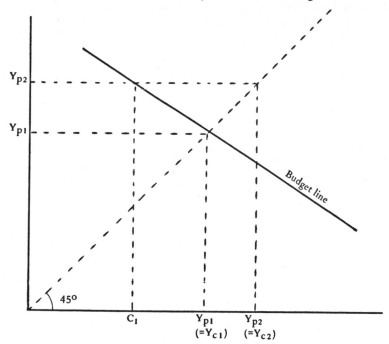

The individual is assumed to have a utility function spanning current consumption and permanent income (consumption). In line with the Friedman symmetry assumption he is assumed to be unwilling to save anything at a zero interest rate (i.e. horizontal budget line) and instead maintains a constant level of consumption equal to his permanent income. In this model savings are dependent on the interest rate, $S = S(i)$. Thus all indifference curves are horizontal when they cross the 45° line representing the equality of current and permanent consumption. The tangency of the budget line with an indifference curve gives current consumption, the proportion of income saved being determined by the utility function and the rate of interest. If the indifference curves are assumed to be homogeneous, at a given interest rate he will save a constant proportion of his (rising) income: $\dfrac{C_1}{Y_{c1}} = \dfrac{C_2}{Y_{c2}}$.

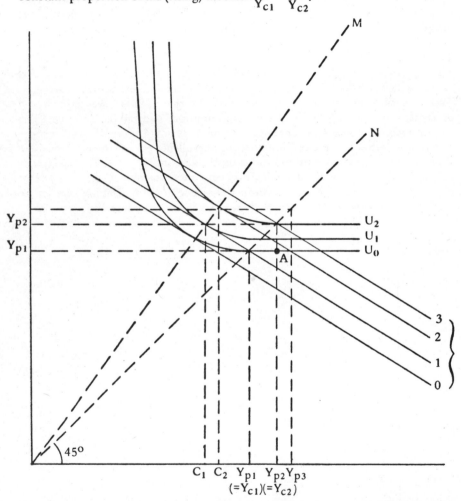

The diagram can also be used to illustrate the concept of transient income and its role in saving behaviour. Suppose the individual is in the permanent income position Y_{p1} and on the 45° line, but receiving a temporary windfall of income $Y_{c2}-Y_{c1}$, so that his actual position is at A off the 45° line. The logic of the diagram might suggest drawing a budget line through U_0 to obtain a tangency to a higher indifference curve on OM. This would imply an increase in current consumption as a proportion of permanent income. The permanent income hypothesis instead asserts that the budget line the individual considers still passes through the original permanent income position on the 45° line (i.e. budget line 1 in diagram). The ratio of consumption to permanent income remains unchanged, and all the windfall extra income $(Y_{c2}-Y_{p1})$ is saved. The justification for this is that there is a lag in the perception of 'windfall' income.

Friedman again

Friedman makes the consumption function depend upon wealth and the rate of interest, $C=j(W,i)$ where wealth can be regarded as the capitalised value of expected future income at the current interest rate $= \sum_{t=0}^{n} \frac{Y_c}{(1+i)^t} = W$. This can be transformed into an annuity $W = \frac{Y_p}{i}$ or $Y_p = iW$. Y_p can be regarded as permanent income as distinct from cash receipts which may fluctuate from one period to another. So we now replace wealth in the original consumption function by the following, $C = f(\frac{Y_p}{i},i)$. As we have the interest rate twice in the function, it can be rewritten, $C = g(Y_p,i)$.

Here, the interest rate must be understood as having two influences on the individual's behaviour: it determines the wealth value of income and influences the allocation of income between consumption and saving.

To complete the picture, we can now use the homogeneity and symmetry assumptions. Initially, we have

$$C = h(W) = h[g(Y_p,i)].$$

We might specify the relationship further by asserting that consumption is a fraction (k) of the level of permanent income, i.e., consumption will increase proportionally with income (homogeneity assumption). The fraction itself will be a function of the rate of interest and people's preferences (u). Thus

$$C = k(i,u)Y_p.$$

This is then our permanent income hypothesis which asserts that, given the rate of interest, consumption will be a constant fraction of permanent income. Permanent income may differ from cash receipts by a positive or negative quantity and Friedman calls this difference transitory income. Similarly, we can divide consumption expenditures into permanent and transitory components, where permanent consumption (C_p, which includes services from durables) is a constant fraction of permanent income for a given interest rate.

$$C_p = kY_p$$

Friedman then uses the hypothesis to explain the conflicts between (i) the observed constancy of saving over the long run and the variability of saving in the short run, and (ii) the higher marginal propensity to consume in the long compared to the short run.

What we actually observe is not permanent income and permanent consumption, but some measured values of these two, i.e.

$$Y_m = Y_p + Y_t, \text{ and}$$
$$C_m = C_p + C_t$$

where m = actually measured, p = permanent, and t = transitory.

To go further, we have to make some assumptions about the relation between these different concepts Y_p, Y_t, C_p and C_t. Friedman assumes no correlation between Y_p and Y_t, C_p and C_t, and Y_t and C_t, i.e.,

$$\rho_{y_t y_p} = 0 \qquad \rho_{c_t c_p} = 0 \qquad \rho_{y_t c_t} = 0$$

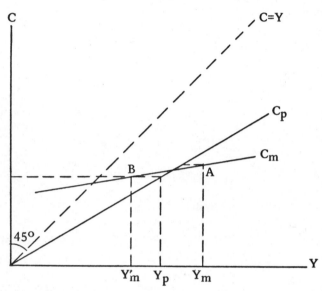

To illustrate, assume we have cross-section samples of people's incomes and consumption behaviour. We plot a 45° line along which income and consumption are equal. Our hypothesis says that, because the interest rate is positive, the actual consumption function will be below the 45° line. Furthermore, consumption is a fraction (k) of permanent income and our function will be $C_p = kY_p$, $k < 1$. But what we actually observe is not permanent income, but some measured value of income which includes permanent and transitory income components. Measured income is going to depart from permanent income in a way which is determined by the sign of the transitory income component. If Y_p is the permanent income of a consuming unit, the actual measured income will be, say, Y_m, with a transitory component which is positive or negative. By the assumption that there is no correlation between the transitory component of income and the transitory consumption factor, what will happen on average is that we observe along with measured income the measured level of consumption (point A on the diagram). So, for individuals with measured incomes above their permanent income, we will find that the consumption point on the average lies below the true relationship. The reason is not that our theory is wrong, but that the assumption that measured and true incomes are equal was false. Similarly, if measured income were Y'_m (below permanent income) and there is no correlation between the transitory components of income and consumption, then, we find a point B (giving consumption corresponding to permanent income Y_p) which lies above the true relationship. Then, if we get a lot of such observations, this gives us a scatter of points and the relationship which fits them (C_m line on the diagram) will intersect the C = Y line at a point which would imply that consumption equals income; below this level there is dissaving, and the proportion of income saved rises as income rises. Friedman uses this argument to show that the consumption function relationship obtained from budget studies or from time-series data during a business cycle is consistent with the true proportional relationship observed over long periods of time (longer than the average business cycle period). Hence the apparent contradiction between cross section and long run time series studies is resolved.

According to Friedman there is a lag in the adjustment of consumption to changes in income because expectations do not adjust immediately: transitory income tends to get saved. The assumption that $\rho_{y_t y_p} = 0$ has been challenged and some Y_t has been found channelled into consumption, which conflicts with Friedman's predictions.

The Life Cycle Hypothesis (Ando, Modigliani and Brumberg)

For the Life Cycle model we use the Fisher diagram on the assumption that the individual receives a single receipt R_1 which must finance his consumption during two periods, one of working for income and one of retirement. His equilibrium point on the budget constraint is E, which gives us C_1^e and C_2^e, the equilibrium levels of consumption in each period. C_2^e is related to the first period decision by the fact that in period 1 he consumes less than his income, i.e., he saves $R_1 - C_1^e$ and he lends it out at the interest rate, so that his total consumption in period 2 is equal to the value of savings accumulated with the interest rate:

$$C_2^e = (R_1 - C_1^e)(1+i)$$

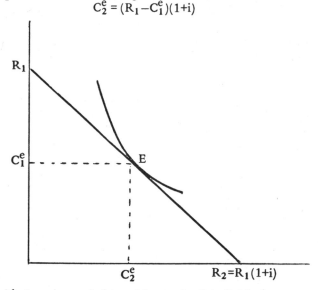

Now considering two period (working, retired) individuals, we can think of a society as composed of n units of 2 individuals of whom one is working and the other is retired. The consumption of workers is some fraction of their wages determined by their preferences between consumption during working and retired life and the rate of interest.

$$C_W = C_1^e = R_1 - (R_1 - C_1^e) = \left(1 - \frac{R_1 - C_1^e}{R_1}\right)R_1 \text{ where } \frac{C_W}{R} \leqslant 1$$

Retired people are property owners (capitalists) and consume

$$C_c = (R_1 - C_1^e)(1+i)$$

This is also the expression for their total income though their actual income as conventionally measured is only $i(R_1 - C_1^e)$ i.e. they use both income and capital to finance consumption.

Note that $\frac{C_c}{Y_c} = \frac{(R_1 - C_1^e)(1+i)}{i(R_1 - C_1^e)} = \frac{1+i}{i} > 1$. If we add C_c and C_W, we have total social income $C_W + C_c = R_1 + i(R_1 - C_1^e)$ where R_1 can be regarded as wages and $i(R_1 - C_1^e)$ is property income. This provides us with a model of national saving behaviour and draws a distinction between the two classes which has been used by many writers for different purposes (e.g. Kaldor's distribution theory).

The theory assumes that people plan to leave nothing for their heirs: this is why it has been called the life-cycle theory of saving. The postulated saving behaviour is fairly consistent with the Fisherian type of model. The theory could however be developed to incorporate positive legacies (a possibility considered by Modigliani-Brumberg). One interesting point about the life cycle theory is that we could have a society with no net saving; each individual who saves is matched by a dissaver. This might suggest that there would be no capital but we could still have a revolving stock of capital. Capital per head is $\frac{R_1 - C_1^e}{2}$

because we have two people, one retired living on his capital and one worker who is saving. The worker would be buying securities or assets sold by retired people. But how could a society like this one generate net saving? For this, we need some exogenous factor which increases the level of income over time. It could happen in two ways.

First, we could have a growing population. In this case, there would be more workers working than retired workers, and this would imply that there are now more people accumulating assets than people running them down. Secondly, population can be constant, but technological progress would increase the income of workers over time. Then each worker would have a larger income than retired workers had and there would be more saving than dissaving. Now, the implication of population or technology growing at a fairly steady rate is that the proportion of income saved will be constant, because it depends on the rate of growth of the economy (assuming a homogeneous utility function). This would give the observed constancy of the long-run savings ratio, not as a consequence of individual saving behaviour at all, but as a consequence of the factors underlying growth.

This is a more interesting theory of saving than the one developed by Friedman, since Friedman does not really give you any reason why an economy as an aggregate should save. In fact, another model, by Spiro, which we are not going to discuss, assumes that people do not want to accumulate capital indefinitely; they will stop when they have reached a satisfactory ratio of total wealth to income. So, in this model again, the realisation of saving in the long run is not a consequence of individual choice, but of the underlying growth of the economy. The Ando-Modigliani model makes more sense than Friedman's because it does not require Friedman's assumption that people will save indefinitely at a positive rate of interest, and the corresponding symmetry property.

The life cycle hypothesis has been tested by taking reasonable parameters about the length of working lives. The wealth position of individuals depends on past saving, present income and expected income. The model produces a consumption function in which consumption is a function of labour income and of property income, with some resemblance to a Marxian analysis: if the population is growing the elderly are small in number and rich. The predictions roughly approximate the actual distributions of wealth and income in western countries, but the model suggests that these distributions are governed by rational choice rather than inequities.

Illustration of the Ando-Modigliani Model

Assume that productivity is growing at the rate g per period; or else that instead of one person in each age group we have many and that each generation is $(1+g)$ times the previous generations. Then, as compared with period one, labour income in period two is $(1+g) R_1$ while capital income is $i(R_1-C_1)$ and total output is $(1+g)R_1+ i(R_1-C_1)$. The consumption from labour income is $(1+g)C_1$, and the consumption from capital income is $(1+i)(R_1-C_1)$; total consumption is $R_1 + g C_1 + i(R_1-C_1)$. This is less than output by $g(R_1-C_1)$, which is the net saving of the economy. Net saving occurs for the economy as a whole, despite the fact that no-one plans to increase the community's total capital stock over his life-time, because of the growth of productivity or population.

The ratio of consumption to income is $\frac{C_1}{R_1} w+\frac{1+i}{i}$, where w and r are respectively the shares of labour and capital in output. Growth causes net saving by the relative share of labour out of which positive savings are made, at the expense of the relative share of rentiers, who dissave.

Example:

1. Let $C_2 = aC_1 = (1+i)(R_1-C_1)$

2. $(1+a+i)C_1 = (1+i) R_1$

3. $\frac{C_1}{R_1} = \frac{1 + i}{1+a+i}$

4. Therefore $C_1 = \frac{1 + i}{1+a+i} R_1$

5. $C_2 = aC_1 = \frac{a(1+i)}{1+a+i} R_1 = \frac{1+i}{i} \cdot iR_1 \frac{a}{1+a+i}$

6. From 1, $C_2 = (1+i)(R_1-C_1) = \frac{1+i}{i} iR_1 [1 - \frac{C_1}{R_1}]$

7. So that $C_2 = \frac{1+i}{i} \cdot iR_1 \frac{a}{1+a+i}$

8. Total Output $= (1+g)R_1 + i(R_1 - C_1)$

$$= (1+g)R_1 + iR_1\left[1 - \frac{C_1}{R_1}\right]$$

$$= R_1\left[1+g+\frac{ia}{1+a+i}\right]$$

9. Labour's share, $w = \dfrac{R_1}{R_1} \cdot \dfrac{1+g}{\left[1+g+\dfrac{ia}{1+a+i}\right]} = \dfrac{1+g}{1+g+\dfrac{ia}{1+a+i}}$

10. Capital share, $r = \dfrac{\dfrac{ia}{1+a+i}}{1+g+\dfrac{ia}{1+a+i}}$

11. The ratio of total consumption to total output

$$= \frac{C_1}{R_1}\,w + \frac{1+i}{i}\,r$$

$$= \frac{1+i}{1+a+i}\cdot\left[\frac{1+g}{1+g+\dfrac{ia}{1+a+i}}\right] + \frac{1+i}{i}\left[\frac{\dfrac{ia}{1+a+i}}{1+g+\dfrac{ia}{1+a+i}}\right]$$

$$= \frac{\dfrac{(1+i)(1+g)}{1+a+i} + \dfrac{(1+i)a}{1+a+i}}{1+g+\dfrac{ia}{1+a+i}}$$

$$= \frac{(1+i)\,(1+a+g)}{(1+g)\,(1+a+i) + ia}$$

12. Ratio of saving to output $= S = \dfrac{ag}{(1+g)\,(1+a+i) + ia}$

This ratio varies directly with the growth rate and the ratio of retirement consumption to working life consumption, and inversely with the interest rate. Suppose retirement consumption equals working life consumption. Then

$$s = \frac{g}{2 \div 2_i + 2g + ig}$$

If $i = 0$, then $s = \dfrac{g}{2(1+g)}$

CHAPTER FIVE

INVESTMENT, BUSINESS CYCLES AND GROWTH

Investment Theory

We start with the Fisher diagram and assume that the individual faces a transformation curve which gives the terms on which he can transform present into future resources. Given technology the economy provides a way to transform present into future resources and this is simply the process of investment. The individual faces a rate of interest in the market which will be represented by a slope (of line AB in the diagram) and his optimal investment choice is at points $P_1 P_2$ because that gives him the highest budget line along which he can maximize his utility. The presence of a market enables him to divorce his investment decisions from his consumption decisions.

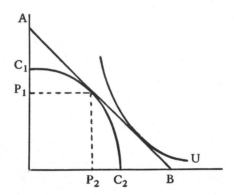

He maximizes utility by choosing the consumption combination that puts him on the highest attainable indifference curve (u). We have a two sided analysis in which the individual first maximizes his wealth (given the interest rate and his transformation possibilities) and then optimizes his consumption subject to that wealth. The condition for wealth maximization is that the line AB, whose slope is $\frac{1}{1+i}$, should be tangent to his transformation curve, which implies that he should carry his sacrifice of present production for the sake of future production to the point where the net marginal increment in total output obtained next period as a proportion of the marginal output sacrificed this period is just equal to the rate of interest, i.e. marginal rate of return on investment = rate of interest. We can use this as an investment rule. It can also be put in another form — maximizing the present value of the investment. At any point on the transformation curve there will be a slope which will imply a certain marginal rate of return on the investment (r). If $r > i$ he should make the investment. Keynes developed this approach making investment a function of i. Hence we have two alternatives — the present value approach and the internal rate of return approach.

Present value

Assume there is an investment which has a single cost (C) incurred in time zero which will yield a stream of net returns $(Q_1 \ldots Q_n)$. The present value approach can be expressed in either of two ways. The Present value of the investment opportunity (V) is:

$$V = \frac{Q_1}{(1+i)} + \frac{Q_2}{(1+i)^2} + \ldots + \frac{Q_n}{(1+i)^n} - C.$$

If $V > 0$ the investment is worth making. Alternatively one can examine the Demand Price (P) an investor can pay for investment goods and still make no loss on the investment.

$$P = \frac{Q_1}{(1+i)} + \frac{Q_2}{(1+i)^2} + \ldots + \frac{Q_n}{(1+i)^n}, \text{ or, } P = V + C$$

If $V > 0$, then $P > C$

Internal Rate of return on investment (or marginal efficiency of capital)

The rate of discount (r) that makes the present value of the annuities given by the returns expected on a capital asset during its life just equal to the current supply price was called the marginal efficiency of capital (MEC) by Keynes.

$$C = \frac{Q_1}{(1+r)} + \frac{Q_2}{(1+r)^2} + \ldots + \frac{Q_n}{(1+r)^n}$$

Solving for r we have the MEC. r is a function of the structure of the investment, namely the initial cost and the stream of returns. This function may yield paradoxical results. Assume we only have two returns and that both are positive.

$$C = \frac{Q_1}{(1+r)} + \frac{Q_2}{(1+r)^2}.$$

Solving for r gives

$$(1+r)^2 = C - Q_1(1+r) - Q_2 = 0$$

$$= \frac{Q_1 \pm \sqrt{Q_1^2 + 4CQ_2}}{2C}.$$

Normalising the Q's by setting $C = 1$,

$$(1+r) = \frac{q_1 \pm \sqrt{q_1^2 + 4q_2}}{2}$$

If Q_1 and Q_2 are both positive, the equation has two real roots, one positive and one negative; only the positive one will be relevant to the evaluation of the investment. If Q_2 is negative, there will either be two positive roots or, if $q_1 < 2\sqrt{|q_2|}$, a negative expression under the square root sign which makes no economic sense. With two positive roots, investment will be unprofitable on the present value criterion at interest rates both above the higher and below the lower one.

This possibility is the source of the 'double switching problem' in growth theory. We expect that as we reduce the rate of interest the economy will become more capital intensive. But that may not be the case. The economy may switch to being less capital-intensive and then to being more capital-intensive as the rate of interest falls. We may then get multiple equilibrium with a given capital stock — which obviously raises problems for a smooth process of capital accumulation.

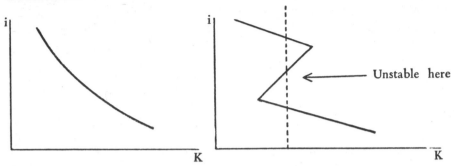

The main difficulty with this approach is that it may not yield a single rate of return on a given project so we cannot proceed with full generality and rank projects by their rate of return (as Keynes did) and thereby construct a schedule which will tell us what the level of investment will be for any given rate of interest.

Interest elasticity of investment

Let P = demand price of capital. Then

$$P = \frac{Q_1}{(1+i)} + \frac{Q_2}{(1+i)^2} + \ldots + \frac{Q_n}{(1+i)^n}$$

$$\frac{\partial P}{\partial i} = -\frac{Q_1}{(1+i)^2} - \frac{2Q_2}{(1+i)^3} - \ldots - \frac{nQ_n}{(1+i)^{n+1}}$$

Using the Marshallian convention we multiply by $-\frac{i}{P}$

$$-\frac{i}{P} \cdot \frac{\partial P}{\partial i} = \frac{i}{1+i} \cdot \frac{\dfrac{Q_1}{(1+i)} + \dfrac{2Q_2}{(1+i)^2} + \ldots + \dfrac{nQ_n}{(1+i)^n}}{\dfrac{Q_1}{(1+i)} + \dfrac{Q_2}{(1+i)^2} + \ldots + \dfrac{Q_n}{(1+i)^n}}$$

If we only have a one period investment we are left with $-\frac{i}{P}\frac{\partial P}{\partial i} = \frac{i}{1+i}$ and since i is going to be a very low fraction, $\frac{i}{1+i}$ is going to be a very low elasticity. But as we get longer lived investment the ratio gets larger and larger (assuming Q's positive). The implication of this is that movements of i will have major effects on long lived investment but not on short lived ones. According to Leijonhufvud's interpretation, Keynes based his analysis of unemployment on liquidity preference and not on the interest inelasticity of investment.

Keynes started by analysing MEC for a particular investment project and then proceeded by aggregation to draw a relation between the rate of interest and the amount of investment. But we must distinguish the demand for capital goods from the theory of investment. Micro theory gives us a theory of the firm's desired stock of capital and its desired utilization of labour in producing the output. It does not tell us anything about investment. The problem is how to get from the optimal capital stock to a theory of investment since, for the purpose of the theory, investment has to be a flow of production of capital goods.

The problem can be handled by a two-stage analysis, first in terms of a theory of the determination of the desired capital stock and then a theory of how changes in the desired capital stock get translated into flows of production of investment goods.

In terms of modern theory, the capital stock desired by a firm (K^*) will be a function of its expected rate of output, the technology available to it, the prices of capital goods and the prices of labour services and other inputs.

For the firm prices and the rate of interest are given. When we move to the economy as a whole we have to recognise that there has to be an equilibrium relationship between the rate of interest and the level of wages (in real terms) and that this relationship will itself determine the cost of capital goods in terms of labour so that the prices and interest rate are not given independently. If any of the elements in the function of the desired capital stock change then firms will change their desired capital stock. The theory does not tell us at what rate they will invest and so does not provide a theory of investment as a process, a flow over time. If we assume that we have perfect competition (the firm facing a perfectly elastic demand curve for its product) then any change in circumstances will lead the firm to adjust its capital stock. But this desired stock approach does not explain how rapidly differences between desired and actual capital stock get converted into actual investment.

There are two approaches to this problem of explaining the rate of investment. Micro-economic analysis concentrates on optimizing decisions of business firms while general equilibrium analysis introduces the supply curve and supply conditions of capital goods industries.

Micro approach to investment

A firm incurs costs when it changes the rate at which it adds to its capital stock. This rising cost is composed of two elements, one internal to firm, the other external. The internal costs arise from plans, decisions, reorganisation etc. entailed by capital stock adjustment. As the firm tries to grow more rapidly it encounters such cost increases and there will be some optimum rate at which it can increase its productive capacity. The external cost increases result from the rising costs of the firm's suppliers as it expands its capital stock.

This second source of cost increases poses problems. For, if we maintain the assumption of a competitive economy, the cost of equipment should be constant for an individual firm. Hence we must add that firms are conscious of each other's existence (at least on the industry level) and collaborate, not necessarily explicitly, but by perceiving that the rate at which they add to their capital stock has implications for the cost of capital goods to the industry as a whole.

The above qualitative approach can be linked with the statistical analysis of investment. The standard method of approaching the theory of investment does not now use this logic. Rather it assumes that deviations of actual from desired capital stock give rise to investment flows which are distributed over time according to a particular formula, namely the standard distributed lag. Let the firm's desired capital stock (K*) be a function of the rate of interest (i) and expected demand for final output:

$$K^* = f(i, D^e)$$

The firm will seek to provide a capital stock which is appropriate to the level of output it expects to sell and to the relation between wages and capital costs which is summarized in the rate of interest (i.e. both the correct level of capital and the correct ratio to output).

$$I_t = K_t - K_{t-1} = \beta(K_t^* - K_{t-1})$$

Investment equals the difference between the capital stock available at time t and at time t−1. It is also related to the difference between the desired capital stock and actual capital stocks available in period t−1. The firm seeks to make good the difference between its desired and actual stock of capital by approximation. If $\beta = 1$, the firm would seek to make good difference between K_t^* and K_t instantaneously. $\beta < 1$ means the firm approaches K_t^* by a series of moves.

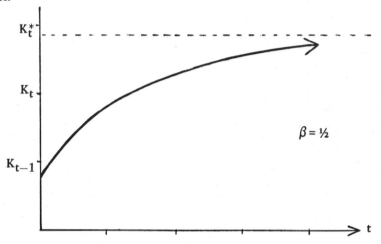

The β factor is a measure of the extent of adjustment of the difference between K_t^* and K_t which the firm makes in any period. This implies exponentially diminishing investment.

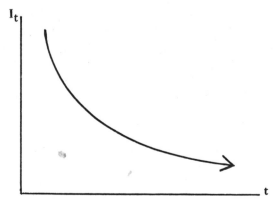

How can one relate this type of empirical approach to investment to any kind of rational optimizing theory? Broadly, the firm's optimizing procedure is to maximise the present value of future profits from investment. A firm distributes investment over time so as to minimize the costs of investment in relation to its contribution to the firm's profits, which can be thought of as a balance between two considerations. If the firm slows down its rate of investment, it reduces the money cost incurred but also postpones its profits. It tries, therefore, to balance these two considerations at the margin.

On that basis, one would expect a pattern of investment in which more is done in the near future and less in the distant because investment done in the near future, even though it may cost more, starts earning profits earlier. The discounted value of the contribution to profits is higher for earlier investments so the firms will optimise by incurring a larger cost (at the margin) in early periods than in later periods to equalise the marginal contributions to present value made by each bit of investment with its marginal cost.

This rationalisation is applicable only for the general shape of the path of investment (as in the second diagram above) but the path will not necessarily be a smooth one (i.e. exponentially declining). It is possible to investigate what path of investment is optimal, given the nature of the cost curve facing a firm, for increases in the rate of investment in any period. In most cases the pattern of investment will be declining in broad terms, although not in an exponential fashion.

Rearranging the equation $I_t = K_t - K_{t-1} = \beta(K_t^* - K_{t-1})$ gives $K_t = \beta K_t^* + (1 - \beta) K_{t-1}$. Looking at it in these terms, what you have is a weighted average (weights summing to one) of actual capital stock and desired capital stock. This can be interpreted as saying that the firm has uncertain expectations about the future and that there are two possible extreme courses open to it. It can leave capital stock as it is ($\beta = 0$) giving zero investment, or it can attempt to build its capital stock immediately up to the level appropriate to the expected future level of demand ($\beta = 1$). $0 < \beta < 1$ then implies that the firm has mixed expectations and is backing them on a probabilistic basis, β representing the weight it gives to making capital stock what is appropriate to its expectation of future needs, the remainder being its hedge that it is better off staying where it is. The standard way of approaching investment analysis empirically can be rationalised in this way in terms of micro theory, although the rationalisation is not water-tight.

Suppose we have an investment function, $I_t = K_t - K_{t-1} = \beta(K_t^* - K_{t-1})$ also suppose that $D_t = g(Y_t)$ where Y_t is the current level of aggregate demand. In forming their expectations of future demand, firms pay some attention to the development of demand in the economy. Expected demand might adjust to the expected level of income $D_t^e = (1 - \alpha)(Y_t) + \alpha Y_t^e$, giving a similarly weighted function as on the investment side. If the level of demand increases above what was expected, this then influences investment through its implications for the expected level of demand on which firms base their calculations. So firms then undertake investment to increase their capital stock. This in turn adds to demand and hence starts a multiplier-accelerator process. Suppose the economy finally gets to a position at which the implications of higher investment for higher demand have less influence on raising the desired capital stock than actual investment has in raising the actual capital stock. We get a closing of the gap between desired and actual capital stock and a fall in the investment rate, which in turn implies a fall in aggregate output which feeds back to the expected level of demand and so to the desired capital stock. We could get a reversal of the process with firms trying to disinvest since their capital stock is too large. We can thus generate a business cycle.

An alternative approach is based on the notion of a propensity of firm's to invest. The idea is that the main influence on investment is the level of profits, which provide funds from which firms can undertake investment. This is not a rational theory, since the fact that a firm is making profits on current capital stock does not imply that at the margin it would make profits by expanding its capital stock. Nevertheless, the theory tends to be popular. Even though the theory does not base itself on any assumed rationality of business behaviour, it will fit the facts fairly well. High investment following disequilibrium between current and desired capital stock will tend to mean high demand, and hence that firms are making abnormal profits. This correlation could be interpreted, wrongly, as meaning that profits determine investment, rather than investment determining profits.

A distinction is often drawn between short-run and long-run investments and between inventory investment, on the one hand, and fixed capital investment on the other, implying that what is involved in inventory investment is investment in particular goods. Since inventories turn over quickly, this is taken to be short-run investment. If looked at more fundamentally, inventories are held as stocks which contribute to firms' productive efficiency. Inventory investment cannot be considered short-term simply because the goods in question are short-lived. It is the stock, not the particular goods, which make the contribution to output. This in turn suggests that efforts to distinguish between two categories of goods and to expect that fixed capital investment would be interest elastic, while inventory investment would not be, are not necessarily correct. However, it is true that inventories can be reduced faster than fixed capital.

One final point is that the rate of interest in the $K_t^* = f(i, D_t^e)$ model of investment does not have a simple connection with the flow of investment, $I_t = K_t - K_{t-1} = \beta(K_t^* - K_{t-1})$. Constructing a simple Keynesian model, we assume there is a downward sloping curve relating I to i. This might be a useful short-run analytical approximation. However, the rate of interest does not act directly on the flow of investment. What is involved is a reduction in the interest rate which operates to increase the desired capital stock which works its way through to a change in investment through the mechanism of change in desired capital stock.

Macro-economic approach to investment

This explanation starts by attempting to give a rationale to the downward sloping curve as a short-run approximation. The Keynesian model involves essentially a stock equilibrium in the assets markets (money and bonds) and a flow equilibrium for supply of and demand for goods. We must disregard long-run effects of the saving-investment process on the stocks of physical assets and the wealth of the public. Over time the economy experiences growth of the physical capital stock as well as in peoples' assets (which essentially are this capital stock but which through financial intermediation are usually held in the form of financial assets or equity claims on capital stock). There is a problem of introducing growth and change into the analysis. This problem has not yet been resolved. Either we take the Keynesian approach, disregarding the movement of the system over time for purposes of short-run analysis, or else we can regard short-run movement of the economy as being dictated by longer-run processes of adjustment. We then regard investment as a matter of adjusting the actual to the desired capital stock, but interpreted from the standpoint of the economy as a whole. Start with the proposition that at a given moment the economy has an actual stock of physical capital which is large relative to the rate at which it can be increased. In this way we can concentrate on the relation between the supply of and demand for the existing stock as determining the rate of flow of additions without having to worry about the influence of the rate of additions back on demand. The economy has a demand curve for the stock, such that for any stock it would have a demand price. This price will depend on various factors, including the rate of interest, expected profitability, etc., as well as the size of the stock. The interaction of the existing capital stock ($\bar{K}$) and the demand curve (D) gives a demand price. The capital goods industry responds to this price (S) until the price of newly produced capital goods equals the price of existing capital goods. Producers adjust the rate of production up to a point where demand price equals supply price. This is a stock-flow relationship on the real side of the economy as distinct from the one concentrated on in the Keynesian model (the financial asset side). The location of the demand curve depends on the stream of earnings which capital goods produce and the rate of interest by which this stream is discounted.

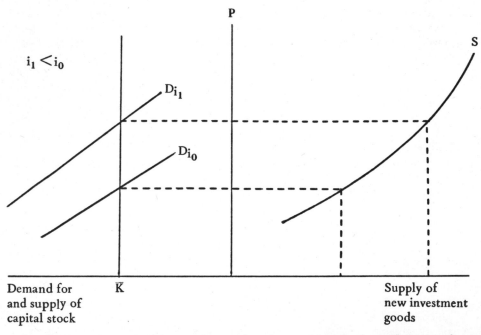

A rise in demand shifts the demand curve up, raising the demand price and the rate of output of capital goods. The relation between the expected demand

and the rate of investment gives the same conclusion: i.e. a rise in demand will have to increase investment via the effects of changes in the demand price on the rate of production of capital goods rather then through a desired capital-stock adjustment mechanism of the type previously analysed.

A fall in the interest rate will raise the demand price of capital goods via a parametric shift of the demand curve. This increases the rate of output of capital goods. How does this relate to the Keynesian curve which says the lower is the rate of interest, the greater will be the rate of investment.This supply-demand mechanism is superior to the Keynesian investment demand supply of saving mechanism since it is a general equilibrium relationship in the market for real capital and the market producing real capital. However the analysis depends on treating the demand for capital as a demand for the existing stock, which is large relative to current production. Hence there is assumed to be no interaction back from production to demand, at least in the short run.

Post-Keynesian work attempting to relate the rate of investment to the interest rate was naive compared with theories relating investment to adjustment of the capital stock to the rate of interest. Demand for investment goods is now most often estimated by measuring demand by changes on order books and by examining investment intentions given by survey data. In general there has been some difficulty in detecting relationships between investment demand or desired capital stock and the interest rate. Recently attempts have also been made to link up the interest rate and the capital stock adjustment process with the consumption of consumer durables.

Rates of return on capital and investment, time preference and savings

A clear distinction must be kept in mind between the marginal efficiency of investment (MEI) and the marginal efficiency of capital (MEC). MEI is the rate of return on investment, which, since it depends on the price of capital goods, decreases as the rate of investment increases $\frac{d\,\text{MEI}}{dP_k} < 0; \frac{dP_k}{dI} > 0$. MEC on the other hand is the rate of return on the capital stock, which is assumed to decrease as the capital stock increases. The rate of return on investment will be lower than the long-run rate of return on the capital stock because the supply price of capital rises when investment increases.

The same short and long-run distinction should be made between the rate of return on saving and the rate of time preference. The rate of time preference is that rate of interest at which the public is just content to hold the existing capital stock. But the rate of return on savings is the return necessary to induce consumers to forego current consumption. As savings increase, the marginal utility of consumption increases, implying that a higher and higher rate of return is required to induce more saving. Hence, from any given long-run capital stock and time preference return position, the rate of return on savings must lie above the time preference curve to allow for this decrease in the marginal utility of savings.

These four concepts can be put together in a model of capital accumulation for an economy with less than the long-run desired capital stock. In the diagram the short-run curves give the equilibrium towards which the economy moves at time t.

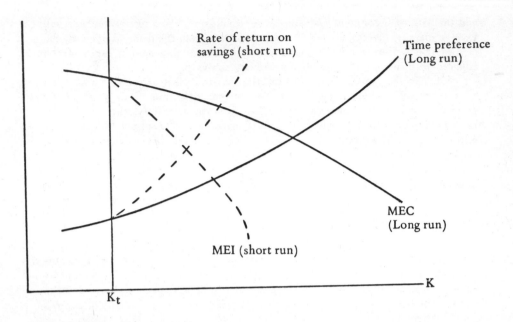

Economic fluctuations and stabilisation policy

Very early writers on the determinants of business cycles attempted to specify a single explanation for cyclical fluctuations, a method which proved inadequate. With the inclusion of General Equilibrium in the economist's tool kit, pre-Keynesian cycle theories erred too much toward equilibrium analysis by assuming full employment, so that cycles had to appear in relative prices and the composition of output rather than in aggregates. The Great Depression proved embarrassingly difficult to explain with such theories. Any good business cycle theory must explain both why shocks are cumulative and why an economy does not collapse completely. (Early theories fell down on the latter point.) Though *The General Theory* was not specifically about business cycles, it did provide a theory of self-limiting fluctuations with the multiplier. Keynes also contributed to the understanding of the cumulative effects of a shock by stressing the role of business expectations in his capital theory. That is, a downturn in present demand lowers expectations of future income from capital, reducing the marginal efficiency of capital, decreasing investment, lowering demand, etc.

The major controversy in business cycle theory, which extended into the 1950's, was over the relationship between changes in investment and changes in income. The two protagonists were the Capital Stock Adjustment Principle and the Accelerator Principle. Both theories drive at the same thing; and the cause of much earlier contention was the relatively primitive mathematical tools available for expressing the quantitative relationships in the accelerator model.

By the late 1930's Kaldor and Kalecki had devised a qualitative, literary theory of the trade cycle using the capital stock adjustment principle. The multiplier explained the exaggerated effects of investment changes on income and cycle limits were explained by capital replacement in the trough and a downturn of investment profits at the peak. The analysis was subtle, but not rigorous. On the other hand several quantitative accelerator theories of the cycle proved unproductive, due to limitations on mathematical tools. Even Samuelson's classic article on the interaction of the multiplier and the accelerator relied on simple relations. A specific theory is formulated, such as:

$$I_t = k(Y_{t-1} - Y_{t-2})$$

$$C_t = cY_t$$

$$Y_t = C_t + I_t = cY_t + k(Y_{t-1} - Y_{t-2})$$

giving

$$(1-c)Y_t = k(Y_{t-1} - Y_{t-2})$$

These second order difference equations were found to give "much richer results": i.e., there were found to be more coefficients to manipulate and more varieties of behaviour of the system than earlier models provided.

But such crude models usually required other awkward assumptions to give them a semblance of reality. For example, with damped cycles, the above model requires 'random shocks', though exactly how nature goes about randomly shocking an economy in a precise manner is never defined. Similarly, with anti-damped cycles, the model requires a ceiling and a floor, the latter supplied in Hicks' formulation by 'autonomous investment', which adds nothing to capacity and satisfies no wants; it is just there.

The assumptions required for quantitative accelerator theories of the cycle were criticised by literary economists, like Kaldor, who pointed out the weakness of the relation involving k in the above model. For, if an increase in output requires an increase in capital, the question remains as to how income could rise before investment takes place. Or, if the relationship defines the behaviour of entrepreneurs, it implies that every time there is an increase in demand, entrepreneurs increase the capital stock. Surely entrepreneurs would be smart enough to know that the increase in capital stock would only be justified if the increase in demand were permanent. Empirical work now follows the principle of capital stock adjustment. It has been found, for example that such a process works better for consumer durables than it does for investment goods.

Economic processes and adjustments take place over time. Macroeconomic theory is now trying to come to grips with this adjustment over time, recent contributions being the permanent income hypothesis, lags-in-investment theory, and lags in the adjustment of the demand for money to changes in interest rates. Such individual structural lags lead to problems in determining how the larger system interacts and, therefore, to critical problems in stabilization policy. Even if the relevant theory is known, the problems of policy implementation are still not small. The government must react quickly enough so that present problems have not been surpassed by other, possibly conflicting, problems by the time a policy is implemented and the government must be able to forecast the effects of its policy changes over time accurately. Without such perfect knowledge of both theory and implementation implications, the chances are that government policies will be destabilizing as often as stabilizing. Recent studies on monetary policy in the UK, US, and Canada have confirmed this and, therefore, to varying degrees urged a scaling down of the short-run aims of policy with more concentration on long-run policy influences. What is needed is an intelligent design of response systems for policy makers who must necessarily work with imperfect knowledge.

A. W. Phillips devised a theory viewing departures from the desired state as *errors*. Policies are then developed to correct for these errors, similar to thermostatic devices in engineering. Yet control is still complicated, since there are three different ways to formulate these errors. If we concentrate on level of error (e.g. the deficit on the balance of payments) the policy should remain in force until the level of error is reduced. But in this way the target is never actually reached, since the end of the error brings an end to the policy, resulting in a partial return of the error. If we study the total accrued error (e.g. total loss of foreign reserves) the problem is overshooting the target. Finally, if the direction in which the error is moving is regarded as of chief importance (e.g. direction of change in the balance of payments) the danger is that a constant error will be sustained. All three formulations have advantages and disadvantages.

Therefore a proper policy system must employ all three formulations. The weights assigned to each will depend on the particular lag structures of the economy. But past experience has been that policy makers tend to react to only one of the above formulations or to different ones at different times.

Fundamentally, Phillips' studies failed to relate control systems to some notion of welfare, which we need to judge efficiency. For example, rapid changes in aggregate demand may be more costly than slow changes; the costs of unemployment may not be proportional to its percentage but rise rapidly as that increases; or a reduction in unemployment may be less costly in terms of inflation if it takes place slowly. But there is no very interesting literature on this problem.

Monetarist theories of fluctuations attribute them to the rate at which central banks adjust the money supply. Proponents are sceptical of the possibilities for fiscal 'fine tuning' and recommend a smooth growth of the money stock to avoid problems posed by lags in adjustments to control instruments.

Central banks may not manage these very difficult problems adequately. Since they operate in money markets they may judge the extent and effectiveness of their actions by their impact on interest rates. But money rates of interest do not reflect the real costs of capital when inflation and expected inflation reduce the real costs of borrowing. (Money rates may rise but less than enough to match the rate of inflation.)

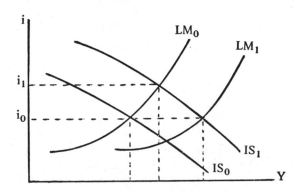

Assume MEC rises with a constant money supply. The IS curve shifts rightward. When i rises as a result, the central bank may think it is being unduly restrictive though there is in fact a normal general equilibrium adjustment in process. An increase in the money supply sufficient to restore i_0 will then be inflationary. For example, in the 1930's the Bank of England prided itself on a cheap money policy designed to overcome unemployment. But the achieved ¼% on Treasure bills and 3% on consols were high in the context of world deflation. Moreover these 'low' money market rates failed to filter through to the mortgage and other markets that determined spending.

A problem with the monetarists' recommendation of a steady growth in the money supply is that, in a regime of fixed exchange rates, it can only be achieved if it is followed by all countries. The implicit requirement for flexible exchange rates has not always been stated.

Economic Growth: the 'Keynesian' model and the Harrod-Domar system

There is a semantic confusion in the idea of a 'macro-economic theory of growth'. The models characteristically take the rate of technical progress and population change as data. (Technical progress may be related to investment in the acquisition of knowledge. But then whatever limits that process must be taken as given.) Savings are treated endogenously and the models concentrate on explaining the path of the economy over time. Hence we have ideas about consistent characteristics of growth rather than theories. The mainsprings of growth in history or in contemporary underdeveloped economies are not explained (especially the transition from Malthusian to contemporary economies where population change and society's willingness to seek and apply new knowledge are economic decisions).

Twenty years ago 'capital' in models of growth and development referred to material equipment and structures. Now we incorporate investment in the training of people.

The Keynesian system was concerned with the short run in which the capital stock (K) is taken as given. Investment's influence on the capital stock was disregarded because in a short period it was small. It enters the system to dispose of output without satisfying demand, so filling the gap between income and personal consumption. This abstraction was fruitful for short term models but left open how investment (and the consequent increase in the capital stock over time) could be digested while the economy grew stably, and under what conditions a rising capital stock was consistent with full employment of labour. (One can envisage a situation in which investment is profitable while unemployment is positive or even increasing.) These problems were posed by R. F. Harrod at the beginning of World War II while E. D. Domar later developed a similar analysis in a less general framework. The main development was Harrod's.

The problem they studied was the rate of growth needed to keep capital (rather than labour) continuously fully employed. Assume full employment of capital capacity at a point in time ($\overline{Y}_t$) and savings constant as a proportion of income ($s_t\overline{Y}_t$). Then savings are given by $S_t = s_t\overline{Y}_t$ and for capacity we also need $I_t = s_t Y_t$, which also gives the ordinary multiplier. Investment adds to capacity so that $d\overline{Y}_t = \alpha_t I_t$ (where α is the marginal increase in output that comes from increasing the capital stock or, equivalently, the reciprocal of the incremental capital/output ratio, $\frac{1}{k_t}$). By substitution we get $d\overline{Y}_t = \alpha_t s_t \overline{Y}_t$ and dividing through by capacity:

$$\frac{d\bar{Y}_t}{\bar{Y}_t} = \alpha_t s_t = \frac{1}{k_t} s_t = \frac{\text{savings ratio}}{\text{capital/output ratio}} =$$

Required rate of growth of output to maintain full employment of the capital stock.

We can think either of the addition to output given by a unit increase in capital or the capital increment required to produce an additional unit of output.

Assuming s_t and $\alpha_t = \frac{1}{k_t}$ are constant over time we can drop the time subscripts and generalise. $s_t = \bar{s}$ is consistent with long run empirical evidence, but $k_t = \bar{k}$ poses problems.

Theory suggests that k_t should respond to changing factor prices and technology. Harrod argued — more plausibly in the 1940's than now — that, since the interest rate could be treated as constant, it would not induce substitutions between labour and capital. He also assumed a constant and 'neutral' rate of technical progress.

Ricardo and Hicks had discussed the impact of technology change on labour. Hicks' definition of neutrality made an innovation neutral if it raised the marginal products of labour and capital in the same proportion (which must raise the return on capital). Harrod's definition made an innovation neutral if, at a given rate of interest, the ratio of capital to output is constant, which would imply that the ratio of labour to output would be falling. Hicks' definition is a point of impact of innovation definition: after the innovation one's stocks of labour and capital are constant and the marginal products of both rise. Harrod's definition assumes that, after the innovation, capital accumulates until the rate of interest returns to its former level. Harrod's innovation is neutral if the ratio of capital to output is then the same as it was before.

The sequence is: an innovation saves labour and capital, initially reducing the ratio of capital to output. The interest rate rises, capital accumulates, the output/capital ratio falls and so does the interest rate. On the labour side an innovation reduces the labour/output ratio, capital accumulates and is substituted for labour, labour per unit of output falls. When the equilibrium interest rate is reached the quantity of labour per unit of output will have fallen.

The importance of Harrod's definition of neutrality is that such technical progress merely saves labour and is therefore equivalent to an increase in the working population. In practice we need not then worry about changes in the ratio of capital to output.

Harrod's equilibrium rate of growth is given by his dynamic 'first fundamental equation' — $g_t = \alpha s = \frac{s}{k}$. He then defines the warranted rate of growth (G_w) which will provide sufficient return on past investment to maintain full employment of capital. C_r describes the capital requirement given by the equilibrium capital/output ratio. He then gets $G_w C_r = s$ and $GC = s$ (where $G =$ actual growth rate and $C =$ actual capital stock). We can write $G = \alpha_t^* s_t = \frac{1}{k_t} s_t$ where $\alpha_t^* s_t = k_t$ and $\alpha^* = \frac{dY_t}{I_t}$, which defines the truism that the capital/output ratio at the margin is the ratio of whatever increase in output occurs to investment.

From the above Harrod derives $G_w C_r = GC$. Therefore if $G_w > G$ then $C_r < C$

(and vice versa). Hence, if private investment is determined by the relation of the actual to the desired capital stock, the equilibrium growth path must be unstable. For if $G_w > G$ and $C_r < C$ entrepreneurs will raise investment, so exacerbating the original situation (and vice versa). (This is the basic message Hicks took from Harrod for his *Theory of the Trade Cycle*.)

Harrod further investigated the relation between G_w and the 'natural rate of growth' which would maintain full employment of labour (G_n). Over time the labour force grows because of rising population and (neutral) changes in technology (which reduce employment for given outputs). The steady rate of advance so determined is $G_n = n + t$. Then if $G_n > G_w$, unemployment will rise over time. (Since G_w is allegedly unstable it makes a poor point of reference for this analysis.) But Harrod suggests that in such circumstances there can be large and sustained booms since there is no labour shortage.

Contrariwise, if $G_n < G_w$ the economy develops to reduce unemployment towards full employment. But labour shortages will not permit continuance of G_w, so the economy may in practice be depressed for prolonged periods because of its inherent instability.

Harrod concluded that the system was in poor shape, but subsequent neo-classicist developments concentrated on the possibility that some natural forces might operate to produce $G_n = G_w$. R. Solow suggested that adjustments in the rate of interest would do so. The 'Keynesian' tradition has concentrated on possible instabilities.

Note that $g_t = \frac{1}{k_t} s_t$ oversimplifies in situations without the reserve pool of skilled labour that Harrod assumed. Development plans have sometimes operated on savings and capital/output ratios but overlooked the absence of an appropriate labour force to service advanced technical investments.

Following Harrod's notion of an unstable growth path 'Keynesian' theorists have concentrated on k. Joan Robinson in *The Accumulation of Capital* was led to re-examine orthodox production theory by relaxing Harrod's assumptions of neutral technical progress and a constant exogenously given interest rate. Kaldor responded to the fact that countries have, in reality, achieved full employment by assuming that the savings ratio adjusts to provide full employment: technology responds to demand so that entrepreneurs batter the technology constraint to achieve the rate of growth they want. In neo-classical models savings are assumed to be invested so that we automatically generate full employment in contrast to the Keynesian tradition. Where $g_t = \frac{1}{k_t} s_t$, g is given by population growth and s is given: hence k adjusts and the Harrod-Domar equation is satisfied consistently with G_n via changes in the marginal product of capital as capital accumulates relative to labour. (In Keynesian models you have s and k given and the problem is whether the implied g is consistent with other desired objectives.) The neo-classical problem then becomes how the economy tracks out to the long run equilibrium growth path over time and what the characteristics of a long-run equilibrium growth path are, if the economy converges on such a path.

PART II

THE DEMAND FOR MONEY

CHAPTER 6

MAJOR ISSUES IN MONETARY ECONOMICS

The essential approach of monetary theory is to formulate economic relationships in terms of the demand for and supply of money. This is to be contrasted with Keynesian theory which is generally couched in terms of expenditure flows, though it can also be formulated in terms of the supply of and demand for money as was done in 'The General Theory'.

Nature and properties of money

Money is an instrument of economic organisation essential for any society which has advanced from the most primitive level. (Anthropologists classify societies by the existence or absence of the several functions of money.) Specialisation and the division of labour, together with activities extending over time, imply exchange and so a means of conducting exchange.

The four most common classifications of money's functions are as a medium of exchange, a measure of value, a standard for deferred payments, and a store of wealth. These can be regrouped into two different classifications. First, we can distinguish by concreteness or abstraction: the second and third functions do not require physical money, only a book-keeping unit; but the first and fourth do require physical money. Second, we can distinguish present functions from functions spanning the present and future. The First and second are instantaneous functions but the third and fourth are means of connecting time periods. However, this distinction must be handled with care, because a medium of exchange must necessarily be a store of value between transactions. It is the concrete functions (medium of exchange and store of wealth) that are of importance in monetary theory since measures of value and standards of deferred payment cannot be demanded. Money also has the unique property of not being demanded for itself but for the fact that it can be used to purchase other things. This has made possible the replacement of precious metals with paper money and bank accounts which are socially more efficient.

Problems arise because some methods of providing money involve social savings and others involve social costs (e.g. the creation of credit cards has resulted in private benefits because the owners are able to borrow without paying interest, but social costs are incurred through the necessary servicing operations). Recently attention has centred on the intricate welfare problem of deciding the optimum supply of money, the creation of which involves zero social cost, but positive social value.

Where money is a physical object it is theoretically possible to separate out the monetary and non-monetary demands, the latter being determined by its uses in other spheres.

Money's property of being desired for its ability to purchase other things results in the property of homogeneity whereby an equal proportionate change in the nominal quantity of money and prices results in no change in behaviour. (This property has been confirmed by empirical work.)

Determinants of Demand for Money

Determinants of demand follow if money is viewed as one of a variety of ways of holding wealth. The demand for money can then be viewed as a function of wealth, relative prices (yields on alternative assets) and expectations of price changes. This last variable is crucial in distinguishing between the quantity theorists and the Keynesians. The Keynesian system often assumes a constant price level; this has theoretical advantages; for it ascribes to money the unique property of safety so that it can be used as the anchor of the system. But if that assumption is not justifiable, then ignoring price expectations will result in faulty analysis and prediction.

A naive approach to the medium of exchange function suggests that institutional factors (such as the distribution of the population between urban and rural areas, or salaried and wage-earning occupations) determine the quantity of money demanded. Deeper analysis suggests that it is the functions of money as a medium of exchange and a store of value that permit the establishment of such institutions. This thesis is supported by evidence from hyperinflations, such as Germany's in the 1920's, where increases in the relative costs of operating with money have resulted in payments of income being made ever more frequently.

The medium of exchange determinants of the demand for money can also be seen in terms of the allocation of wealth: the costs of using money (foregoing interest) are balanced against the convenience of separating sales and purchases.

The Quantity Theory of Money

The medium of exchange formulation of the neo-classical Quantity theory is due to Irving Fisher. The velocity of circulation is the key relationship. The theory can be expressed in the familiar equation:

$$(1)\ MV = PT$$

where M is the nominal quantity of money, P is the nominal price level, V is the velocity of circulation, and T is the number of transactions. The Walras/ Cambridge approach provides the store of value formulation. The desired cash balance (M) is used as the key relationship.

$$(2)\ M = kOP$$

where k is a constant and OP is money income.

(1) and (2) are formally identical but differences exist in their explanatory content and emphasis. The Fisherian approach suggests short-run institutional and objective determination of velocity and so obscures the question of choice in the distribution of wealth. In contrast the Cambridge approach suggests subjective factors are important elements in the demand for money, but it also obscures choice in relation to wealth by concentrating on money in relation to income.

Transactions (which include all sales of intermediate and final goods and services as well as existing assets) present the problem of choosing a suitable price index. Hence they have been replaced by income in the specification of the quantity theory. In modern work some variant of Friedman's permanent income is used which bridges the gap between income and wealth.

Common Variants of Quantity Theory

The naive version of the quantity theory says that, if V and T are constant then P and M must vary in proportion (equation 1). But this variant is devoid of empirical content unless explanations are provided for the assumed constancy of V and T. It may be given by economic conditions. But the Keynesian revolution attacked the assumption of full employment (constancy of T) as well as the constancy of V. (MV = PT is sometimes taken as a truism which merely provides a useful framework for classifying economic phenomena.)

The modern reformulation of the quantity theory is based on the assumption that velocity is a stable behavioural relation derived from the application of capital theory to choice in the allocation of wealth. Don Patinkin in the *Journal of Money, Credit and Banking* volume I, No.1, has recently shown that this development is a new approach and not a continuing oral tradition which has been kept alive in Chicago (as Friedman had suggested). Old Chicago theory was in fact based on a belief in the instability of velocity. Hence the proposal that the central banks' role should be to use the money supply to stabilise the price level and so correct for the instability of velocity.

Definition of Money

Early arguments about the definition of money centred on whether to include bank deposits or to account for them in terms of their influence on velocity. Post-war controversy has been concerned with money substitutes and how they should be treated. The Radcliffe approach, where money is dropped and replaced by 'liquidity', is the most extreme view.

Mechanism of Price Changes

Monetary theorists have proposed two mechanisms for the transmission of monetary changes. In the cash balance mechanics (Cambridge/Walrasian) the demand for money is formulated as a desired ratio of income to money. The mechanism is the attempts by the public to adjust to their desired ratio by varying spending in relation to income. These adjustments in turn influence prices and outputs.

Under the interest rate mechanism, on the other hand, if the nominal amount of money is more than desired, the rate of interest falls. This stimulates investment and possibly consumption, and hence output and/or prices. The cash balance mechanism makes behaviour a result of individual efforts to acquire or get rid of cash. The interest rate mechanism is indirect relying on the market for credit to change the rate of interest.

Each mechanism involves different assumptions about the nature of the system. The cash balance mechanism is best suited to a monetary system where money is created by the government and arbitrary increases are regarded as changes in wealth by the public. The interest rate mechanism is most applicable to a fully developed monetary system where changes in the money supply are brought about by operating in the market for government debt. In this case changes in the supply of money do not result in changes in wealth but rather in changes in the public's asset portfolio which require a change in relative prices (asset yields) before equilibrium is established again.

The interest rate approach grew out of dissatisfaction with the other when applied to a system where monetary changes were not simply the result of arbitrary changes in the gold supply.

Inside and outside money

The above approaches are closely mirrored by the modern distinction between inside and outside money. Inside money is that created by banks against private debts held by the public and changes in it are not changes in wealth but do result in changes in interest rates. Outside money is created by government and is not regarded as debt. Changes in the supply of outside money in real terms are seen as changes in wealth.

CHAPTER 7

CLASSICAL QUANTITY THEORY

(i) I. Fisher

Fisher defines money as anything that is generally acceptable as such, but he narrows the concept to what he considers 'real money' which he divides into 'primary' and 'fiduciary' money. He excludes deposits from his concept of money. His concern is with analysis of the determination of the purchasing power of money: i.e. command over *all* goods that are exchanged (other writers define it as command over *final* goods and services). Purchasing power thus defined is simply the reciprocal of the price level.

He develops his theory by a series of approximations and statements.

(i) The price level depends on three factors: the quantity of money, the efficiency of money (or its velocity of circulation) and the volume of transactions.

(ii) Statement of the quantity theory: the price level will vary proportionally with the quantity of money provided that the velocity and volume of trade are unchanged. This is a truism.

(iii) Fisher develops the equation of exchange, $MV = \Sigma pQ = PT$, i.e. the total quantity of money times its velocity is equal to the total value of transactions.

He proceeds by developing three propositions: First, if velocity and quantities are given then the price level will vary proportionately with the quantity of money. Second, if the quantity of money and of transactions are given, then the price level will vary proportionally with velocity. Thirdly, if the quantity of money and velocity are given the price level will vary inversely with the number of transactions. All of these three propositions are tautologies.

Fisher illustrates the first proposition with three examples — renaming the coins, debasing the coinage and increasing the quantity of money — but he does not yet explain why it is that the price level varies proportionately with the quantity of money. He then extends the analysis to include deposit money: $MV + M^1V^1 = PT$ (i.e. two kinds of money each with its own velocity). Fisher argues that the presence of deposit money (M^1) does not change the connection between 'real' money (M) and prices because there will be a normal relationship between M and M^1 so that the two will move together. He further assumes that bank reserves will have some normal relationship to deposits and that individuals and firms will keep constant the relationship between their cash and cheque transactions and therefore the relationship between the quantity of M and M^1 which they hold.

It is a theory of the determination of the money supply that Fisher is developing at this point since $M + M^1$ will be determined by the amount of base money. If deposits are not related in some stable fashion to base money there is no handle by which to operate monetary control and if the supply of money is not determined by factors independent of demand for money, we have no basis for analysis.

Fisher also states that behind this normal relation between M and M^1 lie what he calls 'considerations of convenience'. They include the state of development of business and the degree of concentration and wealth of the population and it is analysis of these factors that marks the first step in making the quantity relationship a theory rather than a tautology. He then discusses the determinants of P, V, V^1 M and M^1 (though largely in technical terms).

Finally, Fisher gets down to the real theoretical issue which is whether the relationships summarised in the quantity equation are simply definitional or can be regarded as causal. He argues that they are causal because each of the five factors is independent. The two velocities are constant for technical reasons. But they nonetheless rest on individual decisions, which he summarises under the general heading of 'convenience' (embarrassment, fear of robbery, loss of interest from not investing the money. Friedman elaborates the latter in his *Restatement*. Patinkin argues that although Classical writers mention these things, they did not become part of their operational thinking).

By relating M to M^1 and V to V^1 (for technical reasons) and assuming T given at full employment, one concludes that doubling base money will double the price level but will not affect the velocities. The mechanics of this are that, when the money supply doubles people have twice as much money as they find convenient and they try to get rid of it by spending it. They thus transfer their problem to someone else and the process will stop only if prices rise to twice their former level. At that point there is no redundant money and the velocities will be where they were before. Notice that the analysis implies that the demand for money is a real demand. Finally, Fisher assumes that T is given by the resources of the economy and technical conditions (i.e. full employment). By specifying a normal relationship between M and M^1, and taking the determinants of V's and T as given by resources and technical conditions, he arrives at a genuine theory and not a truism.

(ii) Alfred Marshall

Marshall did not produce a full statement of his theory. One has to find it in his evidence to the Gold and Silver Commission and in Chapter IV of his *Money, Credit and Commerce*. He defines money as notes and coins and not deposits. The distinctive feature in his analysis is that there is a demand for money which is for command over an amount of purchasing power and in real terms. He explains that this demand is determined by a balancing of benefits that individuals obtain from holding a stock of money against the disadvantages of locking up resources that could yield a return. The idea is we have a choice at the margin, essentially in capital theory. He gives an example that people will hold in the form of money $\frac{1}{10}$ of their annual income and $\frac{1}{50}$ of their wealth. The significant point is that wealth has some influence on the demand for money.

Marshall argues that, *ceteris paribus*, prices will change proportionately with the quantity of money. He recognises that this relationship is affected by economic changes (population growth, changes in the price level, expectations of inflation, etc.) and criticises the quantity theorists for failing to explain the ceteris paribus conditions surrounding the determination of velocity.

The mechanism by which changes in the quantity of money lead to changes in the price level was provided by Marshall in his evidence before the Gold and Silver Commission. He considers the effect of an increase in the amount of gold in the country assuming that it comes in to the bullion market. There will be a temporary fall in the rate of interest, which induces speculation and rise in prices. People then want more money and this will restore equilibrium: interest rates will return to their previous level. If gold was given to each individual there would be a direct effect on spending and no temporary fall of the interest rate. (He was therefore aware of the difference between interest rate mechanics and cash balance mechanics.) But he does not give a satisfactory explanation of how people acquire this extra money.

(iii) A. C. Pigou

Pigou, like Marshall, defined money to exclude bank deposits. It is 'legal tender' which makes it necessary to bring in the relation between the demand for what PIgou calls 'titles to legal tender' and the demand for legal tender itself.

In Pigou's analysis the demand for money arises because people want to hold a proportion of their resources in legal tender. (He does not say what observable magnitude is meant by 'resources'.)There are two main reasons — convenience (which relates to ordinary transactions) and security (unexpected needs or changes in price level). He then adds that the real value of money is determined by the proportion of resources (R) people want to hold in cash and the nominal value of money: $\frac{1}{P} = \frac{kR}{M}$. Here the Cambridge k is explicitly a matter of personal choice (otherwise the only difference from Fisher is R). He was confronted with the problem of how to bring in bank deposits. (His theory of money supply resembles that of Fisher.)

$$\frac{1}{P} = \frac{kR}{M} [c + h (1 - c)],$$

where c is the ratio of currency to total titles to legal tender and h is the reserve ratio of Banks.

Pigou concludes that the demand schedule for money in real terms will be a rectangular hyperbola, since what is demanded is command over real resources :

$$\frac{M}{P} = kR [c + h (1 - c)] = \text{constant}.$$

The demand for money is determined by k, c and h. He brings in the cost of banking services as one determinant of c; h is determined by banks balancing the advantages and disadvantages of holding cash reserves (which he puts in terms of productivity and convenience). The k factor results from choices at the margin between investment and holding cash (diminishing marginal utility of investment and diminishing marginal convenience of holding cash).

Pigou assumed that the economy tended to full employment and provided no mechanics or stability analysis.

(iv) Knut Wicksell

Wicksell accepted that the quantity theory was not a truism, but he was dissatisfied with the ways in which others had tried to explain how changes in the quantity of money influenced the price level. He was particularly dissatisfied with the cash balance mechanics. He changed the model from a gold and silver economy into one which had a banking system and nothing else. The banking system determines the quantity of money through its willingness to create credit at given money rates of interest. Wicksell's analysis and mechanics distinguish between money and real rates of interest. Differences between them set by the banking system influence the demand for goods and services. If the money rate is less than the real rate it is profitable to borrow from the banks which implies an increase in consumption and investment and reduction in savings. The difference between saving and investment is financed by bank credit creation, which leads to excess demand and rising prices. Since the money rate of interest is fixed in the model, price rises continue cumulatively as long as it is below the real rate. Wicksell also argues that when prices rise people expect them to rise more which leads to more borrowing from the banks at the fixed money rate and so induces a higher rise in prices. If the real rate is below the money rate we have a cumulative downward process.

He also recognised that the price rise might not necessarily be proportional to the increase in the money supply: cumulative movement means that the velocity of circulation can change. With this model Wicksell introduced the income-expenditure approach though he assumed throughout that the economy tended to full employment.

(v) D. H. Robertson

Robertson was concerned primarily with business cycles which he regarded as real phenomena aggravated by monetary disturbances. He also discussed a proper economic policy designed to stabilise the economy. He assumed a central bank intelligent enough to apply the proper policy, so in his system we have a policy maker inside the model.

Given a desired ratio of money to income, suppose the quantity of money increases. Spending will rise and pull up prices. People are forced to save for two reasons: first, the income they receive buys less goods than they had expected and, second, as prices rise and real balances fall they wish to maintain the desired ratio of money balances to income. He called the two effects automatic and induced 'lacking'. When prices are falling there is forced and induced consumption, which he called automatic and induced 'splashing'.

The problem was what would happen if people decided to raise the ratio of money to income (in his terminology, 'hoarding'). As there would be a fall in the price level, people in fact do not accumulate wealth when there is automatic and induced lacking. Robertson wanted to find a way by which the banking system could translate the public's intentions to accumulate wealth into an increase in society's real capital instead of a reduction in the price level. (How could intentions to save be translated, through the Banking system, into actual saving?)

CHAPTER 8

KEYNESIAN MONETARY THEORY:
FUNDAMENTALS OF THE PORTFOLIO APPROACH

Two key assumptions made by writers discussed in the last lecture were rejected by Keynes in the *General Theory*. He did not accept that the economy tends towards full employment in the relevant time period, nor that velocity (or the Cambridge k) is a stable function (or a constant determined by technical conditions). The level of output is determined by effective demand (which is influenced by monetary factors) and the demand for money is a demand for one form of asset and that demand depends on expectations about future movements in prices of other assets. This is a sharp departure from the quantity theory tradition, particularly as developed by Irving Fisher. This tradition emphasised that expectations influenced the demand for money, but the expectations in question concerned movements in the price level, and therefore expectations about the purchasing power of money. Keynes, on the other hand, placed emphasis on expectations about interest rates — the yields on assets competing with money.

Whether or not we regard the first issue (full employment) as a problem in monetary theory, it does not provide us with a basis for discriminating between monetary theories sofar as they deal with the demand for money. We could argue that the question of whether it is legitimate to assume full employment as a long-run tendency or to deal with the short-run (take wages and prices as rigid or sticky) is not fundamental for monetary theory. Once one sees the distinction between time periods (short and long) then either the Keynesian or quantity theories can be used. One could reject the assumption that the economy tends to full employment and still use a classical quantity theory approach to the monetary side of the analysis. Alternatively, one could assume that the economy does tend to full employment and use a Keynesian liquidity preference approach. A great deal of Patinkin's contribution to the integration of monetary and value theory consists in putting the price flexibility assumption, on which the classical full employment tendency rests, back into the structure of the Keynesian model.

The second issue (velocity) on the other hand is a matter of monetary theory.

Keynes presented his theory as an attack on and rejection of the Quantity Theory approach. In large part, that way of formulating the difference produced false issues, because any theory which is going to have money in it at all must incorporate a theory of the demand for money (as well as allowing the quantity of money to influence the economy). What was basically at stake was the insistence that the quantity theory was overlooking some aspects of the problem. Keynes's rejection of the quantity theory approach, which constitutes a large part of the polemics of the *General Theory*, was directed primarily against the Marshallian tradition at Cambridge (the desired money-income ratio) and goes back to his earlier *Treatise on Money*.

The *Treatise* presented a theory of price level determination and movements along income-expenditure lines very similar to Wicksell. The general nature of the model was that the price level moves up or down according to whether entrepreneurial investment is greater than or less than the savings that people would do out of normal income. The difference between investment and saving is windfall profits or losses for entrepreneurs. (In this *Treatise* model savings and investment are not equal and much of the difficulty people had with the *General Theory* was that it insisted that investment and savings must always be equal. The key is that saving is not defined in the *Treatise* as actual saving, but as what people would save out of normal income.)

Money comes into the *Treatise* through its influence on the price level of assets — equities and bonds. The price level of assets then influences investment via the choice between buying old assets and buying new real assets. If the price of existing assets is greater than the cost of production of new assets, new assets are produced. Equilibrium is attained with a rate of investment such that the marginal cost of newly produced assets is equal to the price the market sets on existing assets. Money influences the price level of assets through the fact that people have a choice between holding money and holding these other assets, equities and bonds. If the prices of assets are expected to fall, people will be induced to hold cash; otherwise they will hold assets. The price level of assets must be such that, given people's expectations, the amount of money they wish to hold equals the amount there actually is. In other words, there is substitution between money and other assets which changes their price until people are content to hold both the assets and the existing stock of money.

The *General Theory* switched from this *Treatise* approach (attempting to explain movements in the price level) to one seeking to explain the determination of employment. Keynes dropped equities from the analysis on the monetary side of the model. (They had figured largely in the *Treatise*.) Analysis focuses on the choice between money and bonds. This choice determines the interest rate which, along with the marginal efficiency of capital, determines investment. Through the multiplier, investment determines income and employment. This way of presenting the theory is obviously defective. It is essentially a general equilibrium system, but Keynes initially presented it as a theory of one-way causation from money to interest rates to income.

The Keynesian-Neoclassical split

According to neoclassical writers the demand for and supply of money determined its purchasing power. In Keynesian theory, the demand and supply of money determine the interest rate. Money is not viewed as a commodity but as an asset with a price relative to other assets given by the cost of holding money, i.e. the rate of interest. The 'price' of money is not the reciprocal of the average money prices of other things, but the rate of interest foregone in holding it.

Determinants of Demand for Money in Keynes

Keynes formulated the demand for money chiefly in terms of two groups of motives which determine how much money will be held at a given rate of interest. This corresponds to the two functions of money as a medium of exchange and a store of value.

In dealing with the transaction demand, Keynes was extremely conventional and applied a crude quantity theory approach. Transactions demands were explained by the income and business motives. The income motive would bridge the interval between receipt of income and expenditure (which depended mainly on the amount of income and the length of time between income payments). The business motive bridged the gap between incurring business costs and receiving sales revenue. Robertson pointed out that this is precisely the time that money is not held. The business motive in fact depends on the value of output and degree of integration of the economy whereas the attractions of holding money for business or other transactions depends in part on the cost of borrowing money and the return on cash holding (i.e. interest on bank deposits). Keynes disregarded these in the operational formulations of his theory in which the transaction demand was a constant proportion of income.

Keynes emphasised that the necessary condition for an assets demand for money was uncertainty about future rates of interest. If the rate of interest is never negative, why would anyone want to hold non-interest bearing cash? Keynes answers his own question: if there is certainty about future rates of interest and if these rates are never negative, then this certainty would be reflected in the pattern of interest rates now observable in the market on assets of different maturity. From present rates on different maturities, one could infer the value of an asset at any future point in time. If all future short-term rates were positive, then the value of an asset at any point in future would always be greater than the present price. One would always gain by holding the asset instead of cash.

The future, of course, is not certain and holding an asset involves the risk that the future value will be less than the present cash value. Interest must be high enough to compensate for this risk.

To illustrate (and abstracting from price level changes) take the case where we have one and two year loans. Let r_1 be the interest rate on one year loans and r_2 the interest rate which will prevail for a one-year loan starting a year from now and ending two years from now. Investing in two successive one-year loans gives a return of $(1 + r_1)(1 + r_2)$. Suppose there is also a two year loan, paying interest at the rate of R_1 per year and assume that the interest must be compounded. Then the return on the two-year loan is $(1 + R_1)^2$. An investor would choose the investment opportunity giving the highest return. With perfect certainty, yields would be equal whether one held two successive one year bonds or one two year bond. But in the market we can only at present observe present rates of interest, r_1 and R_1. On the assumption that the market functions rationally, we can infer from the market rates what the implicit rate of interest must be for a one-year loan starting a year from now (r_2).

$$(1 + r_1)(1 + r_2) = (1 + R_1)^2$$

$$r_2 = \frac{(1 + R_1)^2}{(1 + r_1)} - 1$$

If we continue to assume certainty, then we will know the value of a two-year loan after one year with perfect certainty. The capital value of one unit at the end of one year must be $\frac{(1 + R_1)^2}{1 + r_2} = 1 + r_1$, the same as the value of a one-year loan. Hence, under conditions of perfect certainty it does not matter whether an investor buys a one-year loan and gets repayment at the end of the year, or buys a two-year loan and sells it at the end of one year. Assuming interest rates are positive, it will always pay to buy an asset rather than hold cash.

Suppose now that future interest rates are not certain. The value of a two-year loan after one year is then $\dfrac{(1 + R_1)^2}{(1 + r'_2)} = \dfrac{(1 + r_1)(1 + r_2)}{(1 + r'_2)}$. We know with certainty that the value of the loan after two years will equal $(1 + R_1)^2$. The value at the end of one year equals the value at the end of two years discounted back one year by whatever interest rate prevails in the second year. If r'_2, the actual rate that will be earned on one-year loans starting at the beginning of the second year, is less than r_2 (the rate implied now), the individual who buys a two year bond now has made a capital gain at the end of year one by comparison with a person who invested in a one-year loan at r_1. If on the other hand f_2 is greater than r_2, the individual will be worse off over the two years holding a two-year loan than if he holds two successive one-year loans.

This illustrates Keynes's argument and also points to a flaw in it as an approach to the demand for money. A person is always better off holding one-year loans rather than cash. (Recall that the price level is assumed constant.) Therefore, this asset demand is not a good reason for holding cash, but instead for holding short-term rather than long-term loans. Liquidity preference should show up, not in holding cash, but in efforts to substitute short and long loans for one another (i.e. in the pattern of interest rates, Chapter 11 below).

To explain cash-holding, we must introduce one of two assumptions: either the market does not provide securities as short as the period over which people want to be assured about the capital value of their assets, or transaction costs do not make it worthwhile buying short-term securities in preference to holding cash.

Holding cash depends on there being uncertainty about two quite different things — future real interest rates and the point of time when liquidity will be necessary. With only uncertainty about money rates (given the price level), there is no motive for holding cash so long, of course, as we assume that loans can be finely subdivided to match maturities with contingent cash needs.

Keynes called the motive for holding cash due to uncertainty about future rates of interest the precautionary motive. It makes the demand for cash a function of the real interest rate. Consider the borderline case where an individual is no better and no worse off holding a two year asset rather than cash.

$$1 = \frac{(1 + r_1)(1 + r^2)}{(1 + r'_2)}$$

where r_2 is the rate expected to rule in year 2 and r_2 is still the rate that will actually rule in year 2. Thus:

$$r'_2 = r_1 + r_2 + r_1 r_2 \text{ and}$$

$$a = \frac{r'_2 - r_2}{r_2} = r_1 + \frac{r_1}{r_2} = \frac{r_1(1 + r_2)}{r_2}$$

and a is appreciation. If r'_2 is greater than r_2, the individual makes a capital loss. This is the unexpected appreciation of the rate which would leave him worse off holding the asset rather than cash. The degree of appreciation which he is insured against will vary. It will be higher the higher is r_1, lower the lower is r_2, and higher the higher is the general level of interest rates.

The interest rate thus provides the individual with a hedge against the risk of capital loss. The risk will be a function of the general level of interest rates. The higher they are, the greater is the unexpected appreciation of interest rates against which he is protected by holding the asset rather than cash. The higher the level of rates, the smaller the incentive to hold cash and the greater the protection against unexpected changes in the rate.

Finally, we consider Keynes' speculative motive for holding money, which requires the presence of an organised securities market in which assets are continuously revalued in response to people's changing expectations about the future. This market permits speculation in both securities and cash. The speculative demand for money arises from the belief that the current prices of securities are too high and will soon fall, implying that current money interest rates are too low. Whether speculation is profitable depends on whether the gain from buying the lower priced security later outweighs the loss of interest from holding cash in the interim.

There are two ways of formulating this problem. Under what circumstances will the loss of current interest earnings be less than the loss incurred by buying securities now rather than later? And under what conditions does the capital gain from buying securities later compensate for the loss of interest now?

Keynes' speculative demand: further development

The individual's speculative demand for holding money involves certain expectations about the future (given the price level) which he uses to increase his wealth. For example, if a fall in the price of financial assets is expected, then he should delay his asset purchases and hold cash instead. There is a trade-off involved in averting a capital loss which involves the interest payments thereby foregone. Keynes advanced the speculative motive as a theory to explain the conditions under which an individual would forego interest payments to hold cash. Assume that the individual can choose between holding money and a simple financial asset, assumed to be perpetuities promising an income of £1 (say) per period (A), and that he has certain expectations about the future. Then the capital value of the asset is $\frac{£1}{r}$. If he decides to buy the asset, his total income will be the stream of promised payments plus or minus changes in the asset's value, which depend on changes in the rate of interest. The expected gain for one period is then given by

$$E(\text{gain}) = 1 + \frac{dA}{dt} = 1 - \frac{1}{r^2}\left(\frac{dr}{dt}\right)$$

For the individual to be neutral between money and A, any expected capital loss must just be offset by perpetuity payments: i.e. for $E(\text{gain}) = 0$, then $r = \frac{1}{r}\left(\frac{dr}{dt}\right)$

In words, the rate of change of r must equal the interest rate itself; or, the interest rate is expected to rise at a rate equal to itself. If r increases at a faster rate, then the individual is motivated to hold cash.

Graphically this relationship can be represented by a rectangular hyperbola (since rA = 1). Since the perpetuity pays £1 per period, the maximum capital loss which the investor can allow is exactly £1. The diagram shows that he is 'insured' against smaller and smaller absolute and proportional changes in r as the value of A increases; there is thus a greater motivation for him to hold cash

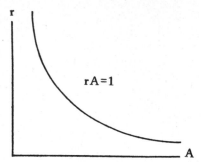

as r falls to lower current levels (if insurance is what he wants). We can also write $E\left(\dfrac{dA}{dt}\right) = \dfrac{1}{r_c} - \dfrac{1}{r_e}$, where r_c is the current rate and r_e is the rate expected in the next period. The investor is then indifferent between cash and bonds when $r_c = \dfrac{r_e}{1+r_e}$ (see Chapter 10).

Keynes used two different theories to derive an aggregate speculative demand curve. First, he assumed many people with different (certain) expectations of r_e, the expected future rate of interest. Thus, as the current rate falls, more and more people will find the relation of r to r_e such as to make them switch to money. This theory involves positive expectations about r_e. Second, he assumed individuals who are uncertain about r_e and who therefore divide their portfolios. Keynes here reintroduced the precautionary demand: individuals are 'insured' against an absolute rise in r equal to r^2, or against a proportional rise in r equal to r itself. No expectations are involved in this theory, just uncertainty. The shape of the speculative demand for money depends both on the degree of unanimity of expectations of individuals and the degree of certainty about those expectations. A great deal of dispersion and uncertainty leads to an inelastic speculative demand.

The total demand for money

Keynes found it expositionally convenient to divide the total demand for money into its three parts and to state that the stock of money left to satisfy the speculative motive equals the stock remaining after the transactions and precautionary demands have been fulfilled. But if we use the speculative curve to determine the interest rate through changes in the money supply, we run into trouble, because changes in the return on capital, propensity to consume, etc., not only affect r but will also affect expectations about r, causing shifts in the speculative demand curve. This is a complicated problem on which not much work has been done.

Suppose the nominal quantity of money can only change in two ways — an open market swap of money for other assets (in which no change in wealth is involved i.e. a movement along a demand curve) or a budget deficit or surplus which does change wealth (i.e. a shift in demand is added to a movement along the demand curve). With pure inside money, the real stock of M is equally affected by an increase in money and a decrease in the money wage rate. But with some outside money there is a difference. An open market operation to increase the money supply is a movement along the demand curve and no wealth effect is involved. But a fall in the money wage rate increases wealth, shifting the money demand curve (and other curves). Under the assumption of outside money and so a wealth effect, the net effect on employment will be greater with a fall in the money wage rate than with an equal increase in money through open market operations.

Keynes' defined three motives for holding M, combined into one total decision:

$$M_1 = M_T + M_P = f(x)P,$$

where M_T is the transactions demand, M_P the precautionary demand and x is real output and P the price level.

$$M_2 = M_{spec} = g(r)$$

Hence income and the interest rate are considered the major determinants in their respective equations. The theory of demand for M_2 includes not only the current interest rate r, but also the expected rate r_e, and implicitly also total wealth. Thus the equation should properly be written:

$$M_2 = h(r, r_e, W)$$

However, following Keynes, we can write

$$M = M_1 + M_2 = L_1(Y) + L_2(r),$$

and L_1 is strictly proportional due to history, demography, etc.

Some of Keynes's presentation implied that his is a one-way causation model, going from the demand for and supply of money to the level of output via the interest rate, investment and the multiplier. Much early work on the Keynesian model — notably that done by Hicks — showed that the model is one of general equilibrium as in the familiar IS-LM conception discussed earlier. The interest rate is therefore not determined just by the demand for and supply of money. But Keynes did devise a model to show how the interest rate could be determined only by monetary factors; and, though it has been criticised, his presentation is legitimate.

Take the usual relations

$$S = S(Y, i)$$
$$I = I(i, Y)$$

and devise a relation between Y and i (via I): $Y = f(i)$. Then, from $L = L_0(i, Y)$ devise $L = L_0[i, f(i)] = L_1(i)$

Thus all the multiplier effects of i on Y via I can be compressed into the demand for money. This is now the demand for all categories of money as a function of the interest rate. This procedure yields the following presentation of general equilibrium.

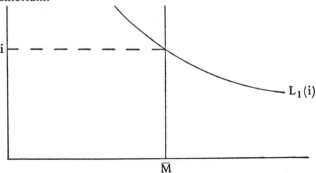

Implicit in $L_1(i)$ is a level of Y which implies equilibrium in the goods market and involves the marginal efficiency of capital and the marginal propensity to consume. And from this formulation one can infer the usual contrast between Keynes and the classics — that in a Keynesian model the money supply ($\overline{M}$) determines the interest rate, while in a classical model it determines the price level.

Changes in the supply of and demand for money

An increase in the money supply implies a decrease in the interest rate, which produces an increase in income and in turn increases transactions and precautionary demands for money. What happens to velocity?

$$V = \frac{Y}{M_1 + M_2} = \frac{Y}{kY + M_2}$$

Thus the change in velocity when income increases depends on the change in the speculative demand, which is given by the elasticity of the demand for M_2, as function of the interest rate. Depending on this elasticity, an increase in the supply of money can therefore either raise or reduce the velocity of circulation.

Analysis of an increase in the demand for money shows this compression of the Keynesian model at its weakest. Such an increase can occur for three reasons: (i) an increase in transactions demand, (ii) an increase in speculative demand (due to a change in the dispersion of expectations), or (iii) an increase in Y at a given i (due to a rise in the marginal efficiency of capital or an increase in the propensity to consume). An increase in the demand for money causes an increase in the interest rate, but we cannot tell much more from there. For in (i) and (ii) the increase in i causes a downturn in income while in (iii) the increase in the interest rate is caused by an increase in income. Thus this particular formulation is not much help in analysing a change in the demand for money.

Thus far, Keynesian monetary theory has been formulated to treat the demand and supply of money as determining the rate of interest rather than the level of prices. Transactions demand for cash (a constant proportion, k, of the level of money income) and speculative demand are collapsed into one demand schedule and can be depicted graphically as follows:

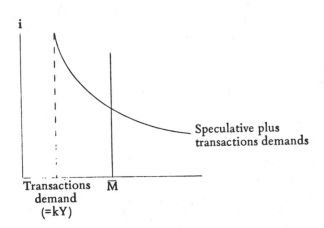

The supply of money ($\overline{M}$) is given exogenously, and, in combination with the demand for money, determines the rate of interest. The implication of this analysis is that any change in the money stock has a direct and permanent influence on the rate of interest.

The supply of money schedule may exhibit some interest elasticity, reflecting a desire by the banking system to economise available cash as the profitability (i.e. a rise in the rate of interest) of lending money increases.

Further, we note that the price level is influenced only indirectly through the product and labour markets. Rising prices with an increase in the level of output and a fall in the rate of interest reflect diminishing marginal productivity of labour.

The classical economists assumed the demand for money to be a constant proportion of money income as well as sensitive to the rate of interest, so the chief result of Keynesian monetary analysis (that a change in the money supply has a direct and permanent effect on the rate of interest) does not require liquidity preference assumptions. Nor are these assumptions necessary for under-employment analysis except when the liquidity preference function 'pegs' the rate of interest at a level that is too high to be consistent with full employment.

The positive contributions of Keynesian monetary theory were (i) to introduce the demand for money as a demand for a particular asset through the influence of expectations; (ii) to analyse the interest rate mechanics of income determination as an alternative to the cash balance, direct expenditure mechanism (later developments along Keynesian lines have, however, re-introduced this mechanism); and (iii) to pose the possibility of a variable velocity factor, i.e. a change in the rate of interest induces more or less demand for cash and this change may be more or less than proportional to the induced charge in income. Subsequently, there have been two interpretations of the last point: the Radcliffe Report's interpretation of extreme volatility of money demand and hence an erratic velocity of circulation; and the interpretation that money demand is determined by stable relationships so that the velocity factor can be satisfactorily explained.

The Short-Run Nature of Keynesian Theory

Several considerations indicate a short-run perspective in Keynesian theory. Money demand is seen to be a function of given expectations of future interest rates which must in the nature of things be reformulated in the light of new evidence. The marginal efficiency of capital schedule is a function of business expectations regarding the profitability of investment, which, in the long run, are likely to be highly volatile. Wages are assumed rigid whereas in the long-run one would want to study the speed of adjustment of money wages. Any savings-investment influences on the stock of the economy's assets is ignored, but a long run perspective would take account of the growth of the physical stock of assets and money wealth through accumulated savings and consider their effect on current saving and consumption.

Are the Keynesian assumptions of any use from a contemporary viewpoint? Ruling out expectations on future movements of the price level may have been appropriate in the late 1930's when, if anything, one would have expected a slow decline in the level of prices. It would seem, however, that a proper explanation of the contemporary short-run situation necessitates introducing expectations of future price level movements. A recent example is the neglect of expectations in analysis of the British devaluation which led to excessive optimism regarding its impact.

Keynesian theory and the price level

Prices can be incorporated in an exposition of the Keynesian model by compressing the determinants of general equilibrium in the markets for goods and assets into a demand curve for output as a function of the level of prices. This demand curve is not the typical microeconomic function whose form depends largely on the presence of goods substitution but rather one deriving its essence from monetary factors.

Consider the following model:

$C = C(X,i)$ consumption function
$I = I(i,X)$ investment function
$L = L(i,X)$ demand for money

$m = \dfrac{M}{P}$ relation of real money stock to nominal stock and the price level.

Notice that the income variable, X, used here is physical output and not the money value of output expressed in terms of wage units as in Chapter 2. Similarly consumption and investment are measured in real terms. Equilibrium conditions of this model are

$L = m$
$X = C + I$, or $X - C = S = I$.

If we combine these equations following the Hicks-Hansen IS-LM analysis we derive an LM function which shifts position as a result of changes in P. (The IS curve is defined in real terms and so does not shift with changes in P.) By varying P we can trace a relationship between the price level and all other functions, and specifically output. In general the demand function $X = X(P)$ is downward sloping.

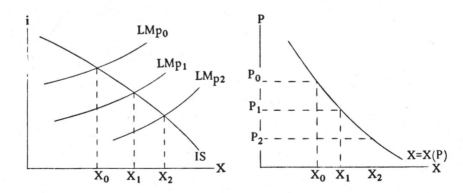

Let us now illustrate the extreme Keynesian and classical systems through the shape of this curve. If there is strict proportionality between the demand for money and the money value of income, the LM curve becomes vertical. We get a rectangular hyperbola relating P to X. Where the LM curve is assumed horizontal (liquidity trap) in the range of the intersection of IS and LM curves, we produce a vertical $X = X(P)$ curve.

To examine the role of the assumption of rigid money wages let us construct a relation between P and X that involves the production and labour (supply) side of the system (with a given production function):

$$X = F(N) \text{ or } N = N(X) \quad \text{production function}$$
$$\text{where N is employment}$$
$$W = P[F'(N)] \quad \text{marginal productivity conditions}$$
$$\text{where W is the money wage}$$
$$P = W/F'(N)$$

Setting $W = W_1$ we have the price level as a function of output from the last equation. In general, P will rise as X increases. The position of this curve (S_{W1}) is determined by the money wage rate. A reduction in the level of the money wage shifts the curve down: $(W_0 < W_1)$:

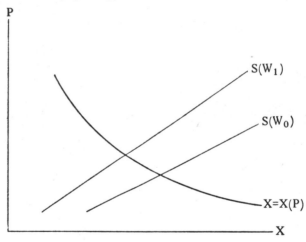

Only in the strict Keynesian case (liquidity trap where $Y = Y(P)$ is vertical) do we have a situation where full employment cannot be achieved by lowering the money wage. We can thus reconstruct Keynesian theory making either the price level or the interest rate a function of demand for and supply of output.

Summary and Conclusion on Keynesian Monetary Theory

The *General Theory* was a step forward in monetary theory. The classical construction was a relation between money and the level of money income established on the basis of a stock (money) yielding a flow of services. The two concepts were difficult to handle simultaneously so Keynes simplified the analysis by making the demand for money the demand for an asset, and hence a problem of capital theory. The argument, however, contained several inconsistencies. The transactions demand for money was treated rather hastily and traditionally formulated with the result that only a part of money demand was a demand for assets. Precautionary demand — the essence of the assets demand — was lumped together with transactions demand. Further, the speculative demand was made to depend on very short-run expectations about interest rates. This last fault was the source of Hicks' criticism that Keynesian interest theory was a bootstrap one, not explaining why the interest rate was what it was.

The narrowing of choice to only two assets made it necessary to treat securities and real assets as essentially the same. Combined with the exclusion of expectations of future prices (from all but the marginal efficiency of capital schedule) this oversimplification precluded the consideration of real versus money rates of return. The two-way classification tends to exaggerate the elasticity of the demand for money because a large part of speculative activity may take place between securities of long and short maturities rather than between money and securities.

Developments since the war have incorporated the Keynesian innovations into frameworks involving more assets. Both quantity theorists and Keynesians have cast the role of money in terms of capital. But there are two major differences. First, quantity theorists tend to give expectations of future prices a central position in their analysis. Keynesians tend to give expectations a residual place and formulate asset choices in terms of a portfolio-balance that maximises the present value of expected returns. Second, quantity theorists treat assets as wealth in the broader context of real and money wealth, non-human and human capital.

CHAPTER 9

INTEGRATION OF TRANSACTIONS DEMAND FOR CASH AND PORTFOLIO THEORY APPROACHES TO THE DEMAND FOR MONEY

Completion of the Keynesian revolution requires an integrated theory of asset demand. Given rational portfolio management (e.g. by institutional investors) the transactions demand may come to be the most important element. Liquidity preference in a market with many assets essentially involves a choice amongst assets other than money. Rational individuals and firms will then minimise the cost of holding the cash they need for transactions and maximise the expected return on assets. This transactions theory involves a motive for holding money that does not attach a utility yield to cash balances. It assumes that utility is generated by consumption of goods and services that the cash balance purchases.

Recently the transactions demand for cash has been developed by Baumol and Tobin following an early discussion by Edgeworth in the late nineteenth century. Cash holdings are regarded as posing a problem in inventory theory. Cash is held to meet unexpected demands without delay, but this imposes a cost in terms of foregone earnings from holding non-return-yielding assets. The problem is to balance the losses against the gains optimally. The uncertainty of future demands, the raison d'être of inventories, is balanced by the cost of holding inventories. Hence we derive the optimum number of times one should convert cash into and out of return-yielding assets in a given period.

We begin by considering a model with no assets other than cash and where there is only one household and one firm. The household is assumed to sell labour services to the firm and to use its income to purchase the firm's product. There are no profits made by the firm — all returns are to labour. Cash payments are made to the household at fixed intervals while sales are made at various times. The fim accumulates cash so that it can pay the household regularly. Hence we have two payments mechanisms — one regular and the other irregular.

Where wage receipts are w per week and the household spends regularly, the household begins each week with w and ends each week with no cash. The average cash holding is therefore (approximately) ½w. As the firm begins each period with zero cash and ends with w, its average holding is also approximately ½w. Therefore total cash holdings are w. (If the household spent nearer either end of the payments period their average cash holdings would differ from ½w as would the firm's. Nevertheless, total cash holdings always equal w.)

With goods produced worth w and cash held equal to w, the income velocity of money is one. Workers spend w and the firm pays out w and the transactions velocity is therefore two.

We have so far been discussing an income circulation period of one week. If we consider a one year period, then transactions velocity is 104 and income velocity is 52. This consideration raises the problem of relating a natural period of velocity to one consistent with empirical necessities (e.g. data are normally available by calendar year).

The world is a far more complex and disaggregated structure than this. The increase in disaggregation especially will affect the transactions velocity: with some firms supplying inputs to other firms, there will be exchanges of money among them as well.

Although modern theory has concentrated on income velocity, transactions velocity may be a more useful concept for analysis.

Transactions Demand for money as a problem of inventory management

Basic Assumptions

(a) Apart from cash assume a single fixed interest yielding asset e.g. time deposits.

(b) the individual receives income at regular intervals and spends in a steady flow; correspondingly the producer receives payments in a steady flow and has to make payment at regular intervals. (The consumer analysis is not important empirically because a consumer does not typically buy and sell assets between income receipts.)

Analysis Assuming income Received in Asset Form

(i) *Key to symbols used*

T = total income in asset form

b = fixed charge per withdrawal from asset holding

k/2 = charge for withdrawal per unit of cash withdrawn

C = size of cash withdrawal

i = interest paid on assets per income period (not a calendar time period)

xi = interest paid for a proportion of this period where x is a fraction of the time period

n = number of withdrawals

c = *average* cash holding = $\dfrac{C}{2}$

y = *net* yield on assets held.

t = *average* transactions balance = $\dfrac{T}{2}$

d = *average* holding of non cash assets = $\dfrac{T-C}{2}$

(ii) *Analysis*

The individual is faced with the choice of holding a large cash balance and avoiding withdrawal charges but losing interest payments, or holding assets earning interest and incurring costs through frequent withdrawals i.e. a problem of maximizing.

(iii) *Proof that withdrawals will be equal*

Let the individual withdraw a proportion x of his assets which will pay his expenditure for a proportion x of the period

Interest on residual $= [(1 - x)T] ix = (ix - ix^2)T$, which is maximised when $x = \frac{1}{2}$ i.e. equal withdrawals equally spaced.

This argument is general for it applies for a period of expenditure financed by any two successive withdrawals whatever their number.

(iv) *Optimum cash holding*

From (iii) above the individual's average transactions balance is

$t = \frac{1}{2}T$

and his average cash balance is

$c = \frac{1}{2}C.$

Therefore:

$d = t - c$

$n = \dfrac{t}{c} = \dfrac{T}{C}$

Cost of providing cash balance $= bn + kt = b\dfrac{t}{c} + kt$

Earnings received $= id = i(t - c)$

Therefore: $y = (i - k)t - ic - b\dfrac{t}{c}$

y is maximised if $\dfrac{dy}{dc} = 0$ and $\dfrac{d^2y}{dc^2} < 0$

$$\frac{dy}{dc} = \frac{bt}{c^2} - i = 0, \quad \frac{d^2y}{dc^2} = -\frac{2bt}{c^3} < 0 \text{ since } b > 0,\ c > 0,\ t > 0.$$

Therefore $c = \sqrt{\dfrac{b}{it}}$

Frequently it is the ratio $\dfrac{c}{t}$ (i.e. relationship between cash and income) that is of interest.

$\dfrac{c}{t} = \sqrt{\dfrac{bt}{i}}$ (Note if $b > it$, then $c > t$ which is economic nonsense).

Therefore it follows that if $b > it$, the individual will withdraw all cash on receipt of T.

These formulas give predictions about the behaviour of the optimum cash balance as a function of the individual's transactions balance and the rate of interest. Using E to denote elasticities

$$E_{ci} = -\tfrac{1}{2} \qquad\qquad E_{ct} = \tfrac{1}{2}$$

$$E_{\frac{c}{t}i} = -\tfrac{1}{2} \qquad\qquad E_{\frac{c}{t}t} = -\tfrac{1}{2}$$

($\frac{c}{t}$ is not the Cambridge k because the latter is defined for a calendar period e.g. one year).

$$k = \frac{C}{2NT} = \sqrt{\frac{b}{2rY}}$$ where Y = NT is income and r = Ni the interest rate for the

calendar period: i.e. the length of the income period does not determine the size of k assuming that the individual has the choice of holding assets. The regularity and frequency of payments will however show up in the size of the transaction assets.

Analysis assuming individual paid in Cash

(i) *Key to symbols used*

B = fixed overhead cost per acquisition

$\frac{K}{2}$ = variable cost, directly proportional to size of asset

a = proportion of transactions money to invest in assets at beginning of period.

(ii) *Analysis*
The problem is to choose a to maximise the net yield which has two parts.

(iii) Net yield on non cash assets during the first part of the period when expenditure is financed from withheld cash. Amount invested is a2t and this remains invested for (1 − a) of period. Hence the interest earned = (1 − a)i (2at). The cost of acquiring this is = B + Kat so that the net yield for the first period = 2a(1 − a)it − B − Kat.

(iv) The net yield on the average transactions balance for the remainder of the period is found from:

$c = \sqrt{\frac{bt}{i}}$. Average transactions balance = at and interest = ai.

Therefore the net yield is = a(ai − k)t − 2a$\sqrt{ibt}$.

(v) The total net yield for the whole period is then:

$$y = 2ait − a^2it − 2a\sqrt{ibt} − a(K + k)t − B$$

For a maximum $\frac{dy}{da}$ = 2it − 2ait − 2$\sqrt{ibt}$ − (K + k)t = 0

i.e. when $(1 − a)t = \sqrt{\frac{bt}{i}} + \frac{\frac{1}{2}(K + k)t}{i} = c + \frac{\frac{1}{2}(K + k)t}{i}$. Hence

$$a = 1 − \frac{\frac{1}{2}(K + k)}{i} − \frac{c}{t}$$

Alternative approach
Apart from fixed overhead charges, ½(K + k) must be paid per unit of cash

invested and subsequently withdrawn. This must be at least covered by the interest earned. Therefore the amount must be invested for a period $\frac{(K+k)}{2i}$ and the cash withheld must be sufficient to finance expenditure of $\frac{(k+K)}{2i}T$.

If this amount is held then cash would have to be withdrawn at the end of the period incurring cost b (which could have been avoided by not investing). Therefore the cash withheld $= \frac{(K+k)}{2i}T+C$ so that the average balance for initial period $= \frac{K+k}{2i} t+c = (1-a)t$. Hence the average cash balance held over a period is a weighted average of the above and the amount held in the second period. The average is weighted by $(1-a)$ and a. The optimum average cash balance is

$$(1-a)^2 t + ac = (1-a)\left(c + \frac{K+k}{2i}t\right) + ac$$

$$= c + \frac{K+k}{2i}t\left(\frac{c}{t} + \frac{K+k}{2i}\right)$$

$$= \sqrt{\frac{bt}{i}}\left(1 + \frac{K+k}{2i}\right) + \left(\frac{K+k}{2i}\right)^2 t$$

Comments

(a) No simple elasticities.
(b) Optimum cash balance varies inversely with i but directly with the average transactions balance.
(c) C is now a function of the period for which expenditure is financed by the initial receipt. This is because the first part of the period, when expenditures are financed from cash received, is independent of the length of the total period; it is a function of costs and i. The remainder of the payment period's length, however, determines the importance of the first period. The shorter is the payments period then the larger is the proportion taken up with zero depositing and withdrawing. If the payment period is frequent enough then no investment takes place.
(d) The major empirical application is therefore to firms who in this model receive a steady inflow of receipts but make discontinuous payments.
(e) The inventory approach makes the transactions demand for money a result of maximising rational behaviour instead of a relationship determined by habit and the institutional setting.
(f) The theory also provides a motive for holding cash without assuming utility from holding cash itself. For cash is a means of minimising costs.

Diagrammatic Representation of First Part

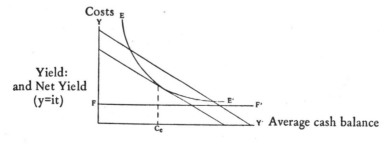

YY' represents gross yield earned on different sizes of average cash holding; at Y' no yield because entire transactions balance is held in cash; at Y yield = it.

FF' represents cost incurred per unit of withdrawal which will be constant and equal to kt.

EE' (a rectangular hyperbola) represents total costs of withdrawal; it consists of the constant kt plus a variable part $\frac{bt}{c}$ which depends on the average size of cash balance held and hence on the number of withdrawals: $\frac{bt}{c}$ = vertical distance between EE' and FF'.

The net yield is the vertical distance between EE' and YY'. This is at a maximum when the slopes of EE' and YY' are equal. An increase in i will increase the slope of YY' and reduce the optimum cash holding. An increase in b will mean that the slope of EE' will equal that of YY' at a larger average cash holding. Similarly for t.

The theory does not appear to be supported by empirical evidence. But this may be because it refers to average cash holdings whereas data refer to cash held at a point of time — an accounting measure (e.g. if a firm's optimum cash holding is one day's cash, then its cash balance as measured at the end of the day would be zero. Further as the period for which cash is held is reduced cash holdings get smaller as transactions increase.)

CHAPTER 10

LIQUIDITY PREFERENCE AND RISK AVERSION

In Keynes's hands liquidity preference largely involved the speculative demand, with some elements of precautionary demand. He considered only two assets, money and bonds, whereas in reality portfolios are diversified. The explanation below follows Tobin's classic article and continues the assumption of price stability.

Recall that Keynes's analysis of liquidity preference led to the derivation of an individual's r_c, a critical rate of interest defined in terms of the expected rate (r_e. See Chapter 8).

$$r_c = \frac{r_e}{1 + r_e}$$

If the actual current $r > r_c$, all investment is in bonds. If the actual current $r < r_c$, all speculative funds are held in cash. An aggregate demand for cash can then be derived by assuming a market of many individual with different r_e's.

A major criticism of this analysis is that it is a bootstrap theory; the interest rate is what it is because it is expected to be something else. What it is expected to be comes from somewhere else which is not explained by the theory. A second criticism is that the argument is only valid for the short-run. Otherwise the monetary authority could keep the interest rate wherever it wished simply by keeping it there, assuming that people's expectations are modified to expect the rate to remain constant. A better theory is required to develop a demand for money based on general uncertainty (precaution) rather than specific expectations (speculation). Tobin's analysis takes our previous discussion of the insurance involved in different interest rate levels even further.

Tobin's approach assumes that an individual's preference system is defined in terms of two aspects of a portfolio — its expected yield and its risk. Holding bonds involves risk, which can be measured by the standard deviation (S) of the expected capital value. This is assumed to be independent of the interest rate. Money, the other portfolio alternative, is assumed to be riskless. The individual then chooses his portfolio mix according to his preference system to give him a combination of risk and expected return.

Let E_r be the expected return (i.e. interest return plus capital gain or loss) and S_r the risk of this return. If S_g is the risk per bond then S_r equals S_g when the whole portfolio is in bonds. Now if the individual holds only cash, he has both an expected return and risk of zero. As more of his holdings are put in bonds, his expected return and his risk increase. At the opposite extreme his total risk is the same as the risk on bonds, and his expected return depends on his budget constraint for buying bonds, OC.

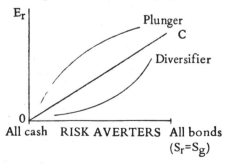

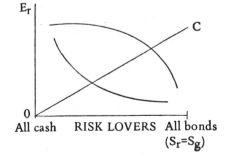

To derive a portfolio mix, we must introduce the individual's preference system. Tobin defines a risk lover as one who gives up income to increase risk (i.e. have a small chance of large capital gains). His indifference curves slope down and he always holds only bonds. A risk averter will only assume more risk for a larger expected return. His indifference curves slope up. A risk averter may be a plunger or a diversifier. A plunger requires decreasing compensation per unit of risk (indifference curves linear or convex upward sloping) and will hold either all cash or all bonds depending on his indifference curves and the budget constraint. There will be a critical interest rate at which he will switch from one to the other. A diversifier requires increasing compensation per unit of risk (indifference curves concave upward). Though he may also have a corner solution only a diversifier will hold a portfolio mix.

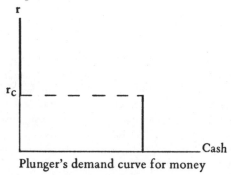

Plunger's demand curve for money

With diversifiers, a smooth aggregate demand for money can be derived. But there is both an income effect and a substitution effect. If the interest rate increases, then the price of bonds decreases, which by the substitution effect implies a reduction of cash holdings. But a higher rate also implies more income for the same risk, so that he may increase his holdings of cash via the income effect. Thus to derive the usual demand for money curve, we have to assume that the substitution effect dominates the income effect.

This analysis rests on the assumption that the standard deviation and the expected return are the only aspects of the portfolio which the individual considers in choosing his mix. In general we cannot assume this, for an individual attempting to maximise utility will take account of aspects other than the standard deviation.

Two alternative assumptions can be made to rescue the analysis. Either one can assume any of a variety of standard distributions of possible outcomes from holding bonds (e.g. a normal distribution), in which cases there is an adequate measure of risk (i.e. the probability distribution is fully specified in terms of its mean and standard deviation), or the individual's utility function can be assumed to involve only S and the expected return of the portfolio. A quadratic utility function has this property: $U(R) = aR + bR^2$ A risk lover has $0 < b < 1$ and a risk averter has $-1 < b < 0$ (which also implies limits to the variation of R, since $MU(R)$ becomes negative). If the individual acts to maximise his expected utility, we derive that $E[U(R)] = aE_r + b(E_r^2 + S_r^2)$ so that only the mean and standard error enter into his choices. However, in general, there is no reason to believe that either of the possible assumptions is valid.

The most important part of Tobin's contribution was to show that if we have a large number of different assets in which the individual can invest, then they can be reduced to one bundle which acts as the bonds did in this analysis, i.e. we can derive a similar budget line of the same shape subject to which the individual maximises his preferences.

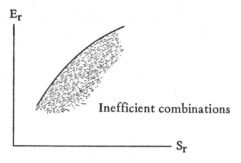

Consider a batch of individual securities, each with some E_r and S_r, measured per unit of investment. Some will be inefficient, offering smaller yield for the same risk. Then we can draw a frontier for the best combinations of risk and yield. But now assume that the risks of different assets may be interdependent (positively or negatively) and the individual can hold mixtures of different assets. Taking one asset pair, if the probable outcomes of holding these assets are perfectly correlated, then a gain on one implies a gain on the other, and a mixture of the two simply gives us a linear combination of the E_r and S_r of the two. But if their outcomes are not perfectly correlated, then we can always increase E_r for a given S_r by taking a mixture of the two, the degree of bowing in the curve increasing the less is the correlation between them.

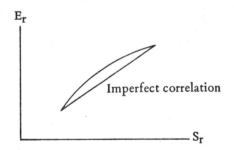

This relation is derived from the following formulae:

$$E_{rc} = aE_{ra} + (1 - a) E_{rb}$$

$$S_{rc} = \sqrt{a^2 S_{ra}^2 + (1 - a)^2 S_{rb}^2 + 2r_{ab}a(1 - a) S_{ra}.S_{rb}}$$

If $r_{ab} = 1$, we get the straight line. If $r_{ab} < 1$, the bowing occurs. Thus we derive a new frontier in which a mixture of risky assets is preferable to holding any single asset.

Now introduce a riskless asset, which may or may not (as in the case of money) have a return. Then we can always find a combination of both a bundle of risk assets and the riskless asset which gives us a better frontier than the one with only the risky assets.

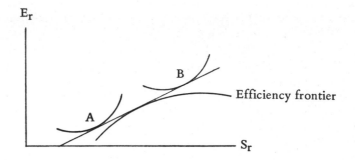

The individual can reach A by mixing some of the safe asset and some of the bundle. B is reached by borrowing in the form of the safe asset and holding more than his net wealth in the form of the bundle. The important point is that no matter how many risky assets there are, as long as there is this safe asset we can always represent the individual's budget constraint as a straight line, which then makes the above analysis more powerful and not restricted to a choice of only a bond or money.

Usually money is assumed to be this safe asset, and without this safe asset the simplification collapses. Should price level changes make money unsafe, the argument can be rescued by assuming that all assets are fixed in money terms. But then an analysis must be added to explain the division of the portfolio between such assets and those fixed in real terms, such as equities and real goods.

Market Equilibrium

How does the assumption of a number of different assets affect market equilibrium? Clearly the prices of assets must be such that all of them are held. That is, on a market frontier curve the bundle will really represent several bundles of different assets, all bundles being equally efficient and such that all of the various assets are held.

The question for asset theory then is to determine the prices and yields on assets, including money and allowing for price level variations. The interesting problems turn out not to be involved with the demand for money, but with prices and returns of other assets. In particular, we are concerned with the effect of monetary policy (here open market policy) on the yields of different assets (Chapter 11 below). The major issue which arises is whether the central bank can differentiate its effects on the economy by dealing in different assets.

Assets have different characteristics, like commodities. Those characteristics are liquidity, maturity, risks, etc. Demands are then for particular characteristics, represented by different assets. Thus the prices and yields of these securities will depend on the demand and supply of these specific, distinguishable assets.

A theory can then be evolved for the relation between the asset market and the economy. Simply, the terms on which people will hold existing assets influence the additions to assets of various kinds, giving the link with the theory of income and employment.

There are two ways of explaining the link between the asset market (including money) and the real economy.

1. The main influence of money is on the shortest rate of interest. This

then penetrates through the market to the rate of return on real investment, and it is at that margin that the policy of the monetary authorities takes hold.

2. The fundamental relation is between money and all other assets taken together so that the quantity of money is the important variable.

One can then construct differing theories of how the interest rate moves the real economy — Hawtrey suggested it was by the effects of short rates on inventories held by traders while Keynes emphasised the influence of the long rate on fixed capital investment. (This controversy has been reviewed recently by Hicks.)

So the basic approach here is to regard assets as commodities. It implies that the central bank can change prices and yields on different assets by changing the relative quantities. A part of the argument is that people are prepared to pay a premium for the liquidity characteristic, so that short-rate should be less than long-rate.

The trouble is that this 'characteristics' approach does not hold up well empirically. Usually there is an inverse relation between the shortest interest rate and the quantity of money relative to other assets, but medium-term securities give results differing from the theory. The contending school explains this by saying that it is incorrect to formulate differences between assets in terms of these characteristics; instead, the essential differences between assets involve time and risk.

CHAPTER 11

THE TERM STRUCTURE OF INTEREST RATES*

In dealing with the problem of uncertainty with respect to future interest rates and its implications, we can distinguish between the Keynesian and the classical approaches. The classical theory treats assets of different maturities as embodying different-length sequences of successive short-period loans; the Keynesian theory treats assets of different maturities in the same way as the theory of value treats different commodities. In this approach, each of a wide range of securities is assumed to have a particular set of more or less desirable characteristics. The relative supplies of these various assets, in conjunction with the preferences of potential holders and their wealth, which acts as a sort of budget constraint, determines the relative prices of the assets and therefore the yields on them.

Keynesian Theory: The Hicksian and Preferred Market Habitat Hypotheses

There are two variants of the Keynesian analysis, the first associated with Sir John Hicks and the Cambridge (England) school of Keynesians, the second being associated with Franco Modigliani of M.I.T. (the other Cambridge) and known as the 'preferred market habitat' theory. The Hicksian variant distinguishes assets according to their degree of liquidity and regards Keynesian theory as predicting the normal existence of a premium on short-term (liquid) over long-term (illiquid) securities. In brief, the short rate will be equal to the long rate minus a risk premium. This formulation is derived largely from the empirical experience of the 1930's when short rates were consistently and significantly below the long rates; it was assumed that this was the natural relation between short and long rates of return. But this situation did not necessarily imply the existence of liquidity preference — a willingness to pay a premium for liquid assets. It can be explained by classical theory: i.e., the market expected short rates to rise in the course of time. Furthermore, empirical evidence on the relation between short and long rates for other periods does not always show an excess of the long rate over the short. However, the Keynesian theory on this interpretation implies the existence of a liquidity premium on short-term securities.

The 'preferred market habitat' approach developed in the postwar II period generalises the Hicksian approach by assuming investor preferences for assets of various types that are not strictly related to the maturity of the assets. It assumes that holders of assets have preferences for particular maturities, but that the preferred assets are not necessarily those with the shortest maturities: investors may for example be prepared to pay a premium for loans with a five-year maturity, over loans with a four-year or a six-year maturity. This hypothesis implies the same general proposition as the other, that the yields on assets of various maturities, given investor preferences, will be a function of the relative quantities of the assets available to hold.

A problem with the Hicksian point of view is that it identifies the average investor with a particular type of investor, namely a commercial bank, whose

---

* A revised version (July 14, 1971) of notes of lectures delivered at the L.S.E. in the session of 1969-70.

business consists of issuing short-term liabilities (deposits) and investing the proceeds in longer-term assets (loans and securities), so that it must show a preference for shorter over longer assets. This form of investment behaviour may be contrasted with that of an insurance company, whose position is one of incurring long-term debt (on an actuarial basis) and being able to invest it in relatively shorter-term assets. This point has been made by Joan Robinson, who distinguishes between two kinds of risks involved in holding a portfolio of securities: a capital risk (the risk of changes in the capital value of the portfolio) and an income risk (the risk of a change in the flow of income accruing to the holder of the portfolio). Different investors will be worried about different types of risk: for example "widows and orphans" will be worried about the income risk and want their portfolios to be as long as possible.

The preferred market habitat theory does not imply such a one-sided view of the mentality of the typical investor: the investor is assumed to have a preferred 'position' in the market that matches his needs. But if such preferences led to the emergence in market interest rates of significant liquidity premia, it would be profitable for arbitrageurs to buy and sell securities of different maturities, so that their activities would offset the influence of the preferences for particular market habitats of the average investors. This criticism also applies to the Hicksian approach. To get a theory which permits rates of interest to vary with changes in the quantities of particular assets one must assume either that some kind of market imperfection prevents arbitrage from performing this function, or that there are substantial transactions costs which make arbitrage unprofitable even though substantial discrepancies exist among the yields on assets of different maturities. Such rationalizations, however, have little substance in view of the very low transactions costs on large dealings that prevail in contemporary securities markets. There are, however, institutional and legal restrictions on the types of assets that particular institutions may hold; and if it is assumed that a small number of large institutions subject to such constraints dominate the market, it is possible to arrive at a plausible justification of the theory that the yields on assets of different maturities are determined by the relative quantities of such assets available.

Empirical work along these lines has generated puzzling and to some extent inconsistent results. The implication that the yield on short-term securities will be inversely related to the quantity of them available has been confirmed by the evidence. On the other hand, the relation between yields and quantities of medium and long-term securities implied by the hypothesis has been contradicted by a variety of empirical evidence. Part of the explanation may be the fact that the data used in the testing are data on government debt only, though the theory ought to include securities of different maturities supplied by the private sector as well. For example, government public debt management operations designed to lengthen the average maturity of the public debt may be largely offset by a private sector switch to short-term financing, so that the net change in the relative quantities of short and long term debt available to the public is negligible.

Classical Theory: The Expectations Approach

The classical theory of the term structure of interest rates is concerned with "pure" interest rates, and therefore with the structure of rates on government debt, since private debt is assumed to involve an element of investor risk. The starting point of the analysis is that a loan for a given maturity can be decomposed into a succession of short-period loans over successive intervals of time from the start of the loan until its maturity date, to which the investor commits himself by purchasing the long-period loan. The hypothesis of the 'expectations theory' of term structure is that the investor will only commit himself to such a series of short-period loans if he expects the yield on each short-period loan to be at least as good as the short-period yield he expects to prevail in the market in each successive period as it arrives. Otherwise, it would pay him not to make that particular short-period loan – which he can do either by buying a security of maturity less than the period in which he expects the market yield to be greater than the yield implicit in the security he could have bought, so that he will have cash to invest for the higher yield he expects in that period, or by combining a sale of the longer-term with a purchase of the shorter-term security, so that he is borrowing instead of lending at the rate he expects to be below the market rate when the future period arrives. Competition in the market should result in the rates for future short-period loans implicit in the structure of rates on loans of different maturities being just equal to the market's expectation of those future rates: and since, in these circumstances, there is no difference in expected yield between an explicitly one-period loan starting from now and a one-period loan starting from now held implicitly in the form of a two-period loan starting from now, there should be no liquidity premium on one-period over two-period securities.

According to this approach, it should be noted, if monetary or debt-management policy changes the relative quantities of safe assets of different maturities available on the market, this should have no influence on the yields of the assets in question unless it changes the market's expectations about future interest rates. Of course one can argue that, since any market position is an average of market views, or more accurately the view of the relevant marginal individual in the market, a change in the relative quantities of assets may shift the identity of the marginal individual and therefore the marginal expectation. But the important point is that a lengthening or shortening of the public debt does not change the quantity of short loans outstanding; one-year debt, two-year debt, and twenty-year debt all involve the same amount of one-year debt implicitly; a switch from one-year debt to two-year debt increases the amount of one-year debt starting one year from now, and a switch from one-year debt to twenty-year debt increases the amount of one-year debt starting two, three, and so forth up to nineteen, years from now. Hence, if there is an effect of such operations on the structure of interest rates, it should work through the rates of interest on future one-year debts implicit in the structure of interest rates on debts of varying maturities.

The expectations theory (the classical theory) thus offers different implications from the liquidity preference theory, and so provides an opportunity for empirical testing.

Formalization of Expectations and Liquidity Preference Hypotheses

For simplicity we assume (a) that all securities mature in an integral number of time periods, and (b) that whatever their maturity all securities pay off the capital sum invested with compound interest at the date of maturity. Let

$_0R_1, _0R_2, _0R_3$ etc. represent the actual interest rates prevailing in the market at time-period zero for securities of one, two, three etc. periods to maturity. That is, if I invest a unit of money in a one-period security, I get back $(1 + _0R_1)$ at the end of one period; if I invest a unit of money in a two-period security, I get back $(1 + _0R_2)^2$ at the end of two periods; if I invest a unit of money in a three-period security I get back $(1 + _0R_3)^3$ at the end of three periods. Let $_0r_1$, $_0r_2$, and $_0r_3$ represent the interest rates expected at time-point zero on one-period loans starting immediately, after one period, and after two periods. Clearly, the actual and the expected interest rates starting immediately must be equal.

As a matter of arithmetic only, the set of actual rates $_0R_1$, $_0R_2$, $_0R_3$ etc. imply a set of rates (forward rates) on one-period loans starting at the beginning of periods 2, 3, etc. (times 1, 2, etc.). By buying a two-year security, I am committing myself to a sequence of two one-period loans, one starting at time zero and one at time one. Let the implied forward rates be represented by $_0i_2$, $_0i_3$, etc. They are determined by the relationships:

$$(1 + _0R_2)^2 = (1 + _0R_1)(1 + _0i_2)$$

$$(1 + _0R_3)^3 = (1 + _0R_1)(1 + _0i_2)(1 + _0i_3)$$

$$= (1 + _0R_2)^2(1 + _0i_3)$$

That is, $\qquad _0i_2 = \dfrac{(1 + _0R_2)^2}{(1 + _0R_1)} - 1.$

$$_0i_3 = \dfrac{(1 + _0R_3)^3}{(1 + _0R_2)^2} - 1.$$

Note that if

$_0R_1 = _0R_2 = _0R_3$, then $_0i_1 = _0i_3 = _0R_1$

$_0R_2 > _0R_1$, then $_0i_2 > _0R_2 > _0R_1$, and vice versa.

$_0R_3 > _0R_2 > _0R_1$, $_0i_3$ may be greater or less than $_0i_2$ because

$$_0i_3 = _0i_2 + \frac{(1+_0R_1)(1+_0R_3)^3 - (1+_0R_2)^2}{(1+_0R_2)^2\,(1+_0R_1)}.$$

The expectations theory maintains that rational individuals will choose among securities of different maturities on the basis of their expectations of future rates of interest on one-period loans. If $_0i_2$ is less than $_0r_2$, they will invest for one period and plan to reinvest in a one-period loan, when the next period begins, rather than invest for two periods now at the rate $_0R_2$; and conversely. Similarly, if $_0i_3$ is less than $_0r_3$, they will invest in either one-period or two-period securities (according to the reasoning just described) rather than invest now in a three-period loan at the rate $_0R_3$; and conversely. The results of the market acting on this basis will be that the implicit forward rates will be adjusted to the expected ones, through adjustment of the rates for one-period, two-period, three-period, etc. loans starting from now, so that $_0i_2 = {}_0r_2$, $_0i_3 = {}_0r_3$, etcetera.

The Keynesian theory of liquidity preference asserts on the contrary that people on the average are willing to pay a premium for liquidity, in the sense of accepting a lower yield on one-period securities than they could obtain by contracting a loan with a longer maturity, i.e. committing themselves to a one-period loan followed by one or more subsequent one-period loans, According to this version of liquidity preference theory, the true yield of a one-period loan starting now is not $_0R_1$ but $_0R_1 + p_0$ where p_0 is the measure of liquidity preference in terms of foregone interest earnings. Hence we have, in contrast to the previous algebra (where the expected and the implicit forward interest rates were hypothesized to be equal):

$$_0r_2 = \frac{(1+{}_0R_2)^2}{1+{}_0R_1+p_0} - 1$$

$$_0r_3 = \frac{(1 + {}_0R_3)^3}{(1+{}_0R_2)^2} - 1$$

where $_0r_2$, which must be less than $_0i_2$, is the 'true' implicit forward rate, which according to the expectations theory gets adjusted to the market's expected forward rate. (Note that liquidity preference is assumed to consist in willingness to pay a premium for one-period securities only; a more complex theory would allow for a premium on two-period over three-period securities, etcetera.)

Note that if the expected yields on future one-period loans were constant over time, we would have $_0R_1 + p_0 = {}_0R_2 = {}_0R_3$ etcetera. That is, we would always have one-period loans starting now (liquid loans) bearing a lower interest rate than longer-period loans, and the actual one-period loans observed as time passed would always bear a lower rate of interest than the rates $_0i_2$, $_0i_3$ etcetera predicted from the past term-structure of interest rates. That is, we would have $_1R_1 < {}_0i_2$, $_1R_2 < {}_0i_3$, and so forth. Hence, on the average over periods when future one-period rates could have been expected equally to rise and to fall, such as the business cycle, we would observe an upward-sloping yield curve (ie. short-period interest rates consistently below long-period interest rates: ie. $_tR_1 < {}_tR_2 < {}_tR_3$ for the average of the starting points t.

Meiselman's Test of The Alternative Theories

One test of the alternative theories has already been suggested — comparison of the average relation between short and long rates. If long rates tend to be consistently above short rates, this would be evidence in favour of the liquidity preference hypothesis. An alternative test, directed at the expectations hypothesis, would be to compare 'holding-period yields' on different securities (i.e. yields on securities of different maturities held over the same short period, allowance being made for capital gains or losses on the longer securities over the period) to determine whether these yields tend to equality as the expectations theory would predict.

These two tests, however, are both weak, because they rest on the assumption that the expectations on which the market acts are correct: and to assert that behaviour is governed by expectations is something quite different from asserting that expectations are accurately formed.

Meiselman's contribution was to drop the assumption that expectations are necessarily correct, and to substitute for it the assumption that if expectations turn out to have been incorrect, they will be revised in a consistent fashion. His work makes use of an error-learning model: incorrect expectations about the immediate one-period rate formed in the past will lead to revisions of expectations about future one-period rates also formed in the past. Specifically, if the actual one-period rate experienced is different from what it was expected to be in the previous period, the market will revise its expectations of future one-period rates in proportion to the degree of error incurred in forecasting the present one-period rate. Note that this procedure does not attempt to explain the term structure itself, and still less the average level of interest rates; instead it explains changes in the term structure over time, by changes in expectations induced by errors in forecasting the level of the short rate.

Let $_t r_n$ represent the expectation formed in period t concerning the interest rate for a one-period loan to be made at a fixed point of time in the future, n. Then $_{t-1} r_n$ is the expectation of the one-period rate at time n formed at time t−1, and $_{t-1} r_t$ is what the market expected this period's one-period loan rate to be in the period before this one. Meiselman's hypothesis is that the one-period rate expected to prevail in period n changes proportionally to the difference between the actual current one-period loan rate and what it was expected to be last period. In symbols,

$$_t r_n - {}_{t-1} r_n = b \,(_t R_t - {}_{t-1} r_t)$$

The equation actually fitted was

$$_t i_n - {}_{t-1} i_n = a + b(_t R_t - {}_{t-1} i_t),$$

where $_t i_n$ is the forward rate implicit in the term structure and the constant term allows for the possibility of liquidity preference. To understand this, suppose there is a liquidity premium (P_O) on current one-year securities, and on these only. Then the above equation for the hypothesis would read

$$_t r_n - {}_{t-1} r_n = b(_t R_t + P_O - {}_{t-1} r_t) = bp_O + b(_t R_t - {}_{t-1} r_t),$$

where $bp_O = a$ is a constant term reflecting liquidity preference.

Meiselman found good correlation coefficients, which he interpreted as evidence in favour of the expectations theory, and constant terms approximately zero, which he interpreted as evidence against the existence of liquidity preference. He was wrong, however, in believing that an estimated constant not significantly different from zero refutes the liquidity preference theory. For suppose that there is a liquidity premium (p_1) on one-period loans starting one period from now, as well as one (p_O) on one-period loans starting now. Remembering that the actual observations are $_0 i_1$, $_0 i_2$, $_1 i_2$, etcetera, and equating $_0 r_2$ and $_0 i_2$, the hypothesis would be

$$_1 i_2 + P_1 - {}_0 i_2 = b(_1 R_1 + P_O - {}_0 i_1 - P_1)$$

But this actual regression is

$$_1 i_2 - {}_0 i_2 = b(_1 R_1 - {}_0 i_1) + bp_O - bp_1 - p_1$$

where the term $bp_O - bp_1 - p_1 = 2$ is the constant term. This term could approximate zero either because $P_O = P_1 = 0$, i.e. the liquidity premia are both zero, or because $P_1 = \frac{b}{1+b}P_0$ by happenstance, and liquidity premia exist but are not caught by the test. This latter possibility is probably best regarded as a curiosum because of the restrictions it imposes on the relative magnitudes of p_0 and p_1.

There are two major problems with the Meiselman type of approach. First, while it does away with the necessity of assuming that expectations are accurate, it still requires a hypothesis about the formation of expectations (the error-learning hypothesis) that may not be correct, or may not be correct in the statistical form given to it. Hence the procedure still involves a test of two hypotheses simultaneously, the expectations theory of interest rate structure and a theory of the formation of expectations. The second problem is that empirical workers, at least so far, are forced to rely on past history when attempting to 'explain' or 'measure' expectations. But expectations may react, rationally or irrationally, to current and expected future conditions on the basis of information and logical processes not readily captured by statistical techniques. For example, it may be argued that expectations of impending war during the 1930's kept long-term interest rates higher than they would otherwise have been. Declines in stock market prices in the past, prompted in the United Kingdom by the death of a monarch or by pronouncements by R. F. Harrod, and in the U.S. by congressional testimony by J. K. Galbraith, suggest that irrelevancy may not be inconsistent with influence and that making sense out of a nonsensical world by assuming simple regularities of behaviour approximates anomaly.

In summary, Meiselman's work constituted an important break-through in empirical work on the term structure of interest rates, but the question of the existence of liquidity preference remains unsettled.

CHAPTER 12

FINANCIAL INTERMEDIARIES

The previous lectures have concentrated on the portfolio approach to the demand for money. In such theories interest centered on bonds of different maturities and hence on the pattern of interest rates.

Recent developments have involved a reformulation of monetary theory to take into account a new problem. This problem is the rapid growth of institutions other than banks which compete by offering assets fixed in money value. The early development of monetary theory in relation to financial intermediaries has largely been the result of work by Gurley and Shaw. (Much of the Radcliffe Report was also based on a belief that traditional monetary theory was mistaken in not emphasising the role of financial intermediaries.) Gurley and Shaw argued that liquidity, defined as the sum of all assets issued by Financial Intermediaries, was the proper monetary variable. Interest also centered on the legal requirements which banks are obliged to meet (e.g. minimum cash ratios) which were seen as restrictions on competition. This issue has been revived in the UK following the Report on Bank Charges issued by the National Board for Prices and Incomes in which it was argued that there should be more competition among banks.

Gurley and Shaw developed a general monetary theory which takes financial intermediaries into account. Although their main concern was with the theories developed by Don Patinkin they also investigated the effects of financial intermediaries on the form and elasticity of the demand for money function.

Very recently the Yale School have published three volumes of work on financial intermediaries (see especially monograph 21 "Financial Markets and Economic Activity" by Tobin and Brainard). They attempt to assert that monetary theory's concern is with assets whose value is fixed in money terms as opposed to real assets; consequently the quantity of money is only part of the problem. This school assumes the price level is fixed and then analyses the financial sector in terms of general equilibrium. This is to be contrasted with the quantity theory approach which makes no such assumption.

The general notion is that there are a number of competing institutions which maximize profits so that marginal earnings are equated with marginal costs; any change in demand or conditions of supply results in a reworking of the system. Money is special only because banks are restricted by legal requirements so that their marginal earnings are greater than their marginal costs. The importance of this last point depends on whether the restrictions are regarded as having operational significance; for example, the legal prohibition in the United States on the payment of interest on current accounts may not be important because it can be avoided by offering various cheap or free services to customers instead.

Assessment of the approach is not easy as a result of the assumed constancy of the general price level. This assumption allows the theory to treat interest determination in the financial sector as one of general equilibrium and then, using these predetermined interest rates, a separate analysis of the real sector is carried out.

Since financial intermediaries pose problems connected with the supply of money as well as the demand the approach is one of general equilibrium.

CHAPTER 13

FRIEDMAN'S RESTATEMENT OF THE QUANTITY THEORY

Friedman starts off by seeing the demand for money as a demand for one kind of wealth. It is therefore determined by the individual's wealth and the yields on other assets as well as the yield from money itself, i.e. the services derived from holding money. Wealth is a budget constraint and can be transformed by means of the identity $W = \dfrac{Y}{r}$ to include income in the analysis (W = wealth, Y = income, r = a general rate of interest determined by the yields on all assets).

This last step introduces, not income as usually measured, but permanent income as used in the consumption theory of Friedman. It does not include transitory elements but should include income derived from holding goods. Friedman attempts to include some of this imputed income, but he excludes that derived from holding money.

The analysis is developed in monetary terms. The individual is seen as facing five different types of asset into which he can place his wealth.

Notation

M_d	=	demand for money
B	=	bonds
r_b	=	rate of interest on bonds
$\dfrac{1}{r_b}\cdot\dfrac{dr_b}{dt}$	=	expected rate of change of r_b
E	=	equities
r_e	=	rate of interest on equities
$\dfrac{1}{r_e}\cdot\dfrac{dr_e}{dt}$	=	expected rate of change of r_e
P	=	price level
$\dfrac{1}{P}\cdot\dfrac{dP}{dt}$	=	expected rate of change of P
H	=	human capital
w	=	ratio of human to non-human capital
g	=	goods

The assets and their yields may be tabulated as follows:

Asset	Yield variable	Comment
Money	P	The services from holding money are derived from the stocks of purchasing power in real terms.

Bonds	$r_b - \dfrac{1}{r_b} \cdot \dfrac{dr_b}{dt}$	—

Equities	$r_e - \dfrac{1}{r_e} \cdot \dfrac{dr_e}{dt} + \dfrac{1}{P} \cdot \dfrac{dP}{dt}$	Equities are not fixed in money value and hence if inflation is expected the yield will be higher than if stable prices are anticipated.
Goods	$\dfrac{1}{P} \cdot \dfrac{dP}{dt}$	(As above)
Human capital	—	Friedman stated that it is not possible to compute the value of H directly. The amount will have been determined by irreversible past decisions. We must therefore allow for the effect of human capital by the use of w, which is assumed constant.

Friedman then states the demand for money function as follows:

$$M_d = f\left[P, r_b - \frac{1}{r_b} \cdot \frac{dr_b}{dt}, r_e + \frac{1}{P} \cdot \frac{dP}{dt} - \frac{1}{r_e} \cdot \frac{dr_e}{dt}, \frac{1}{P} \cdot \frac{dP}{dt}, w, \frac{Y}{r}, u \right]$$

where u is a taste variable.

The following simplifications can be made. First r is not observable but is the weighted average of yields on bonds, equities, goods and human capital; if it is assumed that r varies together with r_b and r_e, it can be eliminated. Second, we can assume that bond and equity rates are expected to be stable: i.e. eliminate $\frac{1}{r_b} \cdot \frac{dr_b}{dt}$ and $\frac{1}{r_e} \cdot \frac{dr_e}{dt}$. Third, one can assume that expectations are perfect so that by competition $r_b = r_e + \frac{1}{P} \cdot \frac{dP}{dt}$ (Friedman did not do this.) After these simplifications the function can be restated $M_d = F[P, r_b, r_e, \frac{1}{P} \cdot \frac{dP}{dt}, w, Y, u]$.

Assume the demand for money is homogeneous of the first degree in P and Y. Then,

$$kM_d = F\left[kP, r_b, r_e, \frac{1}{P} \cdot \frac{dP}{dt}, w, kY, u \right]$$

$$= kF\left[P, r_b, r_e, \frac{1}{P} \cdot \frac{dP}{dt}, w, Y, u \right]$$

Now let $k = \frac{1}{P}$. Then

$$\frac{M_d}{P} = F\left[1, r_b, r_e, \frac{1}{P} \cdot \frac{dP}{dt}, w, \frac{Y}{P}, u \right]$$

$$= g\left[r_b, r_e, \frac{1}{P} \cdot \frac{dP}{dt}, w, \frac{Y}{P}, u \right]$$

$$P = \frac{M_d}{g\left[r_b, r_e, \frac{1}{P} \cdot \frac{dP}{dt}, w, \frac{Y}{P}, u \right]}$$

Now let $k = \dfrac{1}{Y}$.

$$\frac{M_d}{Y} = F\left[\frac{P}{Y}, r_b, r_e, \frac{1}{P}\cdot\frac{dP}{dt}, w, 1, u\right]$$

$$= h\left[r_b, r_e, \frac{1}{P}\cdot\frac{dP}{dt}, \frac{P}{Y}, w, u\right]$$

$$= \frac{1}{V\left[r_b, r_e, \frac{1}{P}\cdot\frac{dP}{dt}, w, \frac{Y}{P}, u\right]}$$

$$Y = M_d.V\left[r_b, r_e, \frac{1}{P}\cdot\frac{dP}{dt}, w, \frac{Y}{P}, u\right]$$

which is similar to the old quantity theory of money except that the velocity of circulation is now a function of several variables.

Keynes had attacked a naive quantity theory which assumed a constant level of real output given by automatically established full employment and a constant velocity of circulation. At its worst this was a trivial identity which stated that if a variable on one side of the equation rose then so must a variable on the other. But Friedman's restatement of the quantity theory is very Keynesian since it treats money demand as the demand for an asset and, through expectations of change, brings in liquidity preference. He also shows that velocity is a stable function of a few variables.

Friedman's quantity theory is not a theory of the price level, nor of income determination. It is only a theory of the demand for money, e.g. if $P = \dfrac{M_d}{g\left[r_b, r_e, \frac{1}{P}\cdot\frac{dP}{dt}, w, \frac{Y}{P}, u\right]}$ is to be a theory of price determination further specification about the determination of income etc is required.

Similarly $Y = M_d.V\left[r_b, r_e, \frac{1}{P}\cdot\frac{dP}{dt}, w, \frac{Y}{P}, u\right]$ is no theory of income determination unless the components of the velocity function are explained.

A determinate theory can be derived by assuming fixity of variables or that the velocity function is very inelastic with respect to its variables.

Friedman states that his theory excludes the possibility of a liquidity or expenditure trap because it assumes well behaved functions.

This new quantity theory is not like the old published theory (see Don Patinkin in 'Journal of Money, Credit and Banking' vol.1, no.1). Friedman's statement that his theory is the old Chicago tradition which had been handed down orally will not do. Nor will his recent attempt to adduce evidence from published sources about how the early theorists conceived the theory. If the argument is about beliefs and thoughts it can only be satisfied by seeing how it was applied to the real world, and, when this is done, it is clear that Friedman's quantity theory is Keynesian economics written in another language. But it has two added advantages. First, it applies capital theory consistently. Second, its emphasis on empirical testing has generated a large volume of very important work. (Part IV below.)

PART III

*INTEGRATION OF MONETARY
AND VALUE THEORY*

CHAPTER 14

THE REAL BALANCE EFFECT

We can pose the central problem of this section of the course as the integration of monetary and value theory (Patinkin's definition) or as the role of money in a general equilibrium model (following Patinkin's work) or as the theory of the real balance effect. Though Pigou's name is normally associated with the last of these formulations, Scitovsky and Haberler also deserve credit.

The Pigou effect begins with a fall in the price level which, by increasing the real value of cash balances held by the community, increases its wealth and ultimately satiates the desire to save. (It was introduced as a reply to Keynes's disciples who had transferred his unemployment equilibrium from the short run to the neoclassical stationary state.) But the argument assumes commodity money (e.g. gold) and not money created largely against private debt as in a modern economy. In the latter case a rise in the real value of money is simultaneously associated with a rise in the value of private debt so that there is no Pigou effect.

Much modern theory has been designed to preserve the Pigou effect against this objection. The crucial assumption is that public debt unlike private debt is regarded as an asset without being regarded as a liability i.e. the public regards government bonds as net wealth even though they are owed by the public to itself. The analysis has been developed with difficulty, initially with the mathematical formulation and more recently as a result of banking and other institutional problems.

Background

As we have seen Classical and neo-Classical monetary theory was formulated either in terms of cash-balance mechanics (whereby an increase in the money supply brought about an excess of actual over desired real balances such that expenditures, and so prices, rose and stabilised where real and desired balances were again equal) or interest rate mechanics (whereby an increase in the money supply lowered the interest rate and so led to an excess of desired investment over desired saving, driving up the price level and restoring equilibrium between real and desired balances when real balances and the interest rate had returned to their former equilibrium level). Which mechanics were stressed depended upon the monetary institutions assumed and how the money supply was supposed to be increased. Monetary ease was normally introduced for cash balance mechanics by free distribution of cash — most recently by helicopter — and by one of two alternatives for interest rate mechanics: (i) Marshall relied on a gold shipment to London; more recent writers employ (ii) open market purchases of securities by the central bank. (The former has both a wealth and substitution effect while the latter has a pure substitution effect.)

Both mechanics imply monetary influences on spending whereas classical and neo-classical value theory assume that quantities demanded and supplied depend on real variables only (real income and relative prices, including the interest rate) and not on the quantity of money. This assumption is embodied in Say's law which excludes monetary theory by denying the influence of money on spending. Hence there is a contradiction in the dichotomy between the classical and neo-classical theories of relative and absolute prices: the monetary theory relied on the influence of money on spending while the real value theory excluded it.

Keynes attacked the real value theory which assumed automatic full employment of resources. He produced an aggregate general equilibrium system with the first monetary model where money influenced real variables (via interest rate mechanics). His claim to have shown that full employment was not normal was attacked first by the argument that his underemployment model depended on wage rigidity. (If wages fall in this model the LM curve shifts rightward so raising the equilibrium level of income.) Keynesians replied that this process might be blocked by a liquidity trap (horizontal LM curve) or by inadequate interest elasticity in the savings and investment functions even when the interest rate fell to zero (inelastic IS curve or such that the highest attainable level of equilibrium income is below full employment).

The Pigou effect reintroduced cash balance mechanics and argued that the location of the IS curve depended also on people's real wealth: a falling price level shifts the IS curve rightward so that the economy gets back to full employment. (Eisner disputed this on the grounds that people may not get satiated with more real balances, but most economists accepted it as a conclusive demonstration that wage and price flexibility must get the economy to full employment.) A highly aggregative integration of monetary and value theory was achieved in this way, but the micro foundations in terms of the general theory of choice remained unexplored.

Towards the end of the 1930's another revolution was developing in the mainstream of English language economics — the absorption of the general equilibrium approach of Walras and Pareto in contrast to the Marshallian partial equilibrium tradition. (The work on monopolistic competition was unaffected by this change.) This development was concentrated at LSE (Hicks and Allen). The general equilibrium approach to value theory, combined with the *General Theory*'s assertion that monetary factors did make a difference at the macro level, along with the social importance of the problems involved, stimulated some hard theoretical work with the rather arid tools of mathematical economic analysis on the need to integrate monetary theory with value and general equilibrium theories. A major effort was made by Lange at the University of Chicago to persuade his colleagues in mathematical language that Keynes did make a difference and Say's law did not make sense. Patinkin's first edition sprang directly from this work and though his book was not the final word, subsequent discussion was about the economics and not the mathematics of the problem.

Money in general equilibrium analysis

There are two problems in formulating a general equilibrium theory of a monetary economy. The first (which is logically prior) arises in fitting the demand for money into a general utility analysis of choice. Money has no intrinsic use or value (except to misers). It is a store of purchasing power which (unlike other stores) is immediately convertible into any goods or securities and which yields services only during the process of exchange. The second problem arises from the nature of equilibrium in a monetary economy and from the effects of monetary changes within a general equilibrium framework. Are the classical propositions then valid? Specifically (i) When can we safely accept the dichotomy between relative price theory and absolute price theory? (ii) Is money neutral or does it affect real variables? (iii) Is monetary equilibrium stable in a general equilibrium model? (The classics assumed it was.)

Money and utility theory

Money is normally (though not necessarily) assumed to bear no interest. (It does yield a return when prices fall.) The demand for money must therefore be for a store of purchasing power which implies also that it is a real demand. The benefits from holding money must be conceived as the flow of services that it yields. What are these services which give utility? It is not easy to translate one's motives for holding money into a flow of services that money can be assumed to yield. The notion of the utility of money must be a shorthand for something far more complex.

It is usually easier not to assume that money yields utility but to make demand for it a consequence of rational, maximising behaviour. For example, consider the Baumol-Tobin model. If exchange was costless there would be no transactions demand for cash. But, given fixed and variable costs of converting cash into earning assets and vice versa, we can derive an optimum number of transactions. Money-holding becomes rational though not directly utility yielding. Similarly in the portfolio balance theory, risk averters require some money though it gives them no direct satisfaction. Patinkin's effort to derive money demand from uncertainty of receipts and payments rests on embarrassment at inability to pay creditors. The motive for demanding money is financial probity and desire for instantaneous ability to pay at any casual street encounter. But this is a strange thing to emphasise in a utility function since not everybody feels that way. Some prefer to skulk in the back alleys. There is no very satisfactory reason for putting money in the utility function.

We can dodge the issue by adopting an 'as if' approach; we assume money yields utility because it is held. This makes utility a function of goods and real balances (where we must not envisage the utility from the latter as arising directly except for misers). Hence we must assume that the flow of services is proportional to real balances held.

This short-cut poses analytical problems. Classical value theory is about flows (utility arises from maximising consumption subject to a budget restraint on the rate at which goods can be consumed). If we put the stock of real balances into the utility function we lose our unambiguous budget constraint. (Archibald and Lipsey and Marty are really concentrating on the nature of the budget constraint implied.)

Monetary equilibrium

The second problem is the formal analysis of general equilibrium in a model including money. The key to understanding here is recognition that, while the public cannot affect the nominal quantity of money which is fixed by authority or other external forces, it can change the real quantity of money by altering its spending behaviour and so changing the price level. Adjustments of actual to desired real balances through price level changes mean that a change in nominal money causes an equi-proportional change in the price level and also guarantees the stability of monetary equilibrium. Moreover, monetary change in this model does not affect real variables so long as there are no other quantities in the economy whose real value varies with the price level. This raises the problems of dichotomy and neutrality.

Can we dichotomise theoretical economic analysis into two parts in this way, dealing exclusively with real variables in one analysis and exclusively with monetary variables in the other? The answer is we can, but only by assuming, first, that nominal money is the only variable fixed in nominal money terms and, second, that changes in the real economy leave monetary equilibrium preserved through appropriate adjustment in the price level.

The assumptions are important in real world policy problems. Real variable analysis of international trade, for example, is largely pro-free-trade; but it assumes that monetary equilibrium is maintained through price level changes. Policy makers, however, are faced with a monetary equilibrium which will not change quickly, and so trade can and does cause monetary disequilibrium.

It is therefore also necessary to ask whether real equilibrium can be invariant (neutral) with respect to changes in nominal money. Again the answer is yes if we make the same two assumptions. Money must be the only variable fixed in nominal terms and adjustments of actual to desired real balances does not affect other variables in the process.

Now we work through several real models of increasing complexity, adding money to each. Following Patinkin and as background to the following discussion we define the accounting prices in an n good economy as $p_1, \ldots, p_{n-1}, p_n$. Then, if the nth good is physical money, the money prices are $\frac{p_1}{p_n}, \ldots, \frac{p_{n-1}}{p_n}, 1$. Finally the relative prices of the n−1 goods in terms of the first good are $1, \frac{p_2}{p_1}, \ldots, \frac{p_{n-1}}{p_1}$ and $\frac{p_n}{p_1}$ (i.e. the number of units of the first commodity that must be given up to acquire one unit of paper money).

Exchange economy without money

First, consider an exchange economy with no physical money but some unit of account for prices. At the beginning of each period an individual has a stock of goods and faces a set of market prices. He attempts to maximise his utility, which is a function of the goods he consumes. His budget constraint is his income which is determined as the quantity of each good in his initial bundle multiplied by its market price.

He chooses an optimal bundle to consume, and any difference between his initial endowment of a good and his desired consumption constitutes his excess demand or excess supply of the good. Obviously, the sum of the money values of his excess demands and excess supplies must be equal, or, if excess supplies are treated as negative excess demands, his total of excess demands must be zero. Thus, if we know his ED for n−1 goods, we know ir for the nth good.

If the price of one or more of the goods changes there is a substitution effect which can be analysed in the usual way, and an income effect, which alters the value of his initial physical endowment. In the general equilibrium context this income effect is just as likely to be negative as positive, depending on whether the individual is initially an excess demander or supplier of the good. Thus $ED_x = f$ (initial endowments, all prices).

An equiproportional change in the accounting price level does not alter the real excess demands or supplies because utility depends only on physical consumption. There is no money illusion. Relative prices and endowments remain unchanged. We can divide by the accounting price of any one good to derive the n−1 relative prices.

To determine the market prices of goods, we add together the derived excess demands of all individuals. These total excess demands and supplies depend not only on initial stocks of goods, but also on their distribution among individuals. Given this distribution, the market excess demand functions can be expressed as functions of the n−1 relative prices.

We want to determine the set of equilibrium prices so that the sum of all excess demand functions is zero so that each individual's utility is maximised. This may sound easy, but when we try to specify the process used, we run into trouble. For if trading is allowed at non-equilibrium prices, then endowments must change and, as a result, so do the equilibrium prices themselves.

Walras avoided this problem by postulating a hypothetical auctioneer and the process of tâtonnement (groping) in which no business is done until all equilibrium prices have been determined. Usually this problem is ignored and it is simply assumed that somehow the market arrives at the equilibrium prices.

Then we determine the equilibrium prices by setting the excess demand for each commodity equal to zero and solving the n−1 independent equations for the n−1 unknown relative prices in terms of the numeraire. For the resulting solution to be unique the n−1 equations must be independent. But, even then, there can still be no solution (or multiple solutions) unless the demand functions are linear in the prices. There is nothing in humanity, introspection, or anything else which insures linearity of demand functions, and so we have to abandon the confidence of Walras for the much less certain hope that there is a unique solution. (See notes by Carl Christ.)

If the solution is not unique then we are in trouble. Non-linear demand curves are particularly possible in this general equilibrium context, due to negative income effects. With such demand curves we can have multiple equilibria, and prediction is made impossible because of discontinuous jumps from one equilibrium to the other whenever an exogenous change is introduced.

Assuming a unique equilibrium does exist, what we are really interested in are the effects of exogenous changes on it. We cannot change prices, for they are all endogenous. Thus the only changes with which we are concerned are in preferences and in endowments (both total and their distribution).

Exchange Economy with Real Money

Assume now that some real fiat money exists which is an asset without being a liability. It does not pay interest and the physical substance of this money is not important.

To provide a motive for an individual to hold money, assume that his utility function is dependent both on real goods consumed and real balances. Note, by the way, that the former is a flow, while the latter is a stock, which causes some analytical problems. Again assume that the individual starts with an initial endowment of goods and nominal money and that he faces accounting prices for goods and money. He maximises his utility subject to his budget constraint.

To assess the effects of relative price changes, his excess demand and supply functions for each good, and money, can be derived as for the no physical money case. Now, however, changes in market accounting prices will have a real balance effect in addition to the (positive or negative) income effect and the substitution effect. A change in relative prices changes the individual's real balances, with his nominal money fixed. However, an equiproportional change in all accounting prices (including money) again has no effect on his real excess demands.

To aggregate the individual functions the market excess demand equations (whose values must again sum to zero) must be set up. The homegeneity of degree zero in accounting prices again allows us to divide all prices by the price of money to derive the $n-1$ money prices. Now however each money price enters each excess demand function in two ways: it influences the relative prices of goods as well as determining the real money balances.

Now an equiproportional change in the $n-1$ money prices does alter the initial endowment of real balances, and so demand adjusts. We are changing something real, the real purchasing power of money, which affects demands for goods either positively or negatively, depending on whether they are substitutes or complements for real balances.

APPENDIX

An Aside on Counting Variables and Equations in Systems of Simultaneous Equations (from Carl F. Christ's lectures at Chicago, 1959)

It is not true that a system of n equations with n unknowns will always yield a unique answer for each variable. Nor is it true that a problem with more equations than variables will always give conflicting answers, or that a system is indeterminate when there are more variables than equations. We shall give several examples.

Case 1. Number of Equations (2) equals number of variables (2).

Case 1a: $y = x + 1$
             $y = -x + 3$

The lines intersect just once, and there is one solution, at $x = 1$, $y = 2$;

Case 1b: $y = x + 1$
             $y = x + 2$

Here there is no solution, for the equations are contradictory. There is no intersection, the lines are parallel.

Case 1c: $y = x + 1$
             $y = (x - 1)^2$

Here there are two solution, one at $x = 0$, $y = 1$ and one at $x = 3$, $y = 4$. The lines intersect twice; one of them is curved (a parabola) rather than straight.

Case 1d: $y = x + 1$
             $2y = 2x + 2$

Here there is an infinite number of solutions; any value of x whatever, together with the value $y = x + 1$, is a solution. The two lines are coincident, so that every point on either of them is on the other one too. Neither equation adds any new information to what the other says, i.e. they are not independent statements.

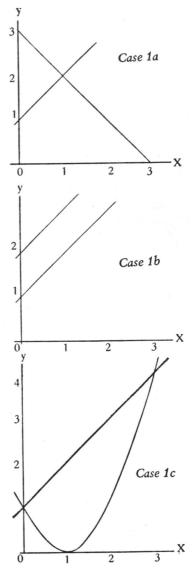

Case 2. Number of equations (1) is less than number of variables (2).

Case 2a: $= x + 1$

Here the diagram looks the same as for Case 1d above. There is an infinite number of solutions just as described in Case 1d.

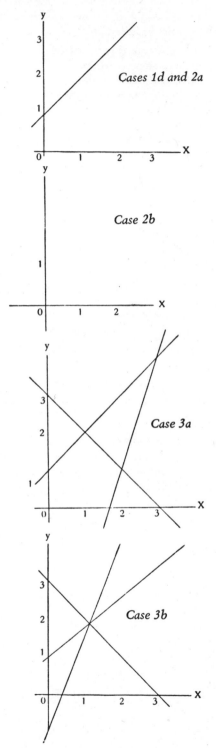

Cases 1d and 2a

Case 2b: $(x-2)^2 + (y-1)^2 = 0$

Here there is one solution, at $x = 2$, $y = 1$. The equation is the equation of a circle with center at that point and a radius of zero.

Case 2b

Case 3. Number of equations (3) is greater than number of variables (2).

Case 3a:
$$y = x + 1$$
$$y = x + 3$$
$$y = 3x - 5$$

Here there is no solution; the 3 equations are contradictory, for the solution of any pair of them does not satisfy the remaining one. The three lines do not have any intersection point in common.

Case 3a

Case 3b:
$$y = x + 1$$
$$y = x + 3$$
$$y = x - 1$$

Here there is one solution, at $x = 1$, $y = 2$. The three lines all intersect at that point. The three equations are not independent, since any one of them is an implication of the other two. For example, if one multiplies the first equation by 2 to get $2y = 2x + 2$, and then subtracts the second equation from this, the third equation is proved to be true as a consequence of the first two.

Case 3b

Case 3c:
$$y = x + 1$$
$$y = (x - 1)^2$$
$$3y = x + 9$$

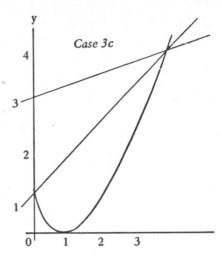

Case 3c

Here there is one solution, at x = 3, y = 4. This is the only point where all three equations intersect. (There are two points where only 2 of the equations intersect, but neither of these 2 points is a solution for all 3 equations.) One of the lines is curved (a parabola), not straight.

We will now summarize the general results that are illustrated by the above examples.

Case 1: same number of equations as variables. If all the equations are *linear* (i.e. each equation is of the form $a+bx+cy+dz+ \ldots = 0$ as in cases 1a, 2a, 1d, 3a, and 3b, with no powers, products, quotients, or other functions involved as in cases 1c, 2b, and 3c) and *consistent* (i.e. not contradictory as in cases 1b and 3a), and *independent* (not dependent as in cases 1d and 3b), then there is a single solution (or as mathematicians say, a unique solution). This solution specifies a single value for each variable. If the equations are linear and consistent but dependent, there is an infinite number of solutions. If the equations are linear but inconsistent, whether independent or not, there is no solution. If the equations are not all linear, no general statement can be made.

Case 2: fewer equations than variables. If all the equations are linear and consistent, whether independent or not, then there is an infinite number of solutions. If the equations are linear and inconsistent, there is no solution. If the equations are not all linear, no general statement can be made.

Case 3: more equations than variables. If all the equations are linear and consistent, they cannot all be independent: the number of *independent* consistent equations can at most be equal to the number of variables. Suppose that the equations are linear and consistent; if the number of independent equations is equal to the number of variables, there is a unique solution; if the number of independent equations is less than the number of variables, there is an infinite number of solutions. If the equations are linear and inconsistent, whether independent or not, then there is no solution. If the equations are not all linear, no general statement can be made.

Regarding each of the models to follow in this course, we shall make the explicit assumption now that the equations are consistent, and that they are either linear, or else nearly enough linear so that if there is more than one solution only one of the solutions will be near the observed values of the economic variables involved, so that it will be easy to tell which solution is relevant to observed phenomena, and which solution or solutions is spurious from the point of view of the real world.

CHAPTER 15

THE REAL BALANCE EFFECT: FURTHER DEVELOPMENT

Summarising the argument so far, a change in any one money price affects the individual's real balances and substitution between this good and other goods. A change in all money prices alters the real value of initial money balances and therefore alters demands for goods. This is the real balance effect. Raise all money prices proportionally and the individual cannot buy the same total of real goods and real balances as before. Consider this as a sort of income effect, though it is more appropriate to call it the budget constraint effect because the equivalent to the income constraint in this model is a mixture of two things — the initial stocks of goods and of money balances. At this point Patinkin introduces the standard distinction between normal and inferior goods.

As the individual's budget constraint increases as a result of a fall in money prices, he will demand more goods and more real balances; his demand for both goods and real balances rises, but not proportionally to the price fall. We have to consider his demands for both real and money balances. His demand for money balances we can think of simply as the price level times the real balances demand ($M = PB$). As the price level falls he demands more real balances which implies that the demand for money balances will fall (since the increase in real balances demanded is not proportional to the fall in the price level). We have a functional relationship between real balances demanded and the price level which will be of less than unit elasticity: as the price level falls the individual demands both more real balances and more goods. If the real balances demand were independent of the price level, money balances demand would vary inversely with the price level (unit elasticity since B constant with respect to changes in P). This is the Classical case illustrated in the charts.

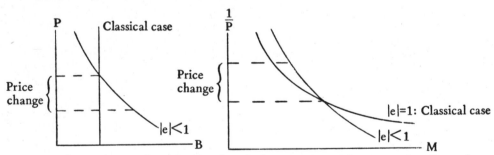

If we change the price level and the money supply proportionally real balances will be constant. It is exactly equivalent to changing all accounting prices in the general equilibrium system. Patinkin criticised Classical monetary theorists and in particular their unit elasticity concept of the demand for nominal money balances which neglects the real balance effect.

We move to market equilibrium (i.e. aggregate to get market excess demand functions) by assuming (i) given accounting prices of goods and money, (ii) one of the market excess demand functions is implied by the others, (iii) homogeneity of degree zero in the accounting prices and (iv) that there is a unique solution of money prices of the commodities as functions of the initial stocks of goods and money balances held by the individuals.

Stability and Neutrality

The real balance effect gives us the stability of both money prices and the price level. If the price level is displaced from its equilibrium position there will be an excess demand or supply of real balances. The consequent excess supplies or demands for commodities will push the price level back to where it started from (if the initial equilibrium is unique). A change in the quantity of money will change the equilibrium money price level in the same proportion. (Strictly, the additional money must be distributed to individuals in proportion to existing holdings.)

If goods are inferior in Patinkin's sense we do not have stability. An increase in the individual's resources (his budget constraint) leads him to raise his money balances more than proportionally. (There is an analytical problem here arising because of the mixture of *stocks* and *flows* of goods in the budget constraint: the relevant budget constraint depends on the length of period chosen, i.e. year or month etc.)

The real balance effect provides for the neutrality of the system with respect to equi-proportional changes in money prices and money balances: the real equilibrium does not change. C. Lloyd has shown that, while the real balance effect is essential for neutrality, it is not essential for stability. You get stability as long as there is a demand for money, but you do not get neutrality unless there is a real balance effect, i.e. unless people demand real balances.

The system can be extended to include bonds by considering more than one period. If we stick to a consumption economy bonds will be issued to finance consumption. People can then borrow in this period and pay next period. Bonds are assumed to be denominated in money terms with the consequence that if we change the price level we will get not only a real balance effect but also what Patinkin calls a real indebtedness effect.

To get neutrality in this extended model both money balances and bonds must change in the same proportion for all individuals.

Post-Patinkin developments

Following the work of Archibald and Lipsey it has been realised that the assumptions on which Patinkin derives neutrality are unnecessarily restrictive (at least in the pure money-goods no bonds model). They showed that if we extend the analysis by allowing for the passage of time then everybody's money balances need not change proportionally to guarantee neutrality. Consider the no bond economy and a non-proportional distribution of money. Assume everyone has the same marginal propensities to spend, so that relative prices are not affected by the distribution of resources among individual. Then those who get additional money balances try to acquire goods with some of their windfall which bids up the price level proportionally to the increase in the money supply. Initially some individuals will have done better than others. (Those who did not receive money will have to cut their consumption.) But if we allow for a second period, those who received the money in the first period will have spent some of it on consumption goods, those who did not receive it will have reduced both their consumption and their real balance but the latter not proportionally to the rise in the price level. So in period 2 we start with people who received the money in period 1, having disposed of some of it for higher consumption. People who did not receive are giving up some of their consumption of real goods to build up real balances. As time goes by there is a gradual adjustment back to the initial equilibrium of real balances. The only effect is a transitory redistribution of real income during these periods. (This mechanism is very similar to Robertson's 'induced lacking' and 'induced splashing'.)

Inflation theory incorporates the notion of a tax on money holders. The non-proportional increase in money balances entails a tax during the period of adjustment on those money holders who do not receive the new money.

One can make the same point by saying that each individual has a desired ratio of real balances to his real consumption and that he is prepared to save or dissave if this relationship is disturbed. For instance, if there is an inflation his real balances fall and he will forego consumption until he accumulates real balances to get him back to his desired ratio. This exposition is similar to Alvin Marty's model where saving takes the form of accumulating real balances. A rational and permanent individual will accumulate real balances until the marginal utility of the services of real balances is zero. The point here is that to accumulate real balances he has to forego consumption for one period. Having done so he will then have real balances which will yield him services for ever. This model synthesises the theory of savings and capital accumulation with the theory of the demand for money. It also yields the classical unit elasticity of demand for money balances.

If we increase the quantity of money nothing real happens in the long run: if we increase the initial stock of goods there is a permanent real change. But both money and goods (initial endowments) enter into the budget constraint. This is the Hahn paradox and its basic source is that we cannot transform real balances into income: real balances are wealth. Since money is the only asset it cannot be converted into another asset namely a flow of consumption goods. All we can do with money is spend it. If we introduce the possibility of converting money (wealth) into a permanent stream of income (by investment) then we have a real permanent change and the neutrality property will disappear.

To repeat, Archibald and Lipsey demonstrated that through a process of excess or deficient transient consumption, a distribution of money in unequal proportions will have no ultimate effect on real variables.

The Diagram illustrates an individual's preference system between a stock of real balances and a flow of goods (as the analysis involves goods and real balances, the price ratio is one to one). With the aid of a budget line that reflects the one to one price ratio plot an income expansion path by points of tangency between individual preference curves and the budget line as real income rises. Assume income is fixed at G_0 in terms of a flow of goods. Initial equilibrium is at b_0, G_0.

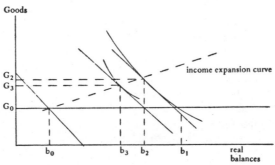

Let the stock of real balances increase to b_1 through a fall in the price level. The individual in period two will then optimize by consuming G_2 and holding b_2. He does so by increasing consumption above the level of permanent consumption (i.e. transforming real balances into goods through the market). The relevant budget line for period 3 is then drawn through (b_2, G_0) and the individual optimizes at (b_3, G_3). This process continues until he has run down his stock of real balances to their old level (b_0) and is consuming at the original rate (G_0).

The analysis admits the possibility of dissimilar preference functions. The disequilibrium period will be typified by changes in relative prices as the preferences of individuals directly affected by the transfer of money are imposed on the market. But this effect is transitory. The final equilibrium price level is higher but relative prices are the same as in the original equilibrium.

The Hahn paradox, that nothing real will be affected in the long-run stems from the fact that, though the individual cannot convert additional money into a permanently increased flow of goods, a change in the flow of goods will permanently alter the accumulation of real balances and the rate of consumption of goods.

This analysis suggests a simple approach to the theory of saving where the stock of assets is adjusted to a desired relation with a flow of goods (income). It differs from our earlier discussions of savings where no allowance was made for the possibility of transforming money into an income flow. Here saving is the accumulation of income-generating wealth. The weaknesses of the approach (which couches its treatment of saving in terms of a stock of assets and a flow of goods) is highlighted by contrasting it with a theory where wealth is treated as part of the choice problem in maximizing future utility. There is no good reason to suppose that a wealth-income ratio is an appropriate way of formulating the problem. The more classic treatment poses the savings-consumption choice as a problem of utility maximisation where wealth is not desired *per se* but as the temporary abode of a permanent flow of income.

Marty's discussion of the problem can be understood by adapting our previous diagram to explain this approach to savings. Looking at the problem in neo-classical terms we recognise again the G is a flow variable and B a stock.

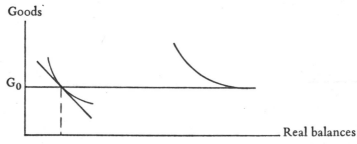

If we are dealing with an individual who demonstrates no time preference in consumption, we can picture him dropping his level of consumption for one period to accumulate wealth or real balances and then returning to his old level of consumption in the next period. He will be better off in perpetuity as a result (higher stock of wealth). A rational individual (who has an expected life-span of infinity) will expand along the horizontal line beginning at G_0 (representing his inflow of goods) to the optimal point where the marginal utility of real balances is zero (he is satiated with real balances). The rate of accumulation makes no difference to his ultimate position: the lower the rate, the longer it will take him to reach the optimum. The situation is similar to the neoclassical world where a society (with no time preference) accumulates capital until its marginal product is zero (either in terms of actual physical output or in terms of its capacity to produce goods to raise total community utility).

Assessment of Patinkin's Contribution

Patinkin's contribution may be viewed both as a criticism of an invalid classical position and development of an alternative to that position. His original theme was that there were basic errors in Classical theory summarised in the invalid dichotomy of real and monetary sectors of the economy. In practice it is difficult to ascertain exactly what the classical writers implied and Patinkin really criticised contemporary writers who assumed that the classical economy can be mathematically compressed into a barter economy determing relative prices, and a quantity equation (MV = PT or M = kOP) determing the level of absolute prices. The procedure involved inconsistency. For example, the "k" of the Cambridge formulation, although put forward as a behavioural relationship, was excluded from the real sector of the model. In other words, no behavioural mechanism was provided to determine monetary equilibrium. The missing piece of the jigsaw must be sought in the real demand equations where the choice between money and goods can be logically expounded.

Patinkin's positive contribution was to show that this logical inconsistency in contemporary monetary theory could be resolved by introducing the real balance effect as a bridge between the money and the real systems. This had the effect of destroying the dichotomy while preserving the essential neutrality characteristic of money in the classical system. In the Patinkin context, however, we can still examine real phenomena (assuming monetary equilibrium has been taken care of, either through movements in the price level or government providing the stabilizing quantity of money). The point is clear in the context of Keynesian economics whose central message was that an economy could equilibrate at less than full-employment. The popular interpretation of this message has been that government policies are necessary to maintain full employment and that such policies can be formulated (through a broad range of monetary and fiscal prescriptions).

There are two implications for traditional analysis (i) To carry the analysis out in a valid manner requires the assumption that government policy is maintaining full-employment and (ii) that, if one assumes full-employment, classical economic problems — the optimal allocation of scarce resources among competing uses, efficiency as a means of increasing per capita output — become relevant. The fundamental implication is that problems of real analysis have to be accompanied by some assumptions or analysis of the appropriate monetary equilibrium. (For some problems of partial equilibrium analysis we may ignore monetary repercussions i.e. assume them to be trivial.)

Patinkin stressed the effects of changes in prices on net wealth: outside money exists so changes in the price level affect peoples' wealth. However, our modern banking system does not work this way. It produces inside money (based on private debt). Even in the case of the old gold standard system a technology for the production of money existed and was based on the profitability of gold production with respect to the world price for gold. Patinkin's analysis proceeds on the assumption of pure outside money or fiat money, and, to make sense of his approach, we must find some empirical equivalent to it. The conventional solution has been to assume a particular form of money illusion on the part of the public when viewing public debt and consider net government debt (bonds or money) as outside money. But as the government, in some sense, is the embodiment of the public, its debts should rationally be regarded as the public's debts to itself and, in consequence, its monetary operations have no net wealth effects.

Criticisms by writers in the Chicago tradition (Bailey, Mundell and Johnson) have proceeded along these lines. They have explained how a rational private sector would realise that, if government debt increases, the public in effect owes more to itself and that the consequent increased present net wealth must be matched against the present value of future increases in taxes necessary to pay interest on the debt. Pure private rationality would then view a change in public debt as a zero change in net wealth.

Metzler, Gurley and Shaw

Another line of criticism questions the construction of the Patinkin model when realistic assumptions (that money is created against debt) yield a more satisfactory representation of the monetary system. Metzler (1950) was the first to employ this analysis. He emphasised the distinction between printed money and debt-based money. The major development was Gurley and Shaw's distinction between inside and outside money and their contention that, although no wealth effect in response to changes in the price level existed in an inside money model, there was a substitution effect. This substitution effect involved the exchange of money for bonds as the stock of money was increased. This was not a direct criticism, however, as the Patinkin analysis did allow for this effect. Gurley and Shaw showed that a substitution effect was sufficient for stability and determinacy in a monetary model. The linkage in the Gurley and Shaw system was the rate of interest so that the dichotomization into real and monetary sectors was valid. The important point is that systems of inside and outside money, although differeing in their monetary mechanics, both preserve the classical neutrality of money.

The Gurley and Shaw approach necessitates a denomination of bonds in real rather than money prices, otherwise a change in the price level would generate analytical problems through a redistribution of real wealth among people. On the assumption that bonds are based on private loans (inside money) it turns out that the redistribution of wealth resultant from a change in the price level will be merely transistory. In the long run the amounts of loans outstanding between banks and individuals, is determined by real factors as only money credit varies with the price level. Allowing for the recontracting of bonds over a sufficiently long time period, a rise in the money supply following an increase in the number of bonds held by banks will change the price level, and subsequently the real value of bonds, leaving us in the same position as before. In effect, we are swapping money for bonds. The interest rate mechanism of monetary adjustment will then change the rate of interest which adjusts the excess demand for goods and leads to a bidding up of the price level. This inside money system, besides preserving the neutrality of money postulate, can be dichotomized into real and monetary sectors.

We may interpret Keynes as having envisaged an inside money model and hence consider him as immune to the criticism of having neglected the real balance effect, unless, of course, an outside money system is the appropriate framework of analysis. There seems to be, however, no *a priori* evidence to make this latter criticism stick.

The real balance effect with inside money

Models using inside money can be contrasted with that of Patinkin. A change in the quantity of inside money also leaves real variables unchanged, but the mechanism is one of substitution between different forms of wealth as opposed to cash balance mechanics. This pure inside money model should also be contrasted with models developed by Metzler and Gurley and Shaw who tried to show that money was not neutral.

The condition necessary for neutrality are best examined through the assumptions in the Patinkin model: (i) redistribution of wealth resulting from changes in the money supply are ignored; this is not a statement about the real world but merely serves to define the level of abstraction; (ii) there is only one variable, the nominal quantity of money, fixed in nominal terms; and (iii) there is a fixed stock of other commodities (Patinkin's manna). In this situation the public can adjust holdings of real balances to any desired level by means of changes in the price level; the reaction to an increase in the nominal quantity of money is to raise the price level via spending of excess balances until the quantity of real balances and all other real variables are the same as the initial equilibrium values.

If there are other variables whose value is fixed in nominal terms or if changes in the money supply alter the amount of a real variable then money cannot be neutral. For example, the introduction of consols whose price is fixed in nominal terms would be sufficient to make money non-neutral, (Nominal bonds which are redeemable would limit the period of analysis since their nominal value is renegotiable.) An increase in the money supply in a consol economy would increase the price level and thus reduce the real value of consols. The increase in the money supply can either be of outside money — the government running a temporary budget deficit financed by an issue of fiat money — or of inside money. In both cases the ratio of money to consols held by the public would change thus necessitating a change in other real variables to restore equilibrium.

Now consider an economy where the nominal value of bonds can be adjusted with the price level. Metzler's model is such an economy; he uses inside and outside money, inside money being money which is issued by the banking system against real bonds; outside money is fiat money.

Consider, first, an increase in the money supply engineered by running a temporary budget deficit and financing by printing money. What happens after the budget has been restored? The price level will rise restoring real money balances to their previous levels. The value of bonds fixed in real terms will adjust to the new price level and therefore there will be no change in real variables.

Contrast this with an increase in the money supply resulting from a bond purchase by the government. The resulting increase in the price level reduces the quantity of real balances to their previous value; but the quantity of real bonds held by the public has been reduced by means of the open market equilibrium. The public has been cheated. Not anticipating the price change they have been willing to swop bonds for money only to find that as a result of this price rise the money part of their wealth holdings has fallen to its previous level. They have surrendered bonds to the government so their net wealth has fallen; a real variable has been affected by changes in the money supply and consequently money is no longer neutral. Real equilibrium is restored because savings are assumed to be an inverse function of wealth and a reduction in wealth stimulates saving, lowering the rate of interest and restoring the full employment equilibrium but with a reduced interest rate and higher savings and investment.

The non-neutrality conclusion depends crucially on Metzler's treatment of the government. G. Haberler was the first to suggest that the analysis involved violating the assumption that there were no net redistribution effects. Properly applied this assumption would note that the government's holdings of wealth had risen by an amount equal to the public's loss and strict symmetry would ensure that the government would react to this and so cancel the public's reaction to the wealth effect.

An alternative approach developed by M.J. Bailey has pointed out that the resulting reduction in government debt (increase in bond holdings) would imply a cut in taxes necessary to finance interest payments; the discounted value of this future stream of tax reductions should be regarded as an increase in wealth equal to the public's loss resulting from the reduction in holdings of real bonds.

R.A. Mundell has refined this analysis by examining the different impacts and incentive effects of reducing corporate taxes on profits and personal income tax. Smaller corporate taxes would be discounted and the value reflected in a rise in the value of equities. Although there is less private holding of real bonds the public will have no net change in wealth following the increase in equity values. But consideration of incentives alters this conclusion. The rise in the value of equities implies that the price of existing capital goods is greater than the current supply price, so there is an incentive to invest. (Alternatively, the net rate of return on investment rises.) The additional investment would tend to increase the rate of interest because savings will not have altered.

If personal income taxes are reduced, Mundell argues that there is no wealth effect because there is no market for human capital. The Metzler analysis still applies but it rests on differences in the impact of taxes. However absence of a capital market does not necessarily rule out human capital as an economic variable; the granting of mortgages and credit cards based on future earning power is evidence that human capital can be a significant economic variable.

The Gurley and Shaw model is similar to that of Metzler in having both outside and inside money: but in contrast Gurley and Shaw's inside money is issued against private debt and these private nominal bonds can be recontracted to maintain their real value. Since pure inside or pure outside models imply neutrality and the price level changing proportionately, in a mixed model equal proportionate changes in both kinds of money will also have the same properties.

Let the total money supply double through inside money being more than doubled and let the price level double so that the real quantity of money remains unchanged. Since only outside money is considered wealth doubling prices lowers the public's wealth holding. The economy cannot be in equilibrium and so the price level will rise less than in proportion to the increase in the quantity of money. Assuming a Metzler savings function, savings will rise and the rate of interest will fall and the neutrality property has gone.

Let the money supply double by more than doubling outside money and let money prices double as well. Since outside money has more than doubled there will be a net wealth effect necessitating a further rise in the price level and also a rise in the rate of interest because with greater wealth saving will fall.

If the simple minded view that more investment means more growth is adopted, then growth can be stimulated via increases in inside money which raises saving, lowers the rate of interest and increases growth. An increase in outside money however is inflationary but not enough to wipe out the wealth effect; thus saving falls increasing the rate of interest and cutting back investment. (The investment/growth link is naive because it ignores the possibility of exhausting limited investment opportunities the growth of which is exogenously determined.)

The non-neutral effects of money in most of the models depend on the form of the savings function and interest theory assumed. If a portfolio balance theory of the rate of interest is adopted, then wealth and the rate of interest will vary together.

The introduction of differentiated securities into a Metzler/Gurley and Shaw model emphasises the non-neutrality of money in the model. If the public respond to different quantities of differentiated securities by changing the interest rates at which they are willing to hold them, then the central bank can alter the interest rate structure via an open market operation aimed at changing the relative proportions of short and long run securties. This will not occur however if an expectations theory of interest rates holds where the long run rate reflects the expected short rates in between (unless the operation affects expectations).

Most analyses have assumed that the crucial distinction to make is that between inside money which is not regarded as net wealth by the community and outside money which is. Pesek and Saving have challenged this contention by arguing that the important economic as opposed to institutional distinction is between interest-bearing and non-interest-bearing money. Thus where there is a prohibition on interest payments banks can earn an excess profit whose discounted value is reflected in the capital of the banks. Raising the money supply increases this stream of profits and therefore raises the capital value of banks. This holds for both inside and outside money (i.e. the wealth effect depends on the non-payment of interest not on the institutional arrangement adopted for creating money).

Pesek and Saving confuse the issue by continuing to argue that interest payments on money would involve money becoming valueless. This muddles two points. First, when interest is paid the public will increase its holdings of money until the marginal utility of money services becomes equal to zero. Second, there is a distinction between the marginal utility of money services and purchasing power. Although an unrestricted competitive banking system would issue money until the marginal cost of creation (assumed zero) was equal to the value of the note (i.e. competition would reduce the value of money to its commodity value) this does not necessarily rule out the possibility of restricting the quantity of money while retaining a competitive banking system paying interest.

Laidler has noted that Pesek and Saving are contradicted by evidence: although there are legal and conventional prohibitions an explicit interest payments in both the US and the UK, there are implicit payments. Yet money is not worthless in either country.

In conclusion it must be recorded that there has been growing dissatisfaction with the general equilibrium approach to monetary theory. Leading this school of thought are R.W. Clower and F. Hahn, who argue that including money in the usual Hicksian general equilibrium equations deprives it of its special attributes unless one resorts, like Patinkin, to using the utility of money approach which depends on individuals going to great pains to avoid embarrassment. The new approach is trying to incorporate money's peculiar feature as an intermediary in exchange into the mathematics of monetary models.

PART IV

EMPIRICAL WORK IN
MONETARY ECONOMICS

CHAPTER 16

THE DEMAND FOR MONEY: ESTIMATION OF STRUCTURAL EQUATIONS

This is not a quick course in statistics. Two of the authors in the readings typify alternative approaches. Harris attempts to find Milton Friedman's 'empirical regularities' in the field of monetary economics, while Laidler more productively, concentrates on testing the reliability of relationships produced by monetary theories. Laidler is not concerned with determining whether everyone agrees on precise quantitative results, but rather whether the broad range of results corroborates the relations of specific theories.

Recall that within the formulation of the general equilibrium system of a monetary economy, we proceed in two stages. First we set up relationships for individuals and the aggregate which gives us excess demand functions for goods and services. Then we solve for the general equilibrium of the system. In the first stage we are interested in the behavioural relationships which influence peoples' demands and in the second, we are interested with how the system reacts to changes in exogenous variables, which for the system as a whole are tastes, technology, and resources.

In the same way there are two ways of approaching the empirical problems of establishing monetary relationships: we can test behavioural relations (i.e. estimate structural equations) or examine how the system reacts to genuinely exogenous changes (i.e. estimate reduced-form equations). The structural approach introduces problems of identification and bias, but most work in the field has been done with structural equations. The argument in favour of this approach comes from the homegeneity postulate that a change in all prices changes nothing in the real system and from the proposition that the public determines the real value of its money balances. If these two adjustments occur perfectly and without lag, then one could argue that all observations are of the real demand function for money. But, if not, we get bias in the estimates. Laidler, however, believes that any bias so far reported does not seem to make much practical difference.

Another preliminary point is that economics produces two kinds of theory: qualitative and quantitative. Most theory is qualitative, only postulating functional relationships between variables, and perhaps their signs. For example, monetary theory tells us that demand for $M = f(r)$, but it does not tell us the size of this relationship, which would be a quantitative prediction.

But there are theories which provide us with testable quantitative limits on the parameters. For example, the Baumol-Tobin inventory approach predicts that both the income and the interest rate elasticities of the demand for money should be less than one. Similarly, we have the Keynesian prediction that, at a low enough interest rate, the demand for money becomes infinitely elastic, which can be translated into the testable hypothesis that as the interest rate falls, the demand for money becomes more elastic.

Issues arising from Keynesian theory (Keynes or Post-Keynes)

The proposition that the demand for money is for real balances is usually assumed, but it is so fundamental that it needs to be tested, particularly since money illusion has been built into models in other areas. Other empirical issues in monetary economics which arose from Keynesian theory include:

(i) that the demand for money is dependent on the rate of interest. This was a major implication of Keynesian theory;

(ii) that the demand for money is related to total wealth;

(iii) Transactions demand implies some demand for money related to current income. While this effect would not be important in general full equilibrium since income, wealth and the interest rate are related in the short run, with wealth fixed, variations in employment and income could influence the demand for money.

(iv) The liquidity trap hypothesis which has been especially important in American empirical investigation.

(v) Keynes hypothesized that

$$M_0 = M_1 + M_2$$
$$= kY + L(r)$$

Much early work by A. J. Brown and James Tobin tried to estimate this equation. Working before regression analysis became popular, they tried to estimate 'k' historically by using the year with the lowest money-to-income ratio. This procedure was highly arbitrary and has dropped out of use.

(vi) The second part of Keynes' above equation contains his speculative motive, which suggests a relation between the general uncertainty of bond yields and the asset demand for money. This relation should be testable empirically.

Issues raised by Friedman's restatement of the Quantity Theory

Several other important issues were raised by Friedman's restatement of the quantity theory. (i) Is the demand for money a stable function of a few variables?

Friedman held up his demand for money function as the difference between Keynesian theory and the quantity theory. This had strategic value in then allowing him to cite any stable demand for money equation as proof of the quantity theory. But of course many Keynesians had been investigating and reporting such equations without feeling "unfaithful" to Keynes and Keynesian theory is consistent with the above stability statement, as the IS — LM analysis implies.

Friedman's emphasis on demand for money may be valid for policy because too often Keynesian "rule of thumb" policy decisions have been made without regard for the money market and based simply on crude multiplier analysis.

One can draw out of Friedman's policy pronouncements an extreme quantity theory view that there is no relation between the demand for money and the rate of interest. But this is contrary to his theoretical work, in which he includes interest rates as determinants of the demand for money. But when he tests his theory empirically he finds that the demand for money is not interest elastic, even though he is careful to state that he expected it to be. With this justification of a vertical LM curve, Friedman is then free to advise policymakers to increase money at a certain rate each year, believing that fluctuations in the IS curve will cause changes in interest rates, but not in employment or output.

(ii) Which wealth concept is appropriate?

Is wealth only a concept of property, or does it include human capital? Friedman's Permanent Income Hypothesis uses the more general human wealth concept, as does Modigliani.

(iii) Is the expected rate of change of prices an important influence on asset choices?

The Keynesian formulation (Yale School, especially) characteristically assumes that prices are stable whereas Quantity theorists emphasise the role of expected inflation. This is currently a major division between the two schools.

Issues raised by Gurley and Shaw and by Baumol and Tobin

The development of financial intermediaries will increase the interest elasticity of the demand for money acording to Gurley and Shaw. Marty, in his review of their book, pointed out that while financial intermediaries might reduce the total demand for money, they might leave this demand resting with those people whose demands are less interest elastic (i.e. you cannot infer from a change in the location of a curve what will happen to its elasticity).

Gurley and Shaw and the Radcliffe view in the UK supported the belief that demand for money would become unstable due to competition between financial intermediaries and banks. This implied that close asset substitution required a broader definition of 'liquidity'. On the other hand it is argued that even with close substitution, if one knows the substituion effects, one can still produce the desired results by controlling the smaller amount of money.

The major issue raised by the Baumol–Tobin inventory theory of the demand for money relates to economies of scale in its use. If there are scale economies in holding money, one would expect a testable decrease in the demand for money relative to the scale variables as wealth increases.

Outstanding practical problems

In addition to these theoretical issues a range of practical problems has been encountered in empirical work. First, what is money? The strong classical or inventory approach defines it as anything which can be used for transactions without any intervening conversion transaction: i.e. currency plus demand deposits (and travellers cheques).

Several writers have tried to define money *a priori* according to institutional data. Friedman and Schwartz have shown that this approach is not correct, the definition of money has to be an empirical question. Once you go beyond the transactions approach, you realise that money is not used only for transactions; it is also held between them so that a capital theory approach cannot be avoided. Once capital theory is introduced, the definitional problem must be faced.

Even though this problem was once thought to be of great importance, it has now been shown that different definitions of money give consistent results so that the definitional problem is not an obstacle to discovering regularities in monetary phenomena.

A further practical problem has been which interest rates to employ. Again *a priori* arguments can be used, but it is essentially an empirical question. One argument is that the appropriate rate is that between money and its closest substitutes in the transactions sense, i.e. use the short-term rate. But a contrary argument is that money is wealth, and since the typical case of wealth is a government bond, the appropriate rate is that of a long-term government bond. However, if one accepts the expectations theory of the term structure, the long rate is a series of short rates; so the bond rate contains all future short rates and is not relevant to money demand, which depends only on the current short rate. In practice, sometimes one rate works well, sometimes the other.

The method of aggregation may foreclose certain important possibilities about which we are concerned. For example, one may want to test that as individuals' wealth rises, they do not increase their holding of money in proportion. Therefore regressions should be run on wealth per capita or income per capita, rather than aggregate wealth. This is because the effects may not be the same for increases in total wealth brought about (i) by an increase in population and (ii) by an increase in physical wealth with population constant. This suggests that the distribution of wealth is also an important variable in the demand for money function.

If the demand for money is formulated as a demand for real balances, then the homogeneity property, which needs to be tested, is being implicitly assumed. Instead regressions should be done in terms of nominal money with the price level as an independent variable to determine whether in fact demand is homogeneous.

In the same way, using a *ratio* of money to wealth or income as a dependent variable involves assuming constant returns to scale. The use of ratios constrains the result to certain proportionalities which may be neither predicted by theory nor what the data actually have to tell you. Much early work on money was not very careful about this sort of thing. For example, the formulation $M/Y = F(r)$ involves the assumption of constant returns to scale in holdings of money as income increases and does not distinguish between increases in income due to increases in average income and due to increases in number.

Much of recent work has been involved in sorting out these problems of earlier research.

Survey of findings

We begin the resume of empirical work with the issues roused by Keynesian theory.

It is now pretty well accepted that the demand for money is homogeneous of degree one in prices. It was assumed by most writers that this was true and they constructed their empirical equations on that assumption. But this procedure provides an indirect test. If the assumption were false the regression results based on it would be very poor. In fact the regression results based on this assumption fit well. Meltzer ran a direct test and his estimates produced an elasticity of nominal money demand with respect to money prices approximately equal to one.

Another strong result relates to interest rates. Laidler's review concludes (his p.97) that: "whether one thinks of the demand for money function as being constrained by income, wealth, or expected income; whether one cares to define money including time deposits, or not; whether one chooses to ignore the identification problem or deal with it; whether one uses a short rate of interest or a long one — there is an overwhelming body of evidence in favour of the proposition that the demand for money is stably and negatively related to the rate of interest. Of all the issues in monetary economics, this is the one that appears to have been settled most decisively."

There is one apparent exception to this which is the finding of Friedman in his article on the demand for money. He could not find any consistent relationship between deviations in the demand for money from the predicted value and movements in interest rates. This is the result of an error in setting up the empirical work. He argued that deviations of interest rates from the normal level are highly correlated with the business cycle and that to get at the demand for money you should get cycle averages of the various variables. He then ran a regression between money and permanent income and discovered (among other things) that income elasticity was 1.8 (money is a luxury good). He took the deviations of interest rates from their average and the deviations of money demanded from that predicted and attempted to find a relationship. It turns out from Laidler's work that, by running his regressions between money and permanent income over the cycle averages without an interest rate variable, he missed the fact that, over the period he was dealing with, there was a slight down trend in interest rates. The results of that omission were both that he did not have a relationship in his original setup between the rate of interest and the demand for money and that (because the influence of the interest rate was absorbed into the influence of permanent income) the predictions he was making were erroneous. Consequently the deviations of the predicted from the actual were erroneous. When you do it properly (as Laidler has) you find a much more consistent relationship between interest rates and the demand for money. The same point was made in a different way by Tobin who also took Friedman's data and ran regressions with the interest rate in them and showed interest elasticity.

The possible presence of a liquidity trap has entered the construction of theories of economic policy (e.g. fiscal policy will be fully effective but monetary policy or wages flexibility will be unsuccessful even if it is possible). The test is that the elasticity of demand for money (with respect to the rate of interest) should increase as the rate of interest decreases. This test is not very satisfactory because Keynesian theory implies that, if the current rate of interest falls relative to the expected rate of interest, then eventually one hits a liquidity trap. The trouble is that we have to discover what the expected rate is before we can tell whether the current rate is relatively lower or not. The tests do not do that. Instead they look at periods of high and low interest rates on the assumption that when the rate of interest is historically low it is also low relative to the expected rate. On that basis no evidence has been found of the elasticity of demand for money increasing as the rate of interest falls.

Is wealth or current income the appropriate variable to use? In principle one can regard current income as corresponding to transactions demand for money. This is to be contrasted with wealth which can be measured either by the value of people's assets or by the permanent income concept. In principle one could expect to bring both into the analysis. This was tested by Meltzer who found he could not get significant results with both variables in the equation. The introduction of one makes the other redundant. Meltzer tries to explain this result by reference to the fact that permanent income has to be the rate of interest applied to wealth: income and wealth are therefore highly correlated. But this is a proposition about permanent income. Current income can deviate substantially from permanent income and it is then theoretically conceivable that significant coefficients could be estimated for both of them. Then we can say that the effort to find a relation with current income is an indirect test of the analysis of demand for money based on its function as a medium of exchange in transactions. If current income does not enter significantly when a wealth variable is included then the emphasis of some writers on transactions demand is called in question. The difference between monetary theorists following the utility maximising approach (wealth) and the monetary theorists following the cost minimising approach (transactions) seems to be resolved by the empirical work in favour of the utility approach. But there is a serious problem here. Permanent income is developed as a lagged function of past values of actual income. It is therefore possible that the finding that permanent income is important and current income is not, simply means that the reaction of demand is lagged against current income, which would be evidence in favour of the transactions hypothesis if corroborated. However it would not be very strong evidence since money is demanded for current transactions and a response related to past transactions is hardly consistent with the hypothesis.

One can get around this difficulty by introducing some variable other than income into the demand for money function and then assuming that if people's reactions are lagged, they are lagged to the same extent with respect to all the variables which influence behaviour. Then we can develop a model allowing for the possibility of different lags in people's actual behaviour between reactions to income and the other variable. If there is then a much longer lag in reactions to income than to other variables (say, the interest rate) there is evidence in favour of the permanent income hypothesis. By assumption the two lags are the same. If one is longer, then people are not just lagging their reactions but also forming expectations. (Edgar Feige found that the lag in the reaction of the demand for money to interest rates is much shorter than the lag in response to income).

To summarise: the evidence is overwhelmingly in favour of the proposition that the demand for money depends on the rate of interest. It is also overwhelmingly in favour of the notion that wealth is an important variable as contrasted to current income. But the hypothesis that transactions demand is related to current income is not supported by the evidence. Finally there is no evidence whatsoever that there is a liquidity trap.

As noted above, one of the major issues raised by Friedman is his contention that stability of the demand for money is the essence of the quantity theory and in contrast to Keynesian theory. But this view is questionable. A good fit does not necessarily mean stability. It has been established that in the USA the demand for money has been stable over the period for which we have data. Specifically, the relation between the rate of interest and the demand for money has been very stable. But this stability does not necessarily prove the Quantity theory better than the Keynesian theory as a theory of money. Keynesian theory assumes that the demand for money is stable in order to arrive at the determination of income. So one may also interpret the evidence on stability as in favour of Keynesian theory, particularly because of the stable relation with the interest rate which was disregarded by earlier quantity theorists. If we have stability then our analysis can go further because fluctuations in the economy may be attributed to the behaviour of the monetary authority and the quantity of money as well as to changes in the real sector.

Contrary to Friedman's contention the evidence is therefore not decisive between one theory or the other but rather moves us ahead of both the old quantity theory and some versions of the Keynesian theory which posit instability of demand for money.

One can approach these issues another way by testing the Keynesian version which tends to get translated into policy — namely the one that assumes implicitly that the LM curve is very elastic (either because the demand for money is highly interest elastic or because the supply of money is variable in response to demand). This is the implicit assumption of those who focus attention on fiscal policy as the major policy instrument. The empirical evidence shows that the demand elasticity for money with respect to the rate of interest is extremely low (= − .15). This is very strong evidence in favour of the quantity theory as applied to economic policy and suggests we are closer to a Classical world (i.e. LM vertical). Certainly the evidence is against the Radcliffe view that velocity can be anything.

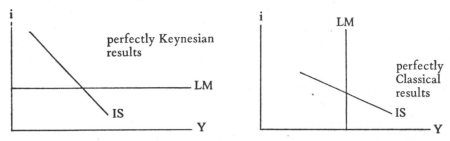

Keynesian theory assumes that prices are expected to stay at the same level, which enables us to develop the theory of portfolio decisions in terms of money with a perfectly certain value and to do all our analysis in terms of real quantities. But if the expected rate of change of prices does enter into people's behaviour it must be added to the consumption, investment and demand for money functions. There is no American evidence that the expected rate of change of prices enters the demand for money function. This poses something of a puzzle because studies of hyperinflation (in other countries) have found that the expected rate of change of prices is a very important variable. This conflict has given rise to the hypothesis of threshold effects: people take the expected rate of change of prices into account only if it is very high.

Another more complicated theory developed by Maurice Allais involves the notion that people pay more attention to current events relative to past events, the more rapidly the situation is changing. He develops one mathematical formulation (the weights given to inflation rise with its rate) and claims to be able to link the behaviour of all countries in one graph.

There is a lot of evidence from observations in the securities market that the public tends to respond rather quickly to changes in the expected rate of inflation and it may be that price expectations enter via the interest rate on monetary assets.

There seems to be slight evidence of economies of scale in the demand for money, but it is shaky and not enough to support the view that the transaction or inventory analysis is superior to that of other writers. Laidler argues that the fact that Meltzer was unable to find any evidence of scale economies from cross-section data is highly relevant. The approach can only apply to firms and other large holders of assets, so cross-section data for firms are much more relevant than evidence on the overall demand for money. (It rarely pays small holders to go in and out of cash.) But Meltzer's finding is not conclusive. Bank balance sheets are struck at the end of the day and so do not reflect accurately the holdings of the firm during the day. Moreover in the USA firms hold deposits with their banks to acquire goodwill.

There is a list of unsettled issues surrounding studies of the stability of money demand. They include (i) whether total wealth including human wealth is a better variable than non-human wealth; (ii) whether currency plus demand deposits is better or worse than currency plus demand deposits plus time deposits; and (iii) the debate on whether the long term rate of interest or the short rate is the relevant variable. (Issues (ii) and (iii) are closely related.)

Feige found very low substitutability between time and demand deposits and the assets offered by financial intermediaries. He therefore argued that the narrow definition of money was preferable to one which included financial intermediaries' liabilities. Laidler concludes that because the post World War II income elasticity of demand for money is less than unity, there is probably something operating that substitutes for money. Evidence from studies of the demand for money in the post-war period, in which the rate of return on financial intermediary liabilities is used instead of the conventional long and short rates, yields better empirical results. The demand for money remains stable though the independent variables are different.

There is therefore some evidence of the importance of financial intermediaries, but it carries none of the implications about instability in the demand function and the need for extended controls which Gurley and Shaw have urged.

CHAPTER 17

KEYNESIAN THEORY VERSUS THE QUANTITY THEORY: REDUCED FORM ESTIMATION

A highly debated empirical article in monetary economics has been the Friedman-Meiselman test of the quantity theory of money and Keynesian theory. The test was a continuation of work done by Friedman and Becker where the error of judging Keynesian theory's usefulness by its success in fitting a consumption function relationship was pointed out: since income is largely composed of consumption, a regression of consumption on income involves regression bias.

The basic methodological premise from which Friedman and Becker worked was that theory should find powerful and stable relationships between sections of the economic system. In this context, a relevant test of the Keynesian theory would be to see how well consumption, and not income, can be predicted from autonomous expenditure. The multiplier is held to be the critical relation of Keynesian economics and a test was performed which found that regressions of consumption on its own past values gave better predictions than the explanation of consumption in terms of investment expenditures.

The work of Friedman and Meiselman represents a stronger test than just the predictive ability of Keynesian theory. It sets up the quantity theory of money as an alternative and potentially more useful approach. In starting from a different methodology than the Keynesians, Friedman and Meiselman could be challenged either on the appropriateness of their scientific method or on the validity of the test itself. Keynesians, until this time, were less familiar with that methodological approach and they regarded economic theory's task as the full exposition of the economy's interdependencies. This point of view led them to construct larger and more disaggregated models of the economy, which attempted to explain how the recently developed aggregates of national income accounts are simultaneously determined in the theoretical terms of Keynes' *General Theory*. Insofar as they distinguished between autonomous and induced elements of the economic structure, the induced elements were held to be reflected by behaviour and not defined by the nature of the aggregates. For example, consumption in the income-consumption relationship may be part autonomous and part induced; the role of Keynesian theory is then, not to determine the relationship between income and the autonomous part of consumption, but to describe how income and elements of consumption fit together.

Friedman and Meiselman redefined the problem as one of explaining changes in induced spending from changes in autonomous spending. In criticising the results obtained from this analysis, the Keynesian would ordinarily return to first (Keynesian) principles to deduce what parts of expenditure are autonomous by their analysis. This procedure allowed quantity theorists to make several criticisms. First, the Keynesians' method was unsatisfactory from a scientific point of view because autonomous elements were identified on *a priori* grounds. Second, different Keynesians carrying out this procedure in different ways would generally not identify the same elements as autonomous whereas no doubt existed but that money supply, however defined, was the relevant autonomous element in the quantity theory. Thirdly, the Keynesians' search for an autonomous element led to a larger and larger definitions of the autonomous aggregate — a *prima facie* shortcoming in terms of the (Friedman) approach whose essence is the prediction of large aggregates from small ones: the larger the autonomous sector, the weaker the Keynesian theory becomes.

The Friedman-Meiselman test compared the Keynesian relation between investment and consumption with the quantity theory relation between the money supply and consumption (i.e. the relative stabilities of the investment multiplier and monetary velocity). They argued that this procedure favoured the Keynesian theory since the quantity theory traditionally explains income and not its consumption component, but their choice of precedure is open to question: investment is probably a small enough proportion of income for any regression bias to be insignificant even though income rather than consumption is what the quantity theory predicts.

Two criteria were established that affected the tests. The equations were calculated on the same data, for the longest period of time possible, and the simplest versions of the theory were tested so that they would be compatible with the fairly simple long-run data available.

$Y = C + A$: income is a function of induced and autonomous expenditure

$C = kY + k'$: consumption is a function of income and a constant term

$C = \dfrac{k}{1-k}A + \dfrac{k'}{1-k}$: consumption is a function of autonomous expenditure and a constant term

Friedman and Meiselman then needed to decide on the relevant C and A. An attempt was made to determine this statistically by starting with investment as autonomous and adding other variables that turned out to be statistically significant in the sense that they behaved more like autonomous than induced expenditure in the context of the model. Net domestic private investment, the government deficit on income and product account and the net foreign balance were finally identified as autonomous.

The statistical procedure has implications for the concept of income applied to consumption. Suppose we have

$\bar{Y} = C + U + A$

Where U is a term representing elements of the national accounts that cannot be identified as either autonomous or consumption (i.e. induced) expenditure. Then we should use $Y - U = C + A$ as the expression for income. Ando and Modigliarni criticised Friedman and Meiselman for this procedure but their criticism was refuted in that any definition of autonomous expenditure implies some definition of income and the fact that U moves with Y means that its addition will not affect the coefficients relating Y (no matter how defined) with C and A. Hence consumption can be legitimately treated as a function of $(Y - U)$ in the Keynesian world.

Three tests of the quantity theory versus Keynesian theory were made:

(i) $C = a_1 + b_1 A$ I

(ii) $C = a_2 + \quad + c_2 M$

(iii) $C = a_3 + b_3 A + \quad + d_3 P$ II

(iv) $C = a_4 + \quad + c_4 M + d_4 P$

$$\text{(v)} \quad C = a_5 + b_5 A + c_4 M$$
$$\text{(vi)} \quad C = a_6 + b_6 A + c_6 M + d_6 P \qquad \text{III}$$

I and II are held to be tests of the alternative hypotheses that autonomous expenditure and money supply determine consumption, in real (I) and money (II) terms, while III tests the same hypotheses in real and monetary terms by comparison of the b's and c's. For annual data between 1897 and 1958 and quarterly data for a shorter sub-period the quantity theory out-performed the Keynesian theory except for the years 1929-1934.

Criticisms of the Friedman-Meiselman test

One might merely accept these findings, concluding that Keynesian theory was relevant to the under-employment, inter-war period, with which Keynes was concerned. But there are several criticisms of the Friedman-Meiselman analysis. The first is that the money supply may be partially induced. For example, it includes the government deficit which may be financed through an increase in the money supply. In that case the influence of autonomous expenditure on income may be picked up as the influence of money. Further, in the US system, the money supply is partially determined (induced) by the private banking system and may therefore respond to changing levels of consumption and autonomous expenditure.

The second and major criticism is methodological. Should one rely upon a single equation that relies on high correlation coefficients as the criterion for a model's predictive capacity? The alternative approach, of course, involves the full specification of the economy's interdependencies. Friedman and Meiselman reply that this is not the name of the game. If we find stable relationships we do not need to know what goes on inside the black box.

A third criticism is of Friedman and Meiselman's identification of autonomous expenditure elements. They isolate the variables using statistical methods and begin by assuming fixed private investment must be exogenous. Observing that shifts between investment and other autonomous elements do not affect consumption, they conclude that the largest correlation coefficient will be between induced expenditure and the sum of all autonomous expenditures. In this way they search for all relevant autonomous elements. But this procedure does not give unambiguous results and is as guilty of *a priori* specification of autonomous expenditure as Keynesian formulations. The basic trouble is that it is quite consistent with the Keynesian system to get a higher correlation on money than autonomous expenditure because it is a general equilibrium model.

The relevant questions for economic theorists are: whether the Friedman-Meiselman methodology is good, or at least acceptable as an operation methodology; and whether the test is a test of anything relevant since the single equation approach precludes full specification of the economy and so the approach that the ordinary Keynesian would take in testing his own theory. An important question here is whether the tests are capable of discriminating between the hypotheses.

The debate is currently continuing in a more reasonable and less assertive fashion in the *Bulletin of the Federal Reserve Bank of St. Louis* in the context of testing whether fiscal policy or monetary policy is more effective in controlling the level and form of economic activity.

PART V

SOME MAJOR POLICY ISSUES

CHAPTER 18

THEORY OF THE SUPPLY OF MONEY

The pure theory of the demand for money assumes a given nominal supply of money which is varied at the discretion of the monetary authorities and government. Demand theory sets out to analyse the effects on general equilibrium of a change in the nominal quantity of money or of a change in demand for money arising from an exogenous change in tastes. (Traditionally the demand for money in the UK has been regarded as stable, but it has not always proved so). This branch of monetary economics also assumes that the authorities can control the nominal quantity of money. In contrast to this view there has always been a school that sees the supply of money responding to demand; it therefore concludes that there is no point in attempting to control the economy by monetary policy. Hence a theory of money, if it is to be consistent, requires that supply be determined independently of the demand for money, and if the theory is to be of use, it must allow that the central bank can control the quantity of money in the hands of the public. It must determine the nominal supply and not real balances: the demand for money is a demand for real balances and the public can determine any quantity of real balances it wishes via the price level. An element of 'money illusion' is usually ascribed to the authorities because their concern is with the price level and so the nominal rather than real quantity of money as such.

This last point is associated with the institutional background of modern banking where paper money is created as zero cost. This situation can be compared with an economy using commodity money with a real cost of production (e.g. the Gold Standard economies). Equilibrium then involves equality of real value with the marginal cost of production of money. In a static society there would be an equilibrium stock of gold such that the value of a unit of gold in terms of goods equalled the marginal cost of producing the first unit of new gold. In this case there would be no monetary authority except in the sense that the government would have the power to alter the nominal value of gold.

Behavioural assumptions and relevant variables

Traditionally money creation has been seen in three ways — as exogenously determined (e.g. by the stock given by past and current production of specie); as created by the central bank by means of open market operations; or, as created by the treasury as a result of a budget deficit financed by printing money. If the quantity of money is the sum of currency and commercial bank deposits the total quantity is given by the liabilities (obligations) of various institutions. Coins are the liability of the treasury, paper currency is the liability of the central bank (occasionally of the commercial banks), and commercial bank deposits are the liability of private profit maximising institutions, backed by cash reserves and earning assets; the latter provide the profit. The cash reserves consist of currency in the tills and vaults of the commercial banks, and deposits of commercial banks with the central bank. Currency and central bank deposits can be aggregated because of the central bank's willingness to provide currency in exchange for deposits.

The money supply includes commercial bank deposits so it cannot be under the direct control of the central authority. Control is exercised through a complex network influenced by two behaviour patterns: (i) the ratio of currency to (demand) deposits desired by the public, and (ii) the ratio of deposits to a given cash base which is determined by the commercial banks.

A third set of behavioural relations is required if a distinction between demand and time deposits is maintained; then two further ratios are necessary. If the money supply is defined to include demand deposits only then the question arises as to how total deposits are divided between them and time deposits. Moreover some assumption must be made as to how the commercial banks alter their reserve ratios according to the ratio of time to demand deposits. Similar problems arise if near moneys (such as building society deposits) are brought into the analysis.

Mechanical theories of money supply

Early theories developed a mechanistic approach which did not allow for the possibility of ratios being behavioural functions of economic variables. This stage of the theory's development is evocative of early quantity theory and Keynesian multiplier analysis.

Assume no difference between time and current deposits nor between currency and deposits of the central bank. Then define

M = currency plus all deposits of commercial banks
B = currency plus deposits of the central bank (known as base money, high powered money or the monetary base)
c = ratio of currency held by public to the total quantity of money
C = total currency held by the public i.e. $C = cM$
D = commercial bank deposits held by public = $(1-c)M$
r = ratio of reserves to deposits of commercial banks
R = reserves of banks = $rD = r(1-c)M$

From these definitions the money multiplier can be derived.

$$B = C + R$$
$$= [c + r(1-c)]M$$
$$\frac{M}{B} = \frac{1}{c + r(1-c)} = m, \text{ the money multiplier.}$$

If c and r are constants the authorities can control the money supply by fixing B; but if B is held constant and c or r change then the money supply does not remain constant.

The large number of bank crashes in the US during the depression led to an increase in the ratio of currency held by the public to the total quantity of money. Customers trusted banks less and therefore held more of their money in cash. The reserve-deposits ratio also rose as commercial banks kept larger reserves to ensure solvency in the face of increased uncertainty. These two developments led to a multiple contraction in the money supply which must have at least aggravated the depression. The results caused some economists to recommend that commerical banks should maintain 100% reserves (i.e. $r = 1$ and therefore $m = 1$ = constant). But this recommendation ignores the fact that reserve ratios less than one are so for economic reasons. The imposition of 100% reserves would result in a growth of near substitutes for bank deposits which would provide the public with the equivalent of money but would not be subject to the controls.

An alternative formulation of the above relationships can be given. Define d as the ratio of currency held by the public to total deposits.

$$d = \frac{C}{D} = \frac{cM}{M-cM} = \frac{c}{1-c}$$

Therefore $c = \frac{d}{d+1}$. Now let

e = ratio of reserves to earning assets

$$= \frac{R}{D-R} = \frac{rD}{D(1-r)} = \frac{r}{1-r}, \text{ and } r = \frac{e}{e+1}.$$

Substitution in the previous formula yields

$$m = \frac{(d+1)(e+1)}{d+e+de}$$

Although both the formulations are identical in a formal sense, availability of statistics and further behavioural assumptions dictate which should be used. For example, a theory based on $d = \frac{C}{D}$ would suggest that as the money supply rose people would increase their holdings of cash and deposits by the same proportion. In contrast Walter Newlyn would argue that currency is kept solely for transactions purposes and that, if the money supply rose, there is no reason to expect currency holdings to rise unless transactions do so too. This would involve adapting the formula for Keynesian transactions demand. $M_1 = kT$ and $\frac{\partial T}{\partial M}$ is the marginal increase in transactions with respect to small changes in money. Then $c = k\frac{\partial T}{\partial M}$ and therefore:

$$m = \frac{1}{k\frac{\partial T}{\partial M}(1-r) + r} -$$

Economic Determination of the Ratios

The cash/deposit ratio can be explained by economic factors (apart from long run considerations such as population growth and other structural changes). There are several determining variables.

1. Relative yields: If a constant price level is expected then currency has no yield whereas deposits carry at least an implicit yield. But the government pays for the cost of maintaining the stock of currency and the public (through bank charges) pays directly for the cost of maintaining deposits. Hence if the reserve ratio is high (earnings of banks low) the servicing charge on depsits will be high and a higher C/D ratio will result.

2. Income: If currency is an inferior good and deposits are a luxury good then a rise in income will lower the C/D ratio. This factor overlaps with a sociological distinction: workers are usually paid in cash rather than by cheque and therefore the C/D ratio depend on the social and occupational structure.

3. Record Keeping: A bank account provides a relatively cheap and convenient way of keeping records and to the extent that this is an advantage it will increase the demand for deposits. But tax evasion and black markets favour means of payment which do not leave written traces. (The marginal rate of taxation has proved a powerful explanatory variable in analysing C/D ratios during wartime.)

4. *Rural vs. Urban:* Rural economies typically depend more on credit and less on currency in contrast to urban communities.

5. *Importance of armed forces:* Since armed forces are paid in cash, war raises the cash-deposit ratio.

6. *Substitutes for currency:* The availability of charge accounts and credit cards lowers the demand for currency.

The factors determining the reserve ratios of banks are therefore closely linked with the institutional and legal structure of the country. Here we confine our analysis to a brief survey of the US and UK monetary systems.

US and UK Banking Systems

The US has a unit banking system with a large number of banks and a legal minimum reserve ratio which until recently was defined in terms of Federal Reserve deposits. This last feature implied that all currency holdings were surplus to this ratio. Since the required ratio was a minimum the banks always had to hold reserves in excess to avoid breaking the law. These excess reserves allowed some elasticity in the money supply.

Like all central banks the Federal Reserve acts as lender of last resort. This makes possible the definition of free reserves as excess reserves minus borrowed reserves. Many financial commentators have used the size of free reserves as an indicator of the tightness of monetary policy. But this criterion ignores that both excess and borrowed reserves are determined by profit maximising behaviour. For example, as the rate of interest rises it becomes profitable to economise on excess reserves and also to increase borrowing; hence free reserves become negative as interest rates rise (mutatis mutandis for a decrease in interest rates).

Consequently free reserves cannot be regarded as an injection of reserves against fixed ratios; instead they reflect banks' behaviour which moves with the business cycle. As indicators of policy they are misleading and would tend to promote pro cyclical behaviour by the central bank (e.g. rising interest rates in the upswing of a business cycle would coincide with negative free reserves and could prompt the authorities to take no action or only partially offsetting action thus aggravating the boom).

The UK banking system is typical of concentrated systems in which a well organised money market allows the few large banks to operate very close to their minimum reserve ratios. These ratios have never been legally set in Great Britain, and until 1945 individual banks kept reserve ratios at whatever level they deemed necessary for confidence. The observed cash ratios were, however, significantly higher than the banks' day to day reserve ratios as a result of 'window dressing'. This practice originated with banks using different days on which to close their books, allowing them to borrow cash from each other on the relevant dates — by arranging their assets to fall due on that day — so as to dress up their assets to appear liquid. (One would expect that window dressing increased in times of tight money.)

Historically the banks held about 20% cash reserves (minus window dressing), though during two periods they reduced their holdings. In the long period of tight money following World War I, as a result of an overvalued pound sterling, individual banks reduced their cash ratios, though, when the authorities reduced the money supply, in the aggregate no one could be better off (except to the extent that earning assets were substituted for cash). And during World War II, when the government pegged interest rates, making government bonds close substitutes for money, cash reserves were further reduced. In 1945, with the nationalisation of the Bank of England, the commerical banks agreed to give up window dressing in return for an 8% cash ratio. They now close their books on the same day.

Today, with the well organised money market, the British banks stay pretty close to their minimum reserve ratios, and one probably would not find as much variation in this ratio as there is in the American data. But the economic behaviour is still similar; one must simply focus on the composition of near-money asset portfolios to derive the banks' reactions to changes in interest rates. In the American data such reactions appear most clearly in changing cash ratios.

Inventory theory, expectations theory, or combinations and additions of other theories can be used to develop explanations of how the banking system reacts to changes in monetary policy.

Further analysis of money multipliers

We begin with a simple model of the money multiplier in which only two ratios are necessary: the public's cash-to-deposits ratio and the banks' cash-to-assets ratio (excess reserves). In the previous analysis these ratios were taken as fixed and the system was therefore mechanistic. But we have now shown that they are in fact variable and adjust as the public's and banks' maximising behaviour responds to changes in other parameters in the system. This simple model can easily be made more complex in various ways.

Time deposits (T), for example, can be thought of as a fixed proportion (t) to M (defined as Cash + Demand Deposits (DD)). Then if r_1 = reserves required against DD and r_2 = reserves required against T, the money multiplier has two forms (corresponding to the two definitions of M given by including and excluding T).

$$\frac{M}{B} = \frac{1}{c + r_1(1-c) + r_2 t}$$

$$\frac{M+T}{B} = \frac{1+t}{c + r_1(1-c) + r_2 t}$$

The higher is the behavioural ratio t (the proportion of simple money which the public chooses to hold as time deposits) the lower is the money multiplier; time deposits absorb cash reserves which therefore are not available to the banking system as either currency or cash base: i.e.

$$\frac{\partial(\frac{M}{B})}{\partial t} = \frac{-r_2}{[c + r_1(1-c) + r_2 t]^2}$$

But if money is defined as M+T, then the effect of a changing t on the money multiplier depends on the assumed values of c, r_1, and r_2: i.e.

$$\frac{\partial(\frac{M+T}{B})}{\partial t} = \frac{c(1-r_1)+r_1-r_2}{[c+r_1(1-c)+r_2 t]^2}$$

The model can be similarly extended to include non-bank financial intermediaries. Assume the amount of financial intermediation (F) is related to the money supply, $F = f \cdot M$, and that intermediaries must hold their deposits at commercial banks. A three tier system emerges. Commercial bank reserves are

$$R_b = r_b[(1-c)M+r_f f]$$

The money base (B) = reserves + cash:

$$B = [c+r_b(1-c)+r_b r_f f]M$$

Thus, $\quad \dfrac{M}{B} = \dfrac{1}{c+r_b(1-c)+r_b r_f f}$, or including F in M,

$$\frac{M+F}{B} = \frac{1+f}{c+r_b(1-c)+r_b r_f f}$$

This simple formulation can add insight to the instability issue raised by Gurley and Shaw. They postulated that the growth of financial intermediaries would lead to instability in the connection between the reserve base and the money supply (however defined). The notion was that changes in intermediaries' reserve ratios could cause substantial changes in the money multipler. However, putting realistic numbers for these ratios in the above equations to estimate the magnitude of possible changes, it is evident that the multiplier is actually pretty stable, since the changing factors are products of fractions.

Theory of Monetary Policy

There are two broad approaches to how monetary policy influences the economic system — through the demand for and supply of money and through the interest rate. Given a single interest rate analysis can be done with Keynesian monetary theory. But with a variety of interest rates the quantity of money itself ceases to be of much interest. A model of an entire financial structure is required, and one must know how monetary policy affects the public's holdings of all types of assets.

As a first approximation assume that the central bank desires to control the total quantity of money. It can do so both because its liabilities are the cash base of the system, and because it is the lender of last resort. However this second function, while it establishes the power of the central bank over the commerical banks, is inconsistent with control of the money supply; for in some circumstances it allows the commercial banks to control what happens.

With a stable money multiplier, we can talk about the central bank controlling any of several quantities, all of which amount to the same thing. That is, the central bank can be thought of as controlling total money, or bank deposits, or total bank credit: with fixed ratios in the multiplier, controlling one controls the others. Of course, when we broaden the model and allow these ratios to be determined by economic maximising behaviour, then the mechanistic interactions may loosen. If the central bank has less than perfect information about the underlying behavioural relationships, it may make some difference whether it tries to control money or for example, total earning assets.

One exception to this approach is found in the British literature in the 1950's. Some Keynesian writers drew a distinction between different types of bank assets and their influence on total spending. It was assumed that an increase in bank loans is immediately spent, while, on the other hand, an increase in bank's holdings of government bonds is not (because the public voluntarily holds the cash it receives). This theory leads to the conclusion that the central bank should control a subset of bank assets. If you add the notion that some people who want to borrow are unworthy, compared to the rest, then quickly you have a system of loan rationing. The traditional objects of contumely have been the consumer and the buyer on hire purchase (regarded as an immoral activity of the working class). This leads to higher interest rates and more refusals to lend to the poor, which is obviously counter to most notions of welfare.

The Central Bank controls the money supply through open market operations, reserve requirements and the rediscount rate. It fixes the size of its liabilities through the amount of assets it holds i.e. open market operations (buying government debt of various maturities to expand the cash base, and vice-versa).

How much extra leverage can the Central Bank get over the system by varying the composition of its assets. Can it affect the structure of interest rates selectively? Usually these endeavours are presented as an attempt to raise the short rate – for balance of payments reasons – while keeping the long rate low – to promote fixed investment.

The economists' answers divide predictably on theoretical grounds. The liquidity preference or portfolio approach to interest rates implies that such 'twists' are possible, while the expectations approach denies it unless the Central Bank can also influence the public's expectations about future rates.

A related issue in policy history is whether the Central Bank should confine itself to the short end of the market – the "bills only" doctrine – for the sake of market stability. This issue was resolved because it was realised that during any expansion or contraction of total assets, it is the expansion or contraction of commercial bank deposits which has the overwhelming influence. The Central Bank's share of the total shift is so small that empirically it makes little difference which assets it deals in.

The Central Bank fixes the terms on which it will act as lender of last resort to the system. It designates what types of assets it will accept and fixes the price which the banks must pay to obtain loans. If the latter policy ("Bank rate" or "Rediscount" policy) is used at all heavily, it must be coupled with some sort of convention through which the commercial banks try to minimise their debt to the Central Bank. This is because with multiple credit expansion the banks may otherwise make a profit by borrowing at what is supposed to be a penalty rate.

In the UK the commercial banks borrow from the discount market, which then borrows from the Bank of England. The tradition is that such borrowing should be kept to a minimum. In the US, the Federal Reserve sets limits to such borrowing — but the arrangement must be looser than that suggests since the Fed is actually owned by its members, whom it is supposed to serve.

To make a change in bank rate effective on other rates in the system, there must be some incentive for others to respond to changes in this rate. The use of bank rate must therefore be supported by open market operations. As in any market, successful price-fixing requires that quantities be fixed to eliminate excess demand or supply, which would otherwise tend to change the price. Thus one cannot contrast a bank rate system with an open market system the two instruments must be used consistently together. The difference lies in which instrument is used to initiate policy changes.

The Central Bank fixes reserve requirements for the commercial banks. Where there is a legal minimum reserve requirement as in the US, then one presumably can legally change it; and the Federal Reserve is empowered to change it within set limits. In systems modeled on the British, where the reserve requirement is a convention, there is a provision for "special deposits" on top of the reserve requirement (developed in Australia). However, in practice changes in special deposits tend to be used as a tax on the banks rather than for monetary control.

Raising the reserve requirement can be used to cut down the money multiplier so that the central bank can influence the money supply with a smaller change in the cash base. But there is no obvious reason why the aim of policy should be to minimise the work that the central bank has to do. Changing reserve requirements can also be used to keep banks sensitive to the central bank's operations. As an example, in the late 1930's, due to an inflow of gold into the US, the banking system was holding reserves far in excess of the Fed's legal minimum. So the Fed raised its reserves far in excess of the Fed's legal minimum. Its alleged purpose in so doing was to "regain control" over the banks. Friedman and Schwartz maintain that the banks were holding these reserves due to their depression experiences, and so when the Fed raised the reserve requirement, the banks contracted credit and the 1937-1938 recession was the result.

The subject of minimum reserves involves some fairly subtle issues, one of them being that reserves held as a legal minimum are *ipso facto* not reserves. Banks cannot use them in an emergency so that they must hold other reserves or liquid assets. Moreover, no interest is paid on legal reserves which are therefore a tax on the commercial banks by the central bank. This is quite a profitable tax as one can judge from looking at the Federal Reserve building in Washington. It also provides employment for economists. The tax raises questions of the appropriateness of its size and its effects on the system.

Other methods which the central banks in many countries use include moral suasion, commercial bank inspection and elgibility rules and direct contacts. Moral suasion, whereby the central bank induces the commercial banks to do what they otherwise would not do, works best with a highly monopolised banking system in which the banking system knows that it is being allowed to earn monopoly profits.

Further discussion of the instruments of monetary policy

In some banking systems the rate of interest has a symbolic significance. By changing the rate of interest the central bank signals its intentions to other financial institutions. But the capacity of bank rate to act as an effective signal is rather dubious and sometimes the Central Bank changes bank rate simply to bring it into line with previous market developments.

Reserve ratios fixed in terms of assets other than money were advocated to control the money supply in the USA. But this can only be successful if (i) the assets are held exclusively by banks and (ii) the authorities can control their supply. Otherwise intervention simply alters the pattern of bank investments.

Which of the tools used by monetary policy is fundamental to control of the money supply? Methods of moral suasion and direct control are not, though they may influence the distribution of loans among different lenders. Reserve requirements, the rediscount rate and open market operations will be discussed.

If banks have some sort of stable function relating their reserves to total deposits, fixed reserve ratios are not necessary. For if they hold more than the fixed ratio then the ratio does not necessarily influence the money supply (at least for small changes). If the required reserve ratio is higher than the banks regard as profitable it entails a tax on them and ultimately on their depositors. The same argument applies to other fixed asset ratios that the banks may be obliged to observe. Banks must hold a less profitable portfolio than they otherwise might and may also lose interest (because by expanding their holdings of particular assets they force down the relevant interest rates).

The rediscount rate is not essential for purposes of monetary policy. Banks can be regulated by imposition of reserve requirements which will induce them to make optimal adjustments by disposal and purchase of assets. Given a reasonably integrated financial market, this process could function easily and smoothly provided the Central Bank is well behaved; there is no need for a rediscount facility. What the rediscount facility offers is an escape hatch for the banking system from the central bank's policy, because it enables them to acquire reserves by borrowing which will offset, say, an open market sale which would otherwise reduce cash reserves. But the high cost of last resort borrowing makes it a transitory loophole.

The rediscount facility does two things which can be regarded as useful. First, it allows banks to protect themselves against arbitrary and sudden changes in central bank policy and, secondly it assists stabilisation of interest rates in the short run. Changes in interest rates relative to the rediscount rate will tend to produce changes in banks' debt to the central bank and the substitution effect will stabilise interest rates.

Open market operations are alone sufficient for control of the money supply. It is through changes in the cash base that the Central Bank influences the total quantity of money supplied. But, because cash reserves bear no interest, the Central Bank implicity uses two instruments — open market operations to control the quantity of cash reserves and a conventional zero rate of interest on cash reserves in the central bank.

If credit is to be rationed it should be rationed by price and not by administrative decision (i.e. controls, moral suasion) for two reasons: (i) controls make the marginal rate of return on credit in different sectors of the economy unequal and (ii) they impose a tax on the banking system, forcing them to lend to borrowers they would not otherwise choose.

Reserve requirements tax the banks both because they are generally larger than commercial purposes require and because they earn no interest. This situation encourages the development of other financial institutions which are not required to hold reserves with the central bank. The efficiency of the system would improve if the central bank would restrain its propensity to issue directives, if reserve requirements were abandoned and if the central bank were to pay interest on commercial bank deposits held with it.

Is monetary control exercised through the cash ratio or the liquidity ratio? This controversy has died out since 1968. Due to pressures from the IMF emphasis has shifted away from two features which previously characterised British monetary policy towards the quantity of money: (i) The practice of stabilising the Treasury bill market which avoided imposing penalties on buyers and sellers, and (ii) Bank of England efforts to maximise the amount of public debt held by the general public. This policy took the form of stabilising operations in the bond market, the central bank attempting to reassure investors by standing by to purchase bonds when the price was tending to fall and selling when it was tending to rise. Insofar as this policy was operated in an environment of rising interest rates it implied a built-in inflationary mechanism.

The theory of control which developed in Britain was that the Bank of England cannot control the quantity of bank deposits through open market operations, but instead controls it by the 'liquidity ratio' and Treasury control of Treasury bills outstanding. When cash contracts, the banks call in loans and the discount market borrows from the central bank which then winds up having recreated cash by loans or purchases of treasury bills. It was therefore argued that the only way to control the money supply was through total liquid assets by restricting the Treasury bill supply.

The essence of this debate is whether treasury bills are perfect substitutes for cash and, if so, whether that is the consequence of Bank of England policy. The traditional idea is that the Bank of England will use the rate of interest to make it expensive for the system to substitute cash for treasury bills.

R.L. Crouch has argued that you can only control the banking system's total assets through a liquid assets aggregate if you have control over that particular aggregate: so long as there are possibilities of substitution then that control is going to be weak. Points of flexibility in the British system of monetary control are: (i) Treasury bills can be bid away from the public; (ii) there is substitution between treasury and commercial bills in the discount market (iii) there is substitution between short loans and outside borrowing in the discount market; and (iv) Call loans and stock exchange loans are substitutes for bills in the liquid portfolios of the commercial banks. Thus total liquid assets are variable even through the total of Treasury bills can be controlled.

APPENDIX

Stylized "liquidity-ratio" model of the determination of the British money supply.

Stylized Accounting Identities (ignoring minor assets and liabilities and own capital of the institutions)

(1) $T = T_E + T_B + T_D + T_O$

The total of Teasury bills outstanding is held by the bank of England, the banks, the discount market, and others.

(2) $C = C_B + C_D$

The total of commercial bills outstanding is held by the banks and the discount market exclusively.

(3) $x = \dfrac{C_D + T_D}{C_D + T_D + C_B + T_B}$

There is some ratio in which the total of Treasury and commercial bills held by banks and discount market is divided between them. Hence:

(3a) $T_B + C_B = (1-x)(C + T_B + T_D)$

(3b) $T_D + C_D = x(C + T_B + T_D)$

(If we assume that the total of Treasury and commercial bills outstanding is constant over a long enough period, that they are all of thirteen weeks maturity, and that the discount market holds all bills 6r a certain number of weeks and then passes them to the banks, x will be 1/13 of the number of weeks for which the discount market holds bills.)

(4) $T_E + B_E = N + R$

Treasury bills and bonds held by the Bank of England equal currency in circulation plus bank cash reserves. (By assumption, R is determined by the banks, through exchange of Treasury bills with the Bank of England at market rate, to maintain the 8 per cent ratio to deposits.)
Hence:

(4a) $R = T_E + B_E - N$

(5) $x(C + T_B + T_D) + B_D = L_B + L_O$

Discount market holdings of bills plus short bonds equal call loans by banks to discount market plus loans by other lenders to discount market.
Hence:

(5a) $L_B = x(C + T_B + T_D) + B_D - L_D$

The total liquid assests of the banks are

$R + T_B + C_B + L_B + S_B$, where S_B represents call loans to the stock exchange. Adding up (3a), (4a), (5a) and S_B we obtain total liquid assets of banks as

(6) $\Sigma L A = T - T_o + B_E - N + C + B_D - L_D + S_B$

Total liquid assets equals Treasury bills outstanding minus those held by outside holders plus Bank of England bond holdings minus currency in circulation plus commercial bills outstanding plus discount market bond holdings minus discount market borrowings from non-bank lenders plus bank call loans to the stock exchange.

Behaviour Relations

The determinants of the total liquid assets, and therefore the money supply, are as follows:

T, the total Treasury bill issue outstanding, is a Treasury (or Treasury-Bank) policy variable.

T_o, outside holdings of Treasury bills, is a private choice variable influenced by the yields on alternative assets, of which one relevant one is interest on bank deposit accounts, and another, call loan rates to the discount market.

B_E, Bank of England bond holdings, is a Bank policy variable; behind the scenes, any change in B_E will influence T_E, Bank of England holding of Treasury bills via the adjustment of bank reserves to conform to the 8 per cent.

N, currency in circulation, is determined by the public but might be influenced by interest rates.

C, commercial bills outstanding, is a private choice variable influenced by the cost of alternative finance, the closest alternative being bank advances.

B_D, discount market bond holdings, is a choice variable for the discount market, influenced by the relation of call loan rates to bond yields.

L_D, outside loans to the discount market, is a private choice variable influenced by the yields on Treasury bills, and on deposit accounts among other alternatives.

S_B is a private choice variable for the stock exchange, influenced by the relationship between yields on stock exchange securities and the applicable call loan rate.

THE BRITISH MONETARY SYSTEM

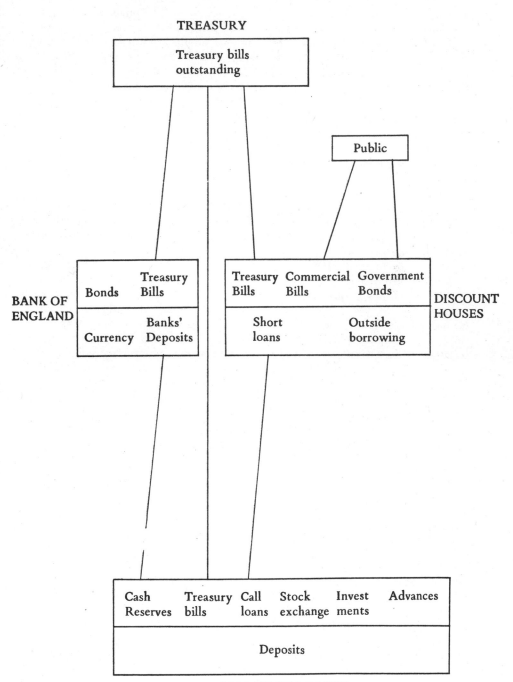

CHAPTER 19

THE THEORY OF INFLATION

A monetary definition of inflation (which focusses on the phenomenon to be explained) is "a sustained upward trend in the level of prices". It may by implication be difficult to detect inflation. Not all upward price movements are inflationary — high interest rates for example, are deflationary not inflationary — and upward price changes may reflect adjustments in demand and supply to disturbances in the economy. Prices may move up after devaluation as demand is switched to domestic production, or a bad harvest, by reducing output, may raise prices if velocity does not change. Price indicators may not adequately reflect an inflationary process either because they weigh relatively stable or insignificant elements too heavily, or if they underallow for improvements in the quality of goods purchased at higher prices. (The Stigler report suggested that the inflation indexed during the late 1950's period of tight money might be due to overstatements of the rate of inflation resulting from such factors.)

Inflation may alternatively be defined by a cause e.g. monetary expansion, deficit financing or excess demand. However, such definitions imply questionable theories of price rise causation and policy prescriptions. In other words, the alleged cause may not be the point at which government policy should be directed. For example, inflation resulting from deficit financing may not be best corrected by balancing the budget.

There are two main approaches to the explanation of inflation. The quantity theory tradition stresses monetary phenomena while the Keynesians have emphasised non-monetary factors. The Keynesian analysis, where expectations of zero price change are assumed, has been chiefly applied to mild inflations while quantity theorists, who have in contrast stressed the significance of expected price changes, have been more concerned with hyper-inflations. Recent American policy dilemmas have brought the two approaches into direct confrontation. The major analytical distinction between the rival hypotheses is between the Keynesian interpretation of inflation as equalising savings and investment and the quantity theory stress on an excess supply of money that continually raises the price level.

Keynesian theories

The Keynesian approach has been developed in two historical phases. The first was in the context of World War II finance problems when concern was generated for building models of the inflationary process. In these models full employment was assumed and adjustments took place via wage and price changes rather than in terms of quantities produced. The second phase was that of the Phillips curve analysis where inflation was related to the balance of demand and supply in the economy. Both phases filled out the original Keynesian system by including mechanisms determining the level of wages and prices.

In examining how wages and prices change, rather than how real output changes, one may distinguish the propensities to save of different sectors of the community. For example, Kaldor's theory identifies the distribution of real income between labour and capital as a function of the rate of investment and differing propensities to save. Extension of the Kaldor model beyond homogeneous labour and capital or two factors of production is impossible.

In Keynesian models inflation is a consequence of a competitive struggle for shares of national income. In equilibrium the income distribution must be such that the savings of the two groups together equal investment, at which point the inflationary process ends. So in the Keynesian models of inflation total savings are equal to total investment as an equilibrium condition; money wages and prices adjust in a lagged manner to previous changes in income distribution and inflation is thus generated that can be either stable or explosive: exact specification of the process depends on the mathematical structure given it. The key characteristic of this and similar models is that inflation results from the behaviour of the economy in working towards an equilibrium distribution of income.

A simpler theory of this form was one developed by Arthur Smithies during World War II. The model assumes a single consumption function and inflation. There is money illusion in the economy. As inflation proceeds the money value of saving rises along AA' until it intersects the line BB' which represents the money value of the real saving required to offset the inflationary impact of government expenditure and private investment.

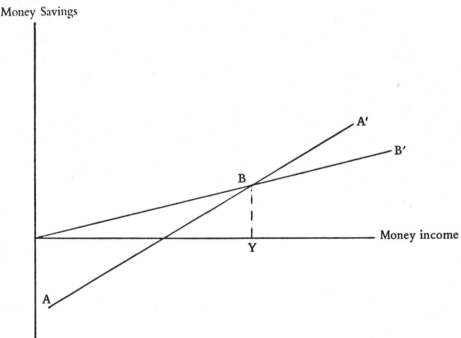

An alternative model assumes an initial equilibrium distribution between labour capital and the rentier class. Further, it assumes a change in the initial distribution of income resulting from (say) war-time destruction. Inflation is then a dynamic sequence generated by the actions of each group in attempting to restore its original real share of national product. The increase in wages and prices continues indefinitely or stops when one group no longer seeks (or cannot get) recompense for its losses (e.g. rentiers get squeezed).

The difficulty with all these models is that their analytics reduce to the same mathematics — first or second order difference equations. A simple model of inflation is:

$$\Delta P_t = ab\,\Delta P_{t-1}$$

or, in terms of wages,

$$\Delta W_t = cd\,\Delta W_{t-1}$$

where the change in prices or wages is some function of last period's change in prices or wages. In the first order difference equation the inflationary process either explodes or converges to zero depending on whether or not ab is greater than or less than one. The coefficient, ab, may correspond to many theories of inflation. It may be interpreted as a single variable representing the presence of money illusion reflected in the marginal propensity to spend out of increments to money income. Or a can represent a 'cost-push' adjustment of prices to previous wage increase and b a 'demand pull' adjustment of wages (or vice versa). All views of the inflationary process may be expressed in terms of these equations where the lags are determined, not by the mathematics, but by the institutional environment (e.g. the duration of wage bargaining processes).

Economically, this approach is not too interesting. The behaviour assumptions are essentially arbitrary, which implies a very institutional form of economics, where, for example, wages may be determined by changes in the cost of living. Further, the approach assumes that people's expectations of future price movements remain unchanged for the duration of the inflation. If the inflationary process is to end, some group must sacrifice real income, so doubt is cast on the economic rationality of the behaviour assumptions implicit in the analysis.

Behaviour is independent of the monetary environment. To predict an interminable inflationary process is to assume either that there is money circulating in the system sufficient to allow the inflation to continue or that the government chooses to finance the inflation. Finally, the mechanism is inconsistent with the observed facts of inflation. A redistribution of real income from labour to capital is predicted, but typically does not take place. Often it is the rentier class, whose wealth is held in non-recontractable assets denominated in money terms, who are squeezed by the inflationary process.

The second phase of the Keynesian analysis of inflation attempted to rationalise the relation of wage and price movements to aggregate demand and supply through the Phillips curve, which postulates a link between variations in employment (capacity utilisation) and price changes. A critical question for this analysis is whether adjustments are made in money or real terms.

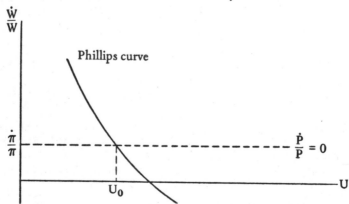

Let $\frac{\dot{W}}{W}$ be the proportional change in wages in one period, $\frac{\dot{\pi}}{\pi}$ the proportional change in productivity in one period, $\frac{\dot{P}}{P}$ the proportional change in prices in one period, and U the level of unemployment. Then the Phillips' curve is described in the diagram by a statistical relationship between the rate of wage increase and the level of unemployment (taken as an index of excess demand for or supply of labour). Price changes equal the wage changes minus the change in productivity and at U_O there is therefore no price inflation. This simple additive model assumes implicitly among other things, that in a growth context factor shares are constant and that technical progress is of the labour augmenting variety.

The analysis has been questioned by a number of economists, most recently by Laidler and Corry, on the grounds that two curves (one for low levels of unemployment and one for high levels of unemployment) may be more appropriate.

The assumption that people bargain about money wages is questionable since the bargaining process characteristically embodies expectations about future price increases. Attempting to get to a point on the Phillips' curve would change expectations and behaviour so that the original curve would shift and no longer be appropriate.

The analysis is useful, however, in making sense out of the distinction between 'cost-push' and 'demand-pull' views of inflation. If we define full employment as that point at which prices have no tendency to rise or fall, all inflation must be 'demand-pull'. If however, we adopt a social norm for unemployment (e.g. Beveridge's 3 per cent maximum) a less that 'full-employment' situation could generate inflation of the cost-push type. Policies might then be introduced to reduce the rate of price increase through improvements in the efficiency of factor markets.

Whatever the alleged 'cause' of inflation the monetary preconditions must be satisfied so that the distinction among Keynesian theories is between different mechanisms of inflation.

The Quantity Theory and inflation

The Quantity theory emphasises the role of money in inflation and therefore assumes a stable demand for real balances when prices are expected to be stable (unit elasticity of price expectations). The demand for real balances is seen as a function of income (or wealth) and the real rate of interest (the opportunity cost of holding real balances). These hypotheses however are common to both approaches; they differ in the role assigned to price expectations which enter explicitly into the Quantity theory whereas the Keynesian approach assumes unit elasticity of price expectations. In particular Quantity theorists treat inflation as a cost of holding money and other assets whose value is fixed in money terms; the difference between money and these other assets is that people can avoid the costs of inflation when holding bonds by being paid a high enough interest rate. Thus if i = money rate of interest, r = the real rate of interest and $\frac{\dot{P}}{P}$ the expected rate of inflation, then people will be persuaded to hold assets whose value is fixed in nominal terms only if $r = i - \frac{\dot{P}}{P}$, or $i = r + \frac{\dot{P}}{P}$. This of course implies that in the long run the authorities do not redistribute income via inflation from those who derive income by holding assets whoe value is fixed in nominal terms to those who do not.

Because there is no close substitute for real balances there is an unavoidable cost during inflation to holding them (equal to $i = r + \frac{\dot{P}}{P}$). If the demand for real balances is a function of this opportunity cost then the effect of anticipated inflation is to reduce peoples' demand for money although not to eliminate it. The similarity of the analysis to the effects of a tax on a commodity has led some to call this an inflation tax.

In long run equilibrium peoples' expectations of inflation adjust to the actual rate.

$$\frac{\dot{P}}{P} = (\frac{\dot{P}}{P})e = \frac{\dot{M}}{M} - \frac{\dot{Y}}{Y}$$

(In most analyses of inflation it is assumed that $\frac{\dot{Y}}{Y} = 0$ and therefore that $\frac{\dot{P}}{P} = \frac{\dot{M}}{M}$.)

In the long run therefore income is redistributed away from holders of money to those who benefit from the monetary expansion — typically the government. But empirical studies in Latin America have shown that the benefits of monetary expansion via budget deficits have been distributed to favoured sections of the community receiving loans at low rates etc. If it is assumed that inflation is correctly anticipated (i.e. consider a long term analysis) then people will adjust the ratio of real balances to income to the alternative opportunity cost of holding money. Then $\frac{\dot{P}}{P} = \frac{\dot{M}}{M}$. Since the ratio of real balances to income can only be held constant by accumulating money holdings, it involves foregoing present consumption (the inflation tax).

Inflation tax and other taxes

In the theory of public finance the revenue collected from a per unit tax on a commodity depends on the elasticity of demand and the waste of resources involved is the costs of collection. In the chart the pre-tax price per unit is 1 and $1 + t$ is the post tax price; q_0 is the pre-tax quantity and q_1 the post-tax quantity. A is the tax revenue and B is the welfare loss (a measure of the waste of resources usually called the collection cost).

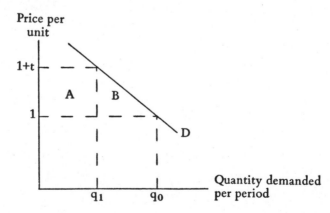

A similar analysis of the demand for real balances is possible using the same familiar diagram. First, assume fully anticipated inflation but ignore the real rate of interest. Now m_0 is the desired ratio of real balances to income when no inflation is expected, m_1 is the ratio when inflation of $(\frac{\dot{P}}{P})_1$ is expected. Then A is the inflation tax revenue as a proportion of national income and the area of the triangle B is the collection cost which depends on the elasticity of demand for real balances.

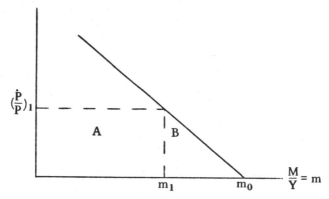

$$\text{Area of B} = \tfrac{1}{2} \left(\frac{\dot{P}}{P}\right) \left[\frac{dm}{d(\frac{\dot{P}}{P})} \left(\frac{\dot{P}}{P}\right) \right] = \tfrac{1}{2} \left(\frac{\dot{P}}{P}\right)^2 \left[\frac{dm}{d(\frac{\dot{P}}{P})} \right] \frac{m_0}{m_0}$$

$$= \tfrac{1}{2} \left(\frac{\dot{P}}{P}\right) \left[\frac{dm}{d(\frac{\dot{P}}{P})} \cdot \frac{(\frac{\dot{P}}{P})}{m_0} \right] m_0 \quad = \tfrac{1}{2} \left(\frac{\dot{P}}{P}\right) \eta \, m_0$$

Here η is the elasticity and it is assumed that $p = 1$ when $(\frac{\dot{P}}{P}) = 0$.

The next stage of the analysis allows for the opportunity cost of holding money $(r + \frac{\dot{P}}{P})$. Before inflation is anticipated there is already a welfare loss equal to B_1 because interest is not paid on money (provided that the social marginal cost of creating money is zero). If inflation is anticipated the demand for real balances falls further and the cost of collecting the inflation tax is $B_2 + B_3$.

Although the cost of inflation may appear small relative to the costs of unemployment when the real rate of interest is ignored, research in Canada suggests that, if B_1, B_2 and B_3 are taken into the account, the costs of unemployment are not much higher than those of the inflation that higher unemployment would prevent. Moreover the analysis shows the cost of collecting the inflation tax is high as a proportion of tax revenue; but in countries where this analysis is especially relevant (less developed countries suffering from acute inflation) the alternative means of collecting revenue may also be very costly.

The quantity theory of inflation implies that income is redistributed from money-holders to others. The Keynesian literature assumes this redistribution is from workers to capitalists, but the quantity approach implies no clear prediction about redistribution among factors of production.

The Dynamics of Inflation

It is rare to have full adjustment to inflation. For example, wartime inflation typically starts off with a gradual erosion of sound financial practices followed by partially successful price controls. Then comes the inflation resulting from the earlier increase in the money supply. This may cause people to continue anticipating price changes even after inflationary pressures have been removed. A similar pattern seen with some frequency in less developed countries is accelerating inflation caused by monetary expansion also aggravated by the formation of price expectations. The outcome is political unrest and possibly a change of power; as the change is based on a promise to halt inflation the new authorities are obliged to impose deflationary measures so large that massive unemployment arises which in turn produces further political change.

A dynamic analysis is essential for such problems. It can be achieved by assuming that expectations are based on past rates of inflation. A simple diagram is also of help here. The horizontal axis measures the ratio of real balances to real national income (or nominal money balances to money national income, $\frac{M}{Y}$). Since real national income is assumed constant an increase in the price level reduces the supply of real balances and the ratio $\frac{M}{Y}$, i.e. a move towards the origin (e.g. form m_1 to m_2). The vertical axis measures the relative change in prices. Furthermore the price level in each time period is normalised to equal one so it cannot fall below -1 and hence the vertical axis stops at -1. (There is no upward limit to the vertical axis).

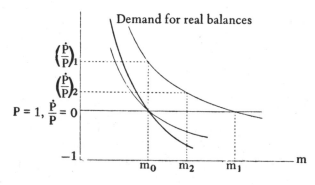

In this diagram a demand for real balances can also be drawn showing the ratio of $\frac{M}{Y}$ desired at varying levels of expected inflation. The intersection m_0 shows the desired ratio of real balances to national income with unit elasticity of price expectations.

Thus any point on the horizontal axis represents a given stock of real balances at a moment of time with an assumed price level of 1. Through any such point it is possible to draw a rectangular hyperbola asymptotic to the vertical axis and the line $\frac{\dot{P}}{P} = -1$. These curves show the amount of real balances available for the next period depending on the inflation that has taken place this period: i.e. $\frac{M_t}{1 \div (\frac{\dot{P}}{P})_t} = M_{t+1}$. Suppose the government expands the money supply so that $\frac{M}{Y}$ changes from m_0 to m_1; m_1 represents the level of real balances before any price rise occurs i.e. at the beginning of time period 1. Through m_1 will pass a rectangular hyperbola showing the amount of real balances available next period (period 2) resulting from any price changes this period. Thus if individuals do not expect any price changes, desire a level of real balances given by m_0, and adjust completely in one time period, then they will travel up the curve through m_1 until they have reduced the stock of real balances to m_0 by an inflation $(\frac{\dot{P}}{P})_1$.

If individuals only reduce half their excess balances in any time period then the movement up the curve will only be until inflation = $(\frac{\dot{P}}{P})_2$; and then m_2 will be the amount of real balances available for the next period (period 2). Now a new rectangular hyperbola through m_2 on $P = 1$ will represent the amount of real balances available for the next period as a result of all possible rates of inflation. Hence prices continue to rise (by $(\frac{\dot{P}}{P})_3$ in period two) even after the increase in the money supply has stopped; but inflation decreases as real balance converge on the desired level m_0.

The analysis changes when unit elasticity of price expectations is dropped.

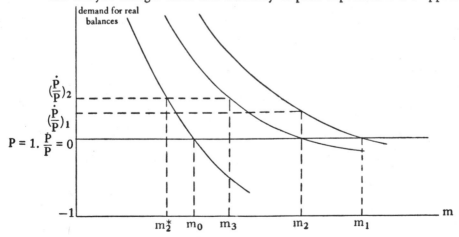

Let the government increase the money supply so that real balances at the beginning of period 1 are m_1. Let half the excess ($= m_1 - m_2$) be eroded by inflation $(\frac{\dot{p}}{p})_1$ so that at the begining of period 2 real balances are represented by m_2. But now assume that peoples' expected inflation in period 2 will be $(\frac{\dot{p}}{p})_1$; desired balances will then be less and can be represented by m_2^* and a higher inflation will be required to halve the new excess real balances $(m_2 - m_2^*)$ than if the excess were $(m_2 - m_0)$. Inflation may be faster for a while after the injection of money stops than initially; and there may be oscillation between inflation and deflation. It is hard, however, to devise expectations assumptions such that eventually the rate of inflation does not converge on the rate of increase of the money supply.

This theory raises the issue of how to stop inflations once there is full adjustment. Suppose such an inflation is taking place but that a plausible government announces that it will halt it. If people believe the announcement then they will start accumulating cash and this effort to increase holdings of real balances, together with government attempts to reduce the money supply, can have a severe deflationary effect. Furthermore, if prices are administered through the industrial and trade union structure, it is possible that they will continue to rise (because negotiators continue to expect inflation) reducing real balances still further and leading to even more drastic deflationary pressures as people try to achieve their desired holdings of real balances. In such a situation it is of course possible to have no price increases despite increases in the money supply greater than during the actual inflation.

The Phillips Curve

The long-lasting, mild inflation in most Western countries has produced a debate between the Keynesian and Quantity theorists on the nature of inflation, and the focus of this debate has been the Phillips curve.

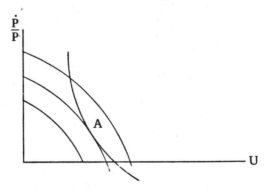

The strength of the Phillips Curve approach was that it seemed to fit the data well, and proved useful in policy discussions. This policy discussion of the Phillips curve has gone through three phases in the 1960's. First it was suggested that policy makers simply find the U_0 which keeps $\frac{\dot{p}}{p} = 0$. Usually this amount of unemployment seemed fairly high: full employment was thought to imply a high degree of inflation. Later policy makers were held to make a choice along a set of indifference curves between unemployment and inflation. (Since both are undesirable, the indifference curves are concave to the origin.) At A, the empirically measured trade off between inflation and unemployment is just equal to the trade off on the policy makers' (or public opinion's) indifference curves. (Tinbergen did the original work in this area, specifying that policy makers must have as many instruments as they have targets if they hope to be effective. In case not all goals can be reached, a policy maker's objective function is used to maximise policy preference.)

This approach is actually weak, because inflation and unemployment are quite different things, not easily represented in a formulation of general welfare. One might instead postulate that what is involved is a social class conflict. Thus the inflation cost falls almost exclusively on the rentiers, while workers bear the cost of unemployment. The effects are not shared and are therefore not general.

Most recently policy makers have been assumed to get behind their trade off and quantify the social costs of both inflation and unemployment. (Study by Grant L. Reuber, JPE, 1964). This is not as easy as it might at first seem. Consider first the unemployment cost. During the Kennedy administration came 'Okun's Law' that GNP increased 3 points for each 1 point decrease in unemployment. Thus, it was argued, unemployment has a high social cost. But this is not a valid analysis, except perhaps in periods of deep unemployment. Presumably the new people who are brought into the labour force with a decrease in unemployment were previously on the margin of indifference between working and not working, so that the extra output they produce has a social value just equal to whatever else they were doing. Thus when peoples' unemployment is voluntary (either usually or temporarily) the output loss is not a valid measure of the social cost: the social cost is substantially less than the output loss.

Analysis of the inflation cost poses similar difficulties.

Unanticipated inflation involves a transfer of income from those who hold assets fixed in money terms to those who issued the assets. There is no waste of resources, simply a transfer. How such a transfer should be weighted as a cost is difficult to resolve. A similar analysis can be applied for an unanticipated end to inflation.

Anticipated inflation involves the cost of the inflation tax on the holders of money. As was shown in our earlier analysis, when no interest is paid on money, the total social cost of inflation is high and is a function of the elasticity of demand for M, r, and $\frac{\dot{P}}{P}$

The Phillips curve was widely applied to policy discussions in the US, but as the problem of inflation persisted, Quantity theorists began to examine and criticise the alleged trade off between inflation and unemployment. Remember that the Quantity theory approach fundamentally assumes that people adjust their demand for money according to expectations of price changes in the light of their past experience, while the Keynesian approach — and with it the Phillips curve — assumes that people have stable price expectations.

Thus the Phillips curve assumes that people do not change their expectations of stable prices, even after a considerable period of price change.

The Friedman-Phelps (and others) argument is that statistical estimates of the Phillips curve are derived from particular historical experience and that the fitted Phillips curve relationship will remain roughly the same only so long as that experience persists. Specifically, since the original Phillips curve was fitted for periods of both rising and falling prices, if you then attempt to operate on a fitted Phillips curve, you will change the historical environment (i.e. raise or reduce inflation) which eventually will affect expectations and shift the curve.

Friedman postulates that there is only one long run real Phillips curve. This is a vertical line (no trade off) intersecting the horizontal axis at the natural real Phillips curve rate of unemployment, U_n. If policy makers attempt to move from U_n, with $\frac{\dot{P}}{P}$ at zero, to A, the inflation caused will induce wage bargaining and other adjustments to inflationary expectations, so that the curve shifts right and we fetch up at B; above U_n with the same unemployment and more inflation.

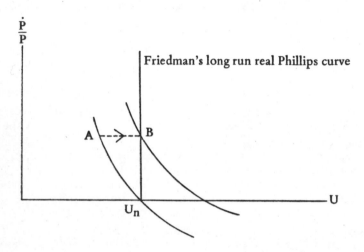

The analysis thus postulates that the only choice open to policy makers is the time path described above, since in the long run U_n is inevitable. The political process usually works to maximise the short-run gain in moving to A, without properly considering the longer-run cost of returning to B. Hence a continually rising rate of inflation is predicted. The analysis is symmetrical for periods of falling prices; people will get used to deflation and modify wage bargaining.

To discredit this analysis on theoretical grounds, one must postulate irrational behaviour i.e. that people ignore the inflation or deflation that is actually occurring. Practically, however, if people learn about inflation and adjust slowly, then Friedman's argument may not be important: people will then behave as if there were no inflation or deflation.

Some people have tried to test the hypothesis for periods of different rates of inflation, expecting to find different Phillip's curves for times in which price change expectations should be forming more quickly. The only supporting evidence found with this method is that the Phillips curve for the UK in the postwar years is higher than for the prewar years.

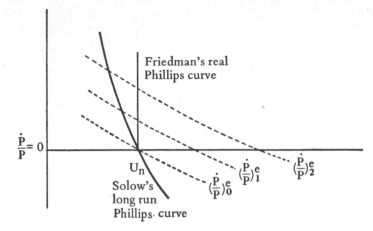

Let price expectations be an independent variable. Then one would have a family of Phillip's curves, each indexed for a particular level of price expectations $[(\frac{\dot{P}}{P})^e_0, (\frac{\dot{P}}{P})^e_1$ etc.]. Then Solow's analysis can be put in the form of three rival theories:

1. Naive Phillips curve. There is only one Phillips curve regardless of expectations.

2. Friedman. There is only one real Phillips curve corresponding to real equilibrium in the labour market with the marginal physical product of labour euqal to labour's supply price. Over time, if the actual rate of inflation is equal to the expected rate, the only points maintainable are those directly above U_n. Thus the rate of unemployment cannot be changed by altering the rate of price change.

3. Solow. People are rational and adjust to inflation, but they are subject to some money illusion and thus do not fully adjust to inflation. This implies a long-run Phillips curve with some trade-off between inflation and unemployment. Solow's generalised equation, which allowed for price expectations, found this long-run relationship.

The mathematics of the analysis is in an appendix based on J. Tobin's exposition. In summary the revised Phillips curve is given by:

$$g_w(t) = a\, g^e_p(t) + b g_m(t) + f[U(t)]$$

where $g^e_p(t)$ is the expected rate of growth of the price level, $g_m(t)$ is the rate of growth of marginal physical product of labour, and $U(t)$ = unemployment rate. Clearly $g_{pt} = g_{wt} - g_{mt}$. When solved for the long-run equilibrium rate:

$$g^e_p(t) = g_p(t) = \frac{f[u(t)] - (1-b)\, g_m(t)}{1-a}$$

The a is the crucial variable. The Quantity theory approach would claim that it is near to 1. In that case, $g_p(t)$ is not solvable — it can be anything. There is only one rate of unemployment ('permanent unemployment') which will prevent accelerating or decelerating inflation and there is nothing to determine the equilibrium rate of inflation. (The Quantity theory implies that this will be the rate of increase of the money supply minus the rate of increase of output.)

Solow found a to be positive but significantly less than 1. Thus the rate of change of prices is determinate, and it is dependent on the unemployment rate as in the original Phillips curve, but the relationship is steeper.

b is an index of the degree of cost push inflation; if it is less than 1, then it might be possible to reduce inflation by increasing the rate of productivity increase.

The Solow-Tobin model with a less than unity implies a 'dynamic money illusion' in the wage-determination process. It does not, however, entail progressive loss of real income share by labour, since by assumption prices rise only in proportion to labour costs.

Rees' contribution

Rees argues, in contrast to Friedman, that there is a range of permanent unemployment rates because of the transactions costs involved in readjusting the real wage rate under inflationary conditions. Specifically, workers will accept a once-over fall in the real wage rate and a corresponding fall in equilibrium unemployment brought about by inflation. Thus workers allow $\frac{\dot{P}}{P}$ to be greater than $\frac{\dot{W}}{W}$ for a while, implying a new, constant but lower marginal physical product of labour (MPP_L) consistent with $W = MPP_L \cdot P$. But once this drop has taken place, wages and prices change together (ignoring productivity changes), keeping U constant. Rees believes that this fall in the MPP_L will be greater, the higher is the rate of inflation. Thus he derives a long run Phillips curve based on rationality — not money illusion — which implies a trade off between unemployment and inflation.

The Phillips curve is useful in analysing the effectiveness of incomes policy. The obvious way to test such policy is to fit the Phillips curve for periods with and without incomes policy to determine if there is a shift to the left with the policy (i.e. a reduction in the rates of inflation consistent with given amounts of unemployment).

David Smith reports such a test in Richard Caves' *Britain's Economic Prospects*. Smith used the simple method of including dummy variables in his regressions (due to a paucity of data). Though he got some slight shift using the wage rate, he got no shift using labour costs. It is therefore probable that no shift took place. The observed shift in the wage regression may be attributable to the common resort to hidden wage increases during times of incomes policy (i.e., better facilities, amenities, etc.) which do not show up in wage bills but do affect inflation.

Lipsey and Parkin, however, have made a recent breakthrough in this analysis. They argue that the aim of incomes policy is not to shift the curve to the left, but to flatten it. An ideal incomes policy would make the Phillips curve perfectly horizontal, in which case the economy could operate at full employment without any additional inflation. Hence they argue that one should look for a change in the slope of the Phillips curve with incomes policy. They found that British incomes policy had in fact been very successful in flattening the Phillips curve, but at the same time, the government had unfortunately introduced policies of demand restraint, which caused more unemployment with no less inflation — a rather sub-optimal way of doing things.

One of the problems with incomes policy is that if the government sets a wage increase limit, everyone will ask for the maximum, even if competition would otherwise bring about a smaller wage increase.

APPENDIX

Notes on the Phillips curve, allowing for price expectations, Feb. 27, 1969 –
Based on J. Tobin, pp.48-54 in Inflation: Its Causes, Consequences and Control,
New York Univeristy, 1968.

Let $g_x(t) = \dfrac{x'(t)}{x(t)}$ be the actual growth rate of a variable x at time t and $g_x^e(t)$ be
the expected value of $g_x(t)$. Also let p be the price level, w the money wage rate,
m the marginal product of labour and u the unemployment rate.

(1) $g_w(t) - g_p(t) = g_m(t)$

(i.e. the rate of wage increase minus the rate of price increase equals the rate of
rise of real wages.)

(2) $g_w(t) = ag_p^e(t) + bg_m(t) + f[u(t)]$

(the revised Phillips curve: the expected rate of inflation, the rate of increase of
productivity and the unemployment rate determine the rate of increase of
wages.)

$$0 \leqslant a \leqslant 1, f'[u(t)] < o$$

(3) $g_p^e(t) = \int_{\tau=-\infty}^{\tau=t} \gamma e^{-\gamma(t-\tau)} g_p(\tau) d\tau$

(the standard expectations function). Then the time derivative of (3), the change
in the expected rate of inflation, is

(4) $g_p^{e'}(t) = \gamma g_p(t) - \gamma g_p^e(t)$

Using (4), (1), (2)

(5) $\dfrac{1}{\gamma} g_p^{e'}(t) = g_w(t) - g_m(t) - g_p^e(t) = f[u(t)] - (1-b)g_m(t) - (1-a)g_p^e(t)$

We set this equal to zero to get the steady state equilibrium; by (4), the expected
and actual rates of price increase are then equal (as asserted by the quantity
school). There are two possibilities for $a \leqslant 1$.

   If $a < 1$, then

(6) $g_p^e(t) = g_p(t) = \dfrac{f[u(t)] - (1-b)g_m(t)}{1-a}$

Inflation accelerates (decelerates) if current unemployment is greater than (less
than) the amount geared to the prevailing inflation and is faster (slower) the
lower (higher) is equilibrium unemployment.

   If $a = 1$, then

(7) $\dfrac{1}{\gamma} g_p^e(t) = f[u(t)] - g_m(t)(1-b)$

(8) $f[u(t)] = g_m(t)(1-b)$ when $\dfrac{1}{\gamma} g_p^{e'}(t) = 0$

There is then only one rate of unemployment ('permanent unemployment')
which will prevent accelerating or decelerating inflation. And there is nothing to
determine the equilibrium rate of inflation. (The quantity theory says this will

be determined by the rate of increase of the money supply minus the rate of increase of output).

The empirical issue between quantity theorists and Keynesians then seems to be whether the a coefficient is approximately zero, in which case the crude Phillips curve approach holds; positive but significantly less than unity, in which case the sophisticated Phillips curve holds; or approximately unity, in which case the quantity theory dismissal of the Phillips curve in favour of the permanent unemployment concept holds.

CHAPTER 20

MONEY IN GROWTH MODELS

There has been a long-standing question of whether or not inflation promotes economic growth. In the Keynesian literature there have been two views each assuming that inflation is expected by only one part of society. One view (Kaldor) is that inflation promotes economic growth because it redistributes income from the rentiers to the entrepreneurs, i.e. entrepreneurs are assumed to expect the inflation while rentiers are not. The entrepreneurs invest the resources they gain.

The opposite view (H. Ellis) is that entrepreneurs do not expect inflation while rentiers do. Hence inflation is bad for economic growth. Both theories depend on an asymmetrical assumption about which class expects inflation and so are questionable because, if inflation persists long enough, then both rentiers and entrepreneurs will come to expect it.

Another approach is based on the notion of inflation as a tax. The government may use the resources raised by this kind of tax to promote economic growth or may put these resources at the disposal of entrepreneurs through low interest rate loans by the banking system.

This raises two questions: (i) Do the government use the inflation tax for promoting economic growth or for other purposes? Much of the evidence shows that the government finances not development but redistribution of income (Latin America); (ii) How big is the inflation tax likely to be? This depends on the ratio of real balances to real income and on the elasticity of that ratio with respect to inflation. (This problem was raised by R. Mundell. The ratio is lower in less developed countries than in developed ones, so the potentialities of an inflation tax in the former are rather small.)

The issue here is whether, by analogy with static theory, money is neutral in the context of growth, or can influence the rate of growth i.e. is money dynamically neutral?

The models of economic growth show that in the long run, the growth rate of the economy will be determined by exogenous factors, specifically the rate of growth of the population and the rate of Harrod-neutral technical change. This in turn means that we cannot ask the question what the influence of monetary expansion on the long-run rate of growth will be. The most we can ask is what will be the influence during the short period in which we are not at the long-run exogenously determined rate of growth but moving towards it, and what will be the influence of a monetary expansion on the characteristics of the steady state growth path.

Recapitulation of models of Economic Growth (without money)

There is a difference between a growth model and a theory of economic growth. A theory of economic growth explains growth in terms of some causal factor. A model of economic growth takes growth as given and simply works out the implications of particular kinds of behaviour (which are postulated but not explained).

Ricardo

Ricardo's chief problem was to explain the distribution of the national product, though he provided a growth model in the real sense. Assume that there is a given quantity of land and that whatever happens to the industrial sector does not really matter but can be regarded as determined by what happens on the land. Then we have average and marginal product curves as a function of the number of people (N) working on the given quantity of land.

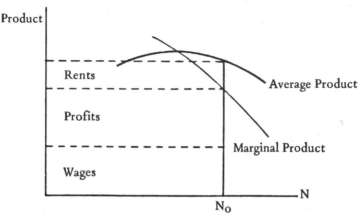

We have two theories determining the number of people working on the land — a short-run theory and a long-run theory. The short-run theory is the Wages Fund theory. The workers have to survive during the production period so there must be a stock of food to keep them at the level of subsistance. The real wage rate is the total wages-fund divided by the number of workers. In the long run workers breed, so the number of workers will be determined by the ratio of the wages-fund to the subsistence wage.

The return to capital will be the difference between the marginal product on the given land and the subsistence wage. The landlords rent will be the difference be the difference between the marginal and the average product multiplied by the number of workers. This position is a semi-short run equilibrium. The size of the wages-fund depends on the accumulative propensities of capitalists and in the long-run there is some minimum rate of return beyond which they will not accumulate any more capital. The rate of return to capital in the simplest model (one period agricultural process) is the ratio of the profits share to the wages-fund. In the long run equilibrium wages are at subsistence, profits at the minimum rate below which capitalists will not accumulate and the remainder (rent) is returns to landowners. This equilibrium is a stationary state. But there can be technical progress and we can drop the assumption that land is fixed. In this model landlords could be regarded as the villains because their rising share reduced development. But the interpretation was questioned by Malthus on the grounds that landlords' expenditures reduced the dangers of underconsumption. A debate emerged, whether in the long run stationary state the interest rate would be positive. Marshall argued that the psychological time preference would mean that the stationary state would arrive at a positive rate of interest because people would discount future as compared with present utility and would therefore stop accumulating at a positive rate of interest. Schumpeter argued that the rate of interest was really not a distributive share but rather a conventional arrangement whereby rentiers were able to extract resources from entrepreneurs, and that it would be zero in long-run equilibrium.

Keynesian dynamic Models: Harrod-Domar equation

In the short run Investment absorbs resources that are saved and income is determined by the amount of Investment in relation to the consumption function. In the longer-run investment now adds to future productive capacity and so reduces the need for future investment. But by adding to capacity investment also increases the amount of investment needed to maintain full employment of capacity. Let $\bar{Y}$ be full employment capacity and assume for simplicity that there is a fixed savings ratio s, then savings of the economy will be $s\bar{Y}$ and that will determine the amount of investment we need to maintain full employment: $s\bar{Y} = I$. Let k = capital output ratio (marginal and average) and then

Then $dY = \dfrac{I}{k}$ and $\dfrac{dY}{Y} = \dfrac{s}{k} = G_W$ the warranted rate of growth.

How should G_W be adjusted to the rate of growth of population? J. Robinson and N. Kaldor rejected the concept of a production function. Kaldor took as a starting point the notion that the economy tends to produce full-employment in the long run by adjustment of the savings ratio. He assumed two classes (capitalists and workers) with different savings ratios. The overall savings ratio gets adjusted to whatever is required for economic growth via changes in the distribution of income.

Joan Robinson's model is concerned mainly with insisting that capitalism is a failure because full employment was not likely.

In general the Harrod-Robinson approach emphasises the instability of the growth process.

Neoclassical Models (Swan, Solow)

The reaction to the Harrod-Robinson analysis reintroduced the notions of the production function, payments of factors according to their marginal productivity and the assumption of full employment. This kind of model can be developed with tremendous complexity but we can get the essential ideas in terms of a one sector growth model (i.e. no distinction between capital and consumer goods).

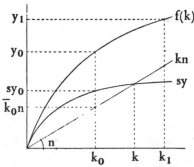

In the simplest kind we have a production function where output is a function of capital and labour. The behaviour of the economy can be summarised by the assumption that a constant proportion of income is saved, there is no technical progress and that population is growing exogenously at a fixed rate, n. If the production function is assumed subject to constant returns to scale and diminishing returns to agriculture are ignored, we can analyse the whole thing in terms of income per capita, savings per capita etc. (i.e. $k = \frac{K}{L}$, $y = \frac{Y}{L}$...). The production function then gives a relation between income per capita (y) and capital stock per capita (k). Savings per capita (sy) is a constant proportion of income per capita. We introduce the notion of a possible long run equilibrium where the stock of capital per capita is kept constant (kn) i.e. the capital requirement line. In the long run the economy must converge to a steady rate of growth n (the rate of population growth). Supposing we start from a position $y_0 k_0$ then saving is sy_0 and the capital requirement is $k_0 n$ lower than sy_0 so in the next period k will increase. Similarly if we start from $k_1 y_1$, $k_1 n > sy$ and the economy will be decumulating capital so we will converge at k where the economy is growing at the rate n. We have a type of stationary state expanding through time by multiplication. But here we do not assume that capitalists save until the rate of interest falls to some minimum: a constant proportion of income is saved. But we could use the same diagram on that alternative assumption. There would be a marginal return to capital corresponding to that minimum rate and people would accumulate up to that point. Savings would be given by the point on the kn line corresponding to the point on the production function where the marginal return to capital equals that minimum rate of interest.

We may not have of course a solution; if sy always lies below kn then the economy just disappears — a possibility that has fascinated some people. Also if sy intercepts the kn line more than once as it may on more complex assumptions about saving or population growth, then there could be multiple solutions.

Consumption per head rises as long as the slope of the production function is greater than the slope of the kn line. Consumption per head is maximised where the two slopes are equal or, putting the same point in another way, wehere the rate of growth equals the rate of interest (marginal product of capital).

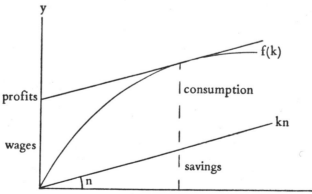

In this case total profits must equal total savings to maximise consumption. From a welfare point of view if we are by chance beyond this Golden Rule position we can always gain by returning to it. if we are to the left of it the only way to get back is by saving more i.e. by sacrificing consumption now for the sake of future higher consumption; whether this is worthwhile cannot be determined without reference to the economy's intertemporal preferences.

The subject is being examined in the context of whether inflation can stimulate economic growth and, if it can, within what limits. There are two issues relating to non-monetary neoclassical growth models: (i) does the system converge on the steady state growth path; and (ii) what is the nature of the long-run equilibrium growth path, focusing on the Golden Rule conditions (the conditions under which consumption per head is maximised over time)? These conditions are that the rate of interest should equal the exogenous growth rate of population or that the savings ratio should equal the share of capital in total production.

Tobin's model

We introduce money in to the apparatus as non-interest bearing fiat money, treated as outside money by the public, and whose growth rate is determined by the monetary authority. This has implications for the trend of prices. With a steady rate of monetary expansion, the public's expectations regarding the change of prices will converge on the rate set by the trend of monetary expansion. The known rate of price change ($\dot{P}/P$) will then be equal to the rate of change of the money stock ($\dot{M}/M$) minus the rate of change of output ($\dot{y}/y$). We must be careful, however, in specifying how the money supply grows. If it is distributed proportionally to existing holdings of money, a form of interest is. being paid on those holdings. In other words, there is some compensation for the inflation which will be higher, in nominal terms, the higher is the rate of price change. Hence, we need to assume that the money is either distributed randomly or according to a fixed rule. Note, too, that the alternative opportunity cost of holding real balances, and hence the demand for real balances, is related to the rate of inflation.

Over time peoples' real balances will be growing regardless of whether nominal money balances are. If the change in the money stock is zero as output increases, the price level will fall at a rate equal to $\dot{y}/y$. The size of real balances held depends, then, on the price of real balances or on the expected and actual rates of inflation. As the growth of real balances is also a change in total wealth, tantamount to a capital gain, we can treat that growth as an addition to real income. Assume that real balances are added to current real output to obtain total income. A fixed savings ratio is applied to this income and, therefore, the income base is larger because of real balances. This, in turn, implies that real savings are higher, the higher the real balances component of total income. However, real balances have to be held and, in consequence, we must deduct increments of real balances held each period from savings available to create real capital stock i.e. for physical investment.

The effect of an increased accumulation of real balances on saving is only a fraction of the increment in the accumulation of real balances, whereas the whole is a deduction from savings (before arriving at a residual for real investment); therefore the higher is the ratio of real balances to output (b) the greater will be the accumulation of real balances and the smaller the net amount left over for real investment. In other words, the higher is b, and hence the higher the accumulation of real balances per period, the lower will be the proportion of output left over for investment. Therefore, in the long run growth equilibrium context the lower will be the capital stock per head (k) and output per head (y).

However, a complication arises from the existence of the Golden Rule conditions. Whereas a higher b implies a lower y it does not necessarily imply a lower level of consumption per head (c). Above the Golden Rule position, a higher b moves us closer to the Golden Rule, whereas if we are below it a higher b implies a lower level of c.

The crucial results of the analysis are these. The ratio of real balances to income (b) is a function of the expected rate of inflation and hence of the rate of increase of the money supply. b is lower, the higher the expected rate of price increase and hence the higher the rate of monetary expansion. As a larger $\dot{M}/M$ implies a lower b, the base to which the savings ratio (s) applies is smaller, and so the smaller is the deduction of real balances from savings and the higher is the ratio of savings available from output for real capital formation. This implies that if the economy is below the Golden Rule position it can move the real savings ratio towards the Golden Rule Rate and c by stepping up the rate of inflation. If the economy is above the Golden Rule position it can move closer by reducing $\dot{M}/M$. While a welfare gain is assured if the economy is beyond the Golden Rule position since we can increase consumption at every moment of time, the gain is not assured if we are below the Golden Rule position as moving towards it implies lowering consumption now and raising it later — to assess whether the move is appropriate necessitates defining an intertemporal utility function.

The argument may be expressed graphically. (y is income per head, k is capital per head, b is ratio of real balances to income, s is savings per head, and n is the rate of growth of population.)

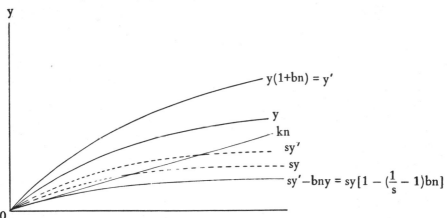

The line y represents the production function relating output per head to capital per head. The total income line y (1 + bn), is composed of y plus the capital gains from the growth of real balances which are related to y through the growth rate of population and the ratio of real balances to output.

Each point in the diagram is a potential long-run equilibrium point, hence n, the rate of growth of population, can define capital needs. If we were starting from a non-equilibrium point and then moved to an equilibrium point, $\dot{y}/y$ would be changing in a manner not represented on the diagram. Here any k implies an equilibrium y.

b is a variable depending on the alternative opportunity cost of holding real balances ($\dot{P}/P$) and possibly per capita income. The capital requirements curve (kn) represents the amount of output needed to be devoted to real investment to equip the growing population with the same amount of capital per head as the old population i.e. the amount of capital necessary to maintain the previous period's level of k. The curve sy' is higher than the savings curve sy as y' is higher than y, but the real savings curve is lower as we must subtract the full value of real balances to be held. In other words y is raised by adding capital gains, this initially raises s by comparison with what it would have been but lowers the real portion of s as real balances must be deducted. This shifts the real s curve downwards by comparison with what it would have been and the shift is greater the greater the value of b.

One is tempted to conclude that the analytical differences between a real and monetary economy in a growth context may be represented as the difference between the intersections of sy and kn on the one hand and of $sy[1 - (\frac{1}{s} - 1)bn]$ and kn on the other. This would imply that in a monetary economy k is lower. However the way money has been added to the model serves only to introduce it as a medium for capital gain. A correct specification would include an economically rational reason for money's existence and for the development of a monetary economy.

In the model, money is assumed neutral in the static sense, i.e. that real, not money, balances are demanded so that the expansion of the money supply does not affect real variables. However it is non-neutral in the sense that a change in $\dot{M}/M$ and therefore $\dot{P}/P$ affects the equilibrium growth path. The higher is $\dot{M}/M$ the higher will be the alternative opportunity cost of holding real balances and so the lower will be b and the higher k and y. We conclude that monetary policy can influence y. We are interested, however, in c and, whereas there is a monotonic relation between y and k, there is not necessarily one between k and c on the steady state growth path. In fact, as we increase k, c first rises and then falls so there is a consumption maximising position on the function. Inflation will increase c if the economy is below the Golden Rule k position. Similarly deflation when the economy is above the Golden Rule k will also increase c.

Is it possible to arrive at the Golden Rule position through the use of monetary policy? Suppose we are short of the Golden Rule position and eliminate real balances by setting $\dot{P}/P$ at a high level (which implies the existence of an asset substitutable for real balances which totally replaces real balances as their price becomes high). Hence, y' approximates y and sy' − bny approaches sy. If sy cuts kn to the left of the Golden Rule then we cannot reach the position; if it cuts to the right it is possible that inflation will get us there.

Suppose now that we are beyond the Golden Rule position and we deflate either without limit or up to a rate such that the rate of return on capital (an asset) equals the rate of return on real balances (a competing asset). If there is a limit to the demand for real balances we may not be able to get to the Golden Rule position as we may not be able to raise b enough. It depends upon the position of the savings line and the flexibility of b. In general, we can move towards the Golden Rule position by appropriate variations of monetary policy, but not always get there. To get there, we might have to change the savings ratio itself.

There is a clear cut policy prescription only when the economy is beyond the Golden Rule position where people are over-saving to keep capital intact. A move to the Golden Rule position from below it implies foregoing present consumption for future consumption.

The analysis fits into the Keynesian line of thought on the desirability of inflation. Some people believe in maximizing the level of total output rather than consumption per head and, as we have seen, we can always increase the level of output per head by inflation.

Further, the analysis fits into some earlier-Keynesian models of inflation. For example, the Metzler-Mundell mechanics of inflation focus on its effect, in a short run context, on the current rate of saving.

Here, a faster rate of inflation implies a lower value of wealth and thus increased accumulation of physical capital, where saving is a wealth adjustment process. In our analysis a higher rate of inflation implies lower wealth (real balances are lower in relation to output). The economy therefore builds up real wealth in the form of material capital. Hence there is a long run influence of the rate of price inflation on the current rate of real saving.

Our creation of a monetary economy has involved adding money to a real system. In this context, however, there is no economically rational reason for this introduction of money. Hence, we must provide a satisfactory explanation of why money is introduced. There are two ways of doing this that correspond to different functions of money: (i) The Chicago (Friedman) "as-if" utility approach says that if money exists it must serve a function and if it is held it must yield utility; (ii) The Yale analysis approaches the problem using the transactions demand for money. Money appears as a means to minimise costs i.e. as a way of increasing output beyond that which the economy would have generated. It is thus a producers' good, an input into the productive process. Both approaches reach the same conclusion — the results of the previous analysis do not hold under the more satisfactory explanation of the monetary economy.

Treating money as a consumers' good we define two productive processes in the economy: the one using capital and labour, the other generating utility from the interaction of consumers and their real balances.Therefore, total output equals real plus psychic output. Treating money as a producers' good we can define a production function relating real output to capital per head and money balances per head where these money balances per head are determined by the real balances to income ratio times the level of output per head.

The above exposition followed Tobins' introduction of money into growth models. The approach was however, somewhat arbitrary and the model lacks any explanation for the inclusion of money; i.e. a motivation for holding money such as the inventory transactions or utility approach is required. There are two alternative for dealing with this problem corresponding to the utility and inventory explanations of money holding.

Further development

If it is assumed that real balances yield utility then this needs to be added to the measure of real output used. But because this is a utility yield these services have to be consumed entirely as services of real balances. The increase in income associated with the presence of real balances must result in more savings being available for real investment. The need to include this yield in a measure of income poses some common national income accounting problems. The usual convention in these is to value goods and services at the prevailing price, the marginal valuation to the consumers. By the same convention real balances should be valued at the alternative opportunity cost (the real rate of return on capital). But if the demand schedule for real balances is inelastic this would result in a fall in real income when the interest rate falls; yet from a welfare point of view they should be better off

This problem is similar to that of valuing government services. J. Buchanan has argued that, as they are free, their value should be zero although by normal conventions they are valued at the cost of supplying them. For growth models however it is desirable to have a measure of income which moves in the same direction as changes in welfare. Such an index would be the area under the demand curve for real balances (i.e. the integral of this function).

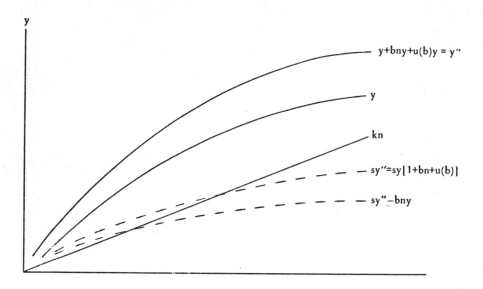

This index can be applied to the diagramatic analysis developed in the last two sections. The y line is the production function relationship in a pure barter economy; $y'' = y + bny + u(b)y$ is the 'augmented' production function. bn is the growth of real balances which takes place either because the authorities expand the money supply so that the price level remains constant or because prices fall as income grows (to provide extra real balances called for by the growth). u (b) is that part of income resulting from the utility yield on real balances. Applying the constant savings ratio (s) to y'' gives
$$sy'' = sy (1 + bn + u(b))$$

From sy" must be subtracted the savings which are used to accumulate real balances, in order to derive the amount available for the accumulation of real capital, i.e.

$$sy'' - bny = sy[1 - (\tfrac{1}{s} - 1)bn + u(b)].$$

In the Tobin model u(b) is absent and consequently the effects of inflation compared with a non-monetary economy are unambiguous, increasing the amount of real saving available for investing in real capital. But the introduction of u(b) makes for uncertainty: on the one hand an accumulation of real balances means that the term $1 - [\tfrac{1}{s} - 1]\,bn$ is reduced $(\tfrac{1}{s}>1)$; but u(b) is increased and there is no a priori way of deciding which will outweight the other. Therefore if the economy is short of the Golden Rule there is no guarantee that inflation will raise output and move the economy towards the Golden Rule position. In fact the Golden Rule analysis is no longer applicable since welfare no longer depends on real goods only. An increase in the consumption of such goods could be associated with a reduction in the yield of services from real balances and it is possible that these could offset each other.

If, for example, the u(b) term dominates then an increase in the rate of inflation will lower the real savings ratio and the utility yield. If the economy is short of the Golden Rule then inflation will lower the consumption of goods and the services from real balances. Thus total consumption falls unambiguously.

Alternatively money can be seen as yielding no utility as such but as reducing the amount of time taken to complete transactions. This releases more labour which increases output. This is difficult to incorporate specifically into the diagrammatics but it can be depicted by considering real balances as an argument of the production function. Thus there is one y' line for each level of real balances (i.e. k includes fixed capital and inventories; money reduces the amount of inventories required to produce a given level of output).

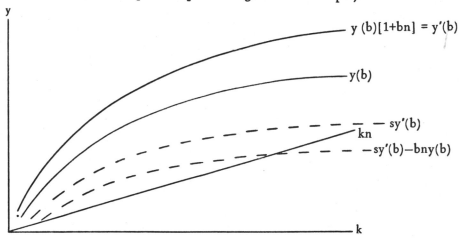

Total income per head is y(b) (1+bn) which allows for receipts of real balances via monetary expansion or deflation in the presence of a fixed nominal quantity of money.

Total savings are fixed proportion of y'(b) i.e. sy'(b). To derive the savings available for accumulation of real capital it is necessary to deduct bny(b). This gives

$$sy(b)[1 - (\frac{1}{s} - 1)bn]$$

The effects of inflation can be divided into two parts:

(i) sy(b) falls as real balances are reduced via inflation: people are led to hold fewer real balances because the alternative opportunity cost rises when inflation is fully anticipated, and this reduces output y(b).

(ii) $[1 - (\frac{1}{s} - 1)bn]$ rises because bn falls. Inflation in this case has the effect of reducing the proportion of saving which is used to accumulate real balances. The net effect is again ambiguous.

The above analysis depends on two assumptions — a constant savings ratio and outside or fiat or non-interest bearing money.

The latter assumption can be dropped. Instead assume that all money is in the form of deposits created by a competitive banking system and bearing interest. The banks are induced to pay interest because they are able to invest in real capital with the resources acquired. It is of course necessary to impose some legal reserve ratios on the banks to prevent money being created to the point where its real value is zero. While the community will be in an optimum position (satiation with real balances) this will not show up in measured wealth.

Assuming that money creation is costless the banks will pay interest equal to the alternative opportunity cost of holding money; this is the sum of the real return on capital plus anticipated inflation which in long run equilibrium will equal actual inflation. If i is the money rate of interest and r the real return on capital, then $i - \dot{P}/P = r$. Money is therefore neutral in this context; a given expansion leads to an equal rate of inflation which leaves real balances unchanged but the increase in i offsets the increased cost of holding balances; thus there is no incentive to reduce holdings. As there are no direct policy conclusions to draw from this governments would probably be advised to aim for price stability which may be desirable on other grounds.

The constant savings ratio assumption can also be replaced by a desired wealth to income ratio; but this has the same effect as the fixed ratio in a Tobin growth model because inflation reduces the amount of real balances held and therefore it is necessary to hold a higher level of real capital to maintain the desired ratio. But this is as arbitrary as a constant s. Instead assume that economic behaviour is determined by time preference and that time preference is not a function of wealth held.

In a static economy with zero population growth, savings will increase so long as the real rate of return on capital is greater than the rate of substitution of future for present levels of consumption (i.e. the marginal rate of time preference). For a static society where everyone is assumed to have an infinite life the question is whether the marginal rate of time preference (MRTP) is positive (Pigou, Ricardo) or zero (Schumpeter). In a growing society the marginal rate of time preference may be assumed to be positive; the effect of population growth is to raise the rate of return on capital and hence this will stimulate savings so as to keep capital per head constant i.e. saving will be undertaken so that MRTP = r. This implies that consumption of goods per head is also constant. As inflation can only influence real balances per head the best policy would be to satiate the demand for real balances by making the alternative opportunity cost zero i.e. by deflating so that $- \dot{P}/P = r$. If the Golden

Rule state prevails and $r = n$ then a constant nominal quantity of money will result in $- \dot{P}/P = n$ and therefore $- \dot{P}/P = r$.

If a competitive interest paying, banking system prevails inflation is irrelevant and the quantity of money is optimised automatically.

If money is non-interest bearing and there is a constant MRTP, then optimality requires $- \dot{P}/P = r$ and $i = 0$, i.e. the money rate of interest will be zero.

Milton Friedman has dealt with this subject in detail in his essay 'The Optimum Quantity of Money' and, contrary to his earlier views, he advocates a deflationary rule (even contemplating a 17% p.a. deflation). This proposal is not realistic. Either the Government is aware of their gain (fiscal in nature) from not pursuing a deflationary policy or they are ignorant of what is optimal. If it is the former it is unlikely that a government would sacrifice such a source of revenue. If it is the latter then persuasion through the usual democratic processes is appropriate.

If the optimum situation is to be achieved via a competitive banking system paying interest on deposits, the difficulty of paying interest on currency remains.

CHAPTER 21

THE MONETARY STANDARD AND INTERNATIONAL MONETARY THEORY

Earlier we dealt with balance of payments policy from the viewpoint of Keynesian theory, which recognises that there are two variables to be kept under control: the level of domestic employment and the balance of payments. In the following exposition we concentrate on monetary theory.

The Monetary Standard

The monetary standard is some commodity or foreign currency in terms of which the value of the domestic currency is fixed by the monetary authority. This means that the authorities undertake to buy and sell the standard at a fixed price. Actually the authority allows a margin between its buying and selling prices which can yield it a profit and which — at least under the old gold standard — deterred unnecessary transactions by imposing a price for them.

The use of the monetary standard had its historical origin in the sovereign's stamp for weight and fineness on the metal coinage. Today the sovereign guarantees that the paper money in use is legal tender, and the money is convertible (though usually not by everyone) into the standard. Under the old gold standard, any citizen could convert his government's paper money into the gold standard. This privilege has largely been revoked now, mainly due to the shortage of gold in the 1920's. But if the citizen is allowed to freely convert at a fixed exchange rate into foreign currency, he can still register his distrust of his government as under the old system. Today the conversion of national currency into gold is restricted to dealings between central banks. Domestic currencies have no real standard; the "fiduciary standard" used in most countries means that the currency is inconvertible.

The importance of a monetary standard is that it places restrictions on the freedom of actions of governments, because they have to maintain their ability to convert their currency into the standard. This means that they have to follow the proper policies.

The advantage of using a commodity as a monetary standard is that to some extent it has automatic stabilising effects. These effects are argued strongly by Hart, Kaldor and Tinbergen, who produced a plan for international monetary reform based on a commodity standard.

The stabilising effects in this system are due to the fact that money can be produced, and its production will respond to changing profitabilities. If people, for example, want to hold more money, this will force prices down — by the ordinary analysis — which will increase the profitability of producing the commodity standard, since its price is fixed in terms of money. Thus more of the commodity will be produced and so satisfy the increased demand for money without such a large fall in prices.

If the supply of the commodity is perfectly elastic, then the price level will be stabilised at a particular level corresponding to the equality of the marginal cost of production of the standard with its monetary value. This statement covers two cases.

In a static economy with perfectly durable money there would be no production of money and the marginal cost in question would be that of producing the next unit of the commodity. In a growing economy, or one using a commodity which physically wears out, then the rate of production equals the growing or replacement need for money, and the marginal cost is that of producing the commodity at that rate.

The automatic stabilisation property, however, obviously depends on the supply conditions of the commodity. From this viewpoint, gold, silver, and almost anything really durable have disadvantages. For instance, in the case of gold, the current rate of production is small relative to the total stock, so variations in production will be even smaller in relation to changes in demand for money. Moreover, the supply is inelastic and gold is a mineral, so its production is governed not only by price, but by the optimising behaviour of mine owners faced with a depleting mineral. Finally, the demand for gold in other uses is fairly small, so that there could be little opportunity for substitution out of other use as a stabilising influence. Thus, while there would be some stabilising influence under a gold system, it would be negligible compared with what would be necessary to make this a strong alternative.

The difficulties with gold have led to proposals for other commodity standards, with better stabilising properties. For example, you can make bricks anywhere, and if it takes too long to bake the bricks, you can dismantle houses. This approximates automatic stabilisation. Hart, Kaldor, and Tinbergen have revised this argument and proposed an international monetary standard based on a basket of typical primary commodities produced by underdeveloped countries. Their aim was to produce a scheme which would channel resources to the less developed countries.

Choosing such a bundle of goods as a standard would provide more stability than a one commodity standard, and everyone would be able to produce his own money.

But the disadvantage of the Hart-Kaldor-Tinbergen model is that, if the commodities chosen were not durable (which they probably would not be), then there would be considerable costs of spoilage, warehousing, etc. This, in effect, involves a negative interest rate on money. This cost has been estimated for their scheme at about 10% of the total money stock per annum, which in the context of our earlier discussions on the optimum holding of money is obviously less than optimal. If one tries to minimise such costs, one is eventually led back to gold as the optimum commodity money.

The arguments against using gold or any other commodity as a monetary standard are these. First, there is not much stabilisation in the short run.

Second, changes in the real costs of producing the commodity would probably occur, due to technological changes, discoveries of new sources, etc. Thus stabilisation of the money price of such a good would not imply a stable price level, but instead a price level with the trends necessary to keep the real cost of the commodity production in the proper relationship with other costs. Thus in the longer run, by stabilising the price of a subset of production, you may actually be destabilising the general price level.

Third, use of the gold standard involves an unnecessary investment of real resources in the money itself. Money circulates because people accept it, not because it embodies physical resources equal to its face value. The economic system has a history of finding less costly substitutes for commodity money (e.g. paper money and bank deposits). This has been a long-run trend in international monetary arrangements: through the nineteenth and twentieth centuries paper money has tended to replace gold as an international reserve. Particularly, at the present time, we are on a U.S. dollar standard, though the presence of gold is retained for symbolic reasons.

Fourth, the purpose of a commodity standard is to put restrictions on governments, and in particular to prevent inflationary policies. But fiat money can be used just as well, and its value retained, so long as governments control its quantity in the proper fashion. In principle the gold standard could produce worse results than intelligent monetary management. In fact, a government will not accept restrictions and will jettison the commodity standard if it gets in the way. Governments maintain fixed exchange rates, but they do not always follow the necessary discipline supposedly imposed: they prefer to devalue rather than face the domestic pressures which would result from a strict policy.

Since World War II most governments have made full employment their main objective; and for a closed economy, at least, this has meant that they have tended to expand the money supply to whatever extent is necessary to meet the full employment aggregate demand. This increased demand, of course, stems from the increases in wages and prices brought about by collective bargaining and industrial price fixing. In the 1950's J. R. Hicks seized on this point and postulated that we are on a labour standard of value. This view, however, has proved false, since governments have had to modify their domestic policy in light of their balance of payments position.

The international system is now on a US dollar standard, not a gold standard, simply because the supply of gold has long ago ceased to be an influence on the system as a whole. We have a fixed exchange rate standard based on the dollar: this means that countries do have to keep their price levels in line, but world price levels are in no way determined by the availability of gold. Instead the world has had a chronic mild inflation, with a monetary expansion. Countries have found substitutes for gold by holding dollar balances and by instituting central bank loans in times of international crises. As a consequence of the subsequent inflation, gold has simply passed out of the system as a standard as the prices of other things have risen. The increasing private demand and the relatively constant supply of gold finally led to the crisis of March 1968, when the link between the monetary system and the private gold market was formally cut.

Why do we have a fixed exchange rate standard based now on the dollar? The general reason is the belief that such a system increases the freedom of international trade and capital movements and so offers the same international benefits as are derived domestically from a national currency. But the system, in important respects, works quite differently. In particular, countries use measures to maintain their balance of payments which in part work toward the disintegration of the world economy. Controls over trade, subsidies to exports, and restrictions on capital movements (not prohibited by GATT) are examples. All of these and other policies involve sacrificing the benefits of international integration for the sake of the international monetary system.

The fixed exchange rate integration ideal is not practical without the same kinds of international assistance policies as are used domestically to aid regions which are hurt by having only one currency.

The Mechanism of International Adjustment

The international economic system can be examined in at least two different ways. We can concentrate on the system, with the nations being simply individual units, like firms, which are constrained and acted upon from the outside. The nation must react to the equilibrium in the system as a whole. Most work until the 1930's was done in this adjustment-to-equilibrium context. Alternatively we can concentrate on the individual nation and the policy choices open to it. We then outline different individual national strategies. This newer approach is therefore centered around policy problems of the individual nation. It was covered in the early lectures; now we turn to the mechanism of adjustment approach.

In the international monetary system, as in any general equilibrium system containing money, there are two kinds of disturbances: monetary disturbances (which we concentrated on earlier in our discussion of the closed economy) and real disturbances. Similarly there are two types of adjustment possible: monetary (price level, quantity of money) and real (relative prices and quantities). While it is thus convenient for analysis to separate these categories; it should be remembered that either type of disturbance in the real world generally requires both types of adjustment; though it is true to say that usually real disturbances primarily require real adjustments, and similarly for monetary disturbances.

This point needs stressing for two reasons. First neoclassical writers generally failed to distinguish between real adjustments and monetary adjustments and tended to concentrate on monetary adjustments for correcting real disturbances. (This stress was probably because they had not worked out a complete general equilibrium system with money, and so tended to work in terms of monetary theory only.) Second, the Keynesian approach emphasises real adjustment through changes in aggregate income and exchange rates. The analysis proceeds in terms of the elasticities of the demand and supply for exports and imports. These elasticities then determine the reaction of the international system to a change in the exchange rate, and this impact effect works on aggregate income through the multiplier process. So it is assumed that exchange rate changes are real changes.

Monetary aspects were brought back into the Keynesian analysis in the early 1950's through the absorption approach. This concept recognises that most economies do not operate with massive unemployment, so that an elementary multiplier analysis applied to a devaluation is too simple. Resources must somehow be freed to meet demand following devaluation, either by policy or by automatic means. Thus elasticities are not the only important elements in adjustment analysis: the relation between the productive capacity of the economy and its aggregate expenditure must also be taken into account.

Adjustment with a Gold Standard

The following analysis is the same for any system with fixed exchange rates and fixed reserves. The simplest model assumes that gold coin is the only money; there are no national currencies. Disequilibrium implies international flows of this gold coin for adjustment. A more complex analysis was worked out at the end of the nineteenth century. Fractional reserve banking systems were introduced to allow for multiple expansion or contraction of the money supply following the gold flows and capital movements were recognized to result from interest rate changes also induced by monetary movements.

The traditional analysis starts with a deficit (which is assumed, and not explained so the analysis may already be in trouble). As a result of the deficit there is a gold outflow which leads to a loss of reserves, a rise in interest rates and short term capital inflows which temporarily finance the deficit and reduce the gold movement. In the long run the higher interest rates lead to domestic deflation and a fall in prices. By a similar mechanism there is inflation in the rest of the world, and together these two influences eventually correct the balance of payments deficit. Keynesians pointed out that the fall in prices may be accompanied by a fall in output and employment, so that the deficit can be corrected only so long as unemployment exists. In any event the balance of payments is only in equilibrium again when prices are at their proper level.

The Keynesian criticism of the gold standard in the 1930's rested on the facts that price adjustments in the short run were sticky and the mechanism had to work through unemployment and therefore was barbarous. But these criticisms were based on the mistaken belief that the British interwar experience was a normal state of affairs. It was not.

There was a prior problem of British adjustment to industrialisation in the rest of the world, which was greatly aggravated by the return to the prewar parity of the pound in 1925. The pound was seriously overvalued, and the mechanism was being asked to adjust to a very large problem deliberately imposed by the government, and to adjust all at one moment. The blame for the subsequent problems should not be on the mechanism, but on government policy.

The 1930's depression was interpreted as reflecting the barbarousness of the mechanism of adjustment. But the depression was greatly aggravated by the failure of monetary policy in the United States. There was a huge contraction of US liquidity which would have required a substantial fall in US prices to restore real balances to their level prior to the bank crashes which the Federal Reserve permitted. This was one of the contributors to the fall in world liquidty, which was exacerbated by the run on the pound sterling during a crisis of confidence. This run shows that the system was not on the pure gold coin standard described above, but had already been substituting (mainly) the pound for scarce gold. So in effect what was required was an extreme fall in world prices. Commodity prices did tumble, but manufactured goods prices did not, which caused unemployment. Thus there was a tremendous problem of adjustment thrust upon the system by a failure of policy by the world's monetary authorities beginning with the US Federal Reserve and going on to other Central Banks. Instead of helping each other, as they would today, they allowed the system to crash because of jealousies in the hope of short run political gains from each other.

Thus, what was at fault in the 1930's was the way the system was operated by the authorities, not the adjustment mechanisms themselves.

Another 1930's Keynesian criticism of the international system was its "deflationary bias". Thus a deficit country would sooner or later be forced to deflate, but a surplus country was under no reciprocal pressure to inflate. Instead a surplus country would accumulate reserves and sterilise their effect by selling securities on the open market. Thus all the pressure of the system was on the deficit country to deflate.

But this criticism also turns out to be an over-generalisation of a particular historical period, for the present argument is that the system has an inflationary bias. That is, countries cannot prevent another country — in particular the United States — from inflating if it wants to. They are instead obliged to import inflation and so finance deficit countries. Surplus countries have to put up with the inflation of deficit countries.

Real and monetary disturbances must be distinguished because they have different consequences.

Suppose we have a world system in equilibrium, in the sense that payments are balanced and prices adjusted. Now introduce a real disturbance in the system, say a reduction in the demand for country's exports. This will result in one of two possible sequences. Either exporters will more or less maintain the prices of their products and respond to the fall in demand by reducing production, which throws people out of work and sets off the usual multiplier process. Or, if prices are fixed competitively, they fall. Money income falls but full employment is maintained.

These reactions to the fall in the demand for exports entail a series of adjustments which reduce the loss of reserves to the country. But this situation will only be temporary. In the long run if the reduction in the demand for exports has lowered the real income of the economy there will be a corresponding reduction in demand for real balances. Getting rid of the excess money balances will meet the deficit and loss of international reserves.

If the disturbance is monetary the major part of the adjustment will be monetary. Suppose for example that there is an increase in one country's demand for goods relative to money. In other words people's desired money to income ratio falls. They will try to get rid of money balances by spending them on goods which will cause a deficit in the balance of payments reflected either in a reduction of exports or an increase in imports. The deficit will continue until we reach a new equilibrium at the new desired money to income ratio. The process will involve general world inflation.

There are two parts of the equilibrating mechanism, the movement of money and the rise in prices which serve to restore balances to the desired level in the countries receiving the money. One of the propositions involved here is that the level of money prices throughout the world economy will be kept in line through these combinations of real and monetary adjustments. This is the Purchasing Power Parity Principle developed by Cassel. The principle can be applied either to a fixed exchange rate system to predict what the domestic money prices will be, or to a floating exchange rate system to predict what the exchange rate will be. J. Viner sharply criticised the principle. He claimed that real factors will change the purchasing power relationship. Cassel however was using it to predict the results of monetary movements in the very short run. The Keynesian approach was developed in terms of elasticities of exports and imports. Lately there has been a revival of the monetary approach and it makes an important difference which approach one adopts when analysing a particular problem.

Now we concentrate on the effects of alternative policies beginning with some basic algebra relating to growth.

$$G_{AB} = G_A + G_B$$

$$G_{\frac{A}{B}} = G_A - G_B$$

$$G_{A+B} = \frac{A}{A+B}G_A + \frac{B}{A+B}G_B$$

$$G_{A-B} = \frac{A}{A-B}G_A - \frac{B}{A-B}G_B$$

Assume a country on a fixed exchange rate system, that the public adjusts its money holdings to the desired level (always and instantaneously) through spending or not spending, that there is a high degree of substitutability between the goods of this country and those of the rest of the world, that the world price level is constant, and money demanded is a multiple of income ($Md = KY$). Then the money supply existing at any time will be the sum of the assets backing the domestic money supply (international reserves and domestic credit $Ms=R+D$). The basic assumption is that the money supply must always equal money demanded ($Ms=Md$). This means that through its domestic policy the monetary authority (by operations on D, through open market operations) does not determine the money stock. The money stock is determined by demand. What the authority determines is the size of the reserves, through the relation $\Delta R = B = \Delta Md - \Delta D$, or, in dynamic terms:

$$\frac{B}{R} = G_R = \frac{M}{R}G_y - \frac{D}{R}G_d = \frac{1}{r}[G_y - (1-r)G_d]$$

where r is the reserve ratio ($=R/M$). So the behaviour of the balance of payments is determined by the growth rate of the economy (assumed exogenously given) and the growth rate of domestic credit. To improve the balance of payments one must restrict the growth of domestic credit.

We now move from a single country to a world system and for simplicity we assume that we have only one kind of money. For the system as a whole there will be a fixed amount of nominal money and countries' demands for real balances have to be reconciled through changes in the world price level.

$$\frac{M_i^d}{P} = k_i y_i \qquad : \text{i'th country's demand for real balances}$$

$$\sum_i \frac{M_i^d}{P} = \sum_i k_i y_i \qquad : \text{aggregated demands for real balances}$$

$$G_{\frac{m^d}{P}} = \sum_i m_i G_{yi} \qquad : \text{the growth rate of the demand for real balances is equal to the weighted sum of the income growth rates where } m_i \text{ is the initial share of nominal money stock}$$

$$G\frac{m^s}{P} = Gm^s - G_p = G\frac{m^d}{P} \quad : \quad \text{growth of world supply of real balances}$$

growth of world supply of real balances equals growth of world demand for real balances.

Then

$$Gm_i^d = Gy_i + G_p = Gy_i + Gm^s - \sum_i m_i Gy_i,$$

and if m^s is constant (i.e. $Gm^s = 0$), then

$$Gm_i^d = Gy_i - \sum m_i Gy_i$$

We get a relationship between the growth rate of output for country i and the average growth rate of the world determining the growth rate of the demand for and actual supply of money balances for economy i (provided $Gm^s = 0$). The assumption of one world money supply is not very realistic. There are two developments one could make. Either one can distinguish between international reserves and domestic money supplies or alternatively it can be assumed that one of the currencies is a reserve currency for the other countries. Under the first assumption (i.e. $M^s = R + \sum D_i$) we get

$$G_{R_i} = \frac{1}{r_i} Gy_i - \frac{1-r_i}{r_i} Gd_i + \frac{R}{R+\sum_i Di} G_R + \frac{\sum_i D G_{d_i}}{R+\sum_i Di} - \sum_i m_i G_{y_i}$$

Under the second assumption the money supply is also $M^s = R + \sum_i D_i$, but the change in the reserves of the reserve country includes another term representing foreigners' demand to hold the reserve currency. This analysis has some implications drawn by Mundell. If we do not have an adequate rate of growth of international reserves (G_R), then somebody has to provide them by a deficit. Also a country with a Gd relatively high in relative to its Gy will have a deficit in the balance of payments.

The traditional theory of devaluation deals with it as having the effect of changing the prices of a country relative to foreign prices and thereby setting in motion (through the elasticities of demand for imports and exports) changes in trading patterns. The more sophisticated version recognises that we have to combine with this some sort of expenditure control policy to avoid inflation. For things to happen this way we have to assume that there is low substitutability between home and foreign goods. Let us suppose, as the monetary approach does, that there is a high degree of substitutability between goods produced in different countries. Then devaluation must have only a temporary effect; domestic prices and wages will rise over time into line with those elsewhere.

What is actually achieved by devaluation is exactly what could have been done by contracting the domestic money supply. Devaluation reduces the purchasing power of domestic money in terms of foreign goods and increases the purchasing power of foreign money in terms of domestic goods. Real balances are deflated in the domestic economy and inflated in the rest of the world; there is an initial real balance effect followed by accumulation of real balances in the economy and spending in the rest of the world until the desired real balances are again achieved. Prices in the domestic economy rise into line with foreign prices. The essential point is that there is a temporary real balance effect and that devaluation is equivalent to contracting the domestic money supply.

This approach yields different results from traditional theory about the relation of devaluation and the terms of trade. Traditional theory claims that as a result of devaluation the terms of trade turn against the country. It arrives at this result through the elasticities approach under the assumption that imports have a perfectly elastic supply while exports have an imperfectly elastic demand. The monetary approach claims that movements in the terms of trade depend on the relative marginal propensities to spend in the country and the rest of the world on their respective goods, so the result of devaluation for the terms of trade will be indeterminate.

APPENDIX

AGGREGATE DEMAND AND SUPPLY RELATIONSHIPS IN A SIMPLE KEYNESIAN MODEL

by

MARCUS H. MILLER

London School of Economics

Introduction

The purpose of this Appendix is to demonstrate the use of the aggregate demand and supply curves of Chapter 8 in analysing the impact of changes in fiscal and monetary policy, and of wage cuts, on the level of aggregate price and output in a simple Keynesian model with a fixed money wage rate.

Since the demand relationship is derived from the IS and LM curves which give the equilibrium conditions in the goods and money markets, consequently changes in fiscal and monetary policy shift this aggregate demand schedule. Likewise, the supply relationship being derived from equilibrium in the labour market, changes in the conditions governing the supply of labour or its productivity shift the aggregate supply schedule. Thus the effects of changes in any of the parameters mentioned can be analysed by shifting either the demand or supply relationship, but not both, with implications for the level of output and prices that are relatively easy to determine. Students preparing for the M.Sc. (Economics) course at the London School of Economics have found this presentation helpful in understanding the predictions of Keynesian macro-models.

In what follows the characteristics of the aggregate demand and supply relationships are derived diagrammatically for a simple Keynesian model (with no 'Pigou effect'), and the properties ascribed to these schedules are also determined algebraically. Given these properties, the 'comparative static' effects on output and the price level of changes in fiscal and monetary policy and of a wage cut are traced by shifting the aggregate demand and supply schedules, and again these results are confirmed algebraically.

The implications of including the Pigou effect (Chapter 2 above) for the slope of the demand schedule and for the efficacy of monetary policy and of cuts in the money wage are indicated in the next section. The Appendix concludes with a numerical exercise and notes on sources and further reading.

For convenience the variables used are listed here

Exogenous variables   G   rate of government spending in real terms
                              M   nominal quantity of money
                              W   money wage rate

Endogenous variables   X   real national output and income
                              N   employment of labour
                              i   rate of interest
                              P   nominal price level

A subscript attached to the name of a function denotes the derivative of the function with respect to the subscript variable, thus

$$L_X \equiv \frac{d}{dX} L(X,i)$$

No notation for variables measured in wage units is required as the LM and IS relationships are expressed in terms of real money balances and real income only.

The aggregate demand relationship between output and the price level implied by equilibrium in the goods and money markets.

Assuming no money illusion in the goods and money markets, the equilibrium conditions in these markets can be expressed by constructing the IS and LM curves with the rate of interest, i, and real output, X, measured along the axes, as in the top part of Diagram 1. For the given stance of fiscal and monetary policy (G_0, M_0) and any given price level, P_0, the intersection of these two curves determines the equilibrium quantity of output demanded, X_0, at the given price, P_0, and these co-ordinates are plotted as one point on the aggregate demand relationship DD in the lower part of Diagram 1.

With no change in G or M but with a lower price level, P_1, there will be a higher level of real balances and the LM curve will be further to the right, leading, under normal assumptions, to a lower rate of interest, i_1, and a higher level of investment demand. Since a higher level of aggregate demand, X_2, is associated with a lower level of prices, P_1, the demand relationship has a negative slope. If either the IS curve is vertical or the LM curve horizontal, so that in the absence of the Pigou effect an increase in real balances fails to raise aggregate demand, the demand relationship will, however, be vertical.

By definition, 'expansionary' policy measures by the authorities may be expected to increase aggregate demand at any price level, i.e. shift the DD schedule to the right. Thus with the LM curve given by M_0 and P_0 as in Diagram 1, an increase in government spending (with no change in the stock of money) sufficient to shift the IS curve to the right till it intersects the LM curve at the higher interest rate, i_2, will increase aggregate demand at the same price level, P_0, to X_2; thus the DD curve will shift to the right as shown by the arrow in Diagram 1. Similarly, with the IS curve given by government spending at the rate G_0, an increase in the supply of money (with no change in government spending) sufficient to displace the LM curve to the right and to lower the rate of interest to i_1 will also increase demand at the same price level, P_0, to X_2.

Of course if fiscal policy affects only the rate of interest because the LM curve is vertical, then there will be no shift in the demand relationship following a change in government spending. And where the demand relationship is a vertical line (see above) it will not shift in response to changes in the money supply.

Algebraic derivation of the properties of the aggregate demand relationship.

Equilibrium in the goods and money markets, with no money illusion in either market, can be expressed by the IS and LM relationships thus

(1) $X - C(X) - I(i) = G$ assuming $1 > C_x > 0 > I_i$

                                        (and $C_i = I_x = 0$ for simplicity)

(2) $P L(X, i) = M$ assuming $L_x > 0 > L_i$

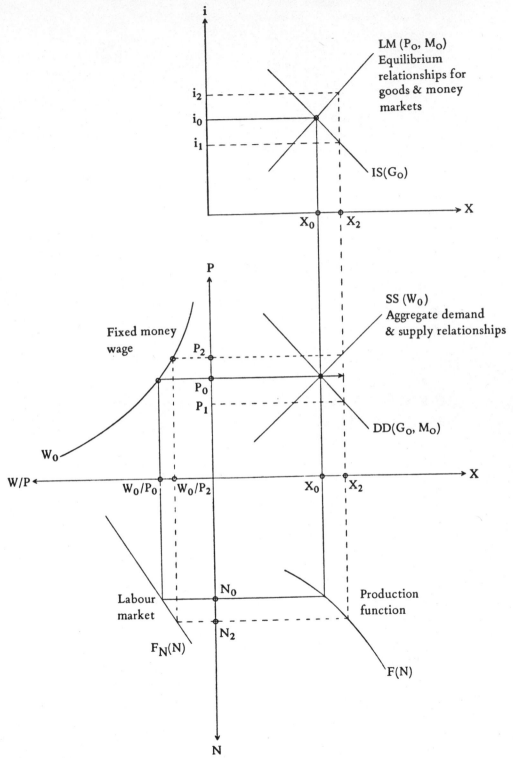

Diagram 1. Derivation of the Aggregate Demand and Supply Relationships.

In principle a demand relationship of the form

(3) $X = D(P, G, M)$

can be obtained by eliminating i from (1) and (2) by substitution. The required partial derivatives of this relationship can, however, be obtained without substitution by first writing out the differential equations of (1) and (2)

(4) $\begin{bmatrix} 1-C_x & -I_i \\ PL_x & PL_i \end{bmatrix} \begin{bmatrix} dX \\ di \end{bmatrix} = \begin{bmatrix} dG \\ dM - LdP \end{bmatrix}$

and then solving for dX in terms of dP, dG and dM by the application of Cramer's Rule

(5) $$dX = \frac{\begin{vmatrix} dG & -I_i \\ dM-LdP & PL_i \end{vmatrix}}{\Delta_1}$$

where

(6) $\Delta_1 = (1-C_x)PL_i + PL_x I_i < 0$

Equation (5) gives the differential of the demand relationship (3) and the coefficients of dP, dG and dM are the required partial derivatives.

Thus the slope of the demand relationship, measured with reference to the P axis, for given values of G and M is

(7) $\dfrac{\partial X}{\partial P} = \dfrac{-LI_i}{\Delta_1} < 0$

and the shifts of the demand function given the price level as a result of fiscal and monetary policy are

(8) $\dfrac{\partial X}{\partial G} = \dfrac{PL_i}{\Delta_1} > 0$

(9) $\dfrac{\partial X}{\partial M} = \dfrac{I_i}{\Delta_1} > 0$

The above results (7), (8) and (9) apply to the standard Keynesian case shown in Diagram 1. In the special Keynesian cases, where either $I_i = 0$ or $L_i \to -\infty$ or both, then both $\dfrac{\partial X}{\partial P}$ and $\dfrac{\partial X}{\partial M}$ are zero and $\dfrac{\partial X}{\partial G} = \dfrac{1}{1-C_x}$, the Keynesian multiplier.

A demand relationship having a zero slope with respect to the P axis would of course appear as a vertical line in Diagram 1.

The aggregate supply relationship between output and the price level implied by equilibrium in the labour market.

Before tracing out the supply relationship, we describe the other functions graphed in the lower part of Diagram 1. First the production function in the short-run, when the stock of capital and the state of technology are given, is shown by the function F(N) at the bottom right. Next the marginal product of labour, $F_N(N)$, a decreasing function of the amount of employment, is plotted at the bottom left, and constitutes the demand curve for labour under competitive conditions.

For the purposes of this Appendix it is assumed that the labour force is never fully employed and that it suffers from money illusion as the supply of labour is perfectly elastic at an historically-given *money* wage rate, W_0. Thus for any given price level, say P_0, the rectangular hyperbola labelled W_0 indicates, on the horizontal axis, the *real* wage, W_0/P_0, at which labour will be elastically supplied.

The point on the aggregate supply relationship corresponding to a price of P_0 may be traced by finding the competitive level of employment, N_0, demanded at this real wage, W_0/P_0, and plotting the output, X_0, produced by such a level of employment. With no change in the conditions of production or the money wage, a higher price level, P_2, will lower the real wage at which labour is supplied and so increase employment to N_2 and output to X_2, as shown in the Diagram. The higher level of output resulting from a higher price gives a positive slope to the supply relationship between X and P. As can be seen, the less the marginal product of labour falls with increased employment the more price elastic is this positive supply response.

The effect of a cut in the money wage demanded by labour is to shift the supply schedule SS to the right. Thus if the money wage were to fall to W_1 and shift the rectangular hyperbola showing the fixed money wage so that, at the price level P_0, the real wage, W_1/P_0, were equal to W_0/P_2, then the level of output produced at this real wage, namely X_2, will be associated with the price level P_0, so the SS curve will shift to the right as shown by the arrow in the Diagram.

Algebraic derivation of the properties of the aggregate supply relationship.

The short-run production function, together with the conditions for competitive equilibrium in the labour market given a fixed money wage, can be expressed as

(10) $X - F(N) = 0$ $\qquad$ assuming $F_N > 0$

(11) $P F_N(N) = W$ $\qquad$ assuming $F_{NN} < 0$

In principle a supply relationship of the form

(12) $X = S(P,W)$

can be obtained from (10) and (11) by eliminating N. The partial derivatives of this relationship are obtained without substitution, as before, by writing the differential equations of (10) and (11)

(13) $\begin{bmatrix} 1 & -F_N \\ 0 & PF_{NN} \end{bmatrix} \begin{bmatrix} dX \\ dN \end{bmatrix} = \begin{bmatrix} 0 \\ dW - F_N dP \end{bmatrix}$

and solving for dX

(14) $dX = \dfrac{\begin{vmatrix} 0 & -F_N \\ dW - F_N dP & PF_{NN} \end{vmatrix}}{\Delta_2}$

where

(15) $\Delta_2 = PF_{NN} < 0$

The coefficients of dP and dW in (14) are the required partial derivatives of the supply relationship (12). Thus the slope of the supply relationship, measured with reference to the P axis, is

(16) $\dfrac{\partial X}{\partial P} = \dfrac{-F_N^2}{\Delta_2} > 0$

and the shift of the supply function, given the price level, as a consequence of supply changes in the money wage is

(17) $\dfrac{\partial X}{\partial W} = \dfrac{F_N}{\Delta_2} < 0$

The effects of fiscal and monetary policy and of wage cuts on output and the price level.

Using the demand and supply curves derived above, the effects of *expansionary* fiscal and/or monetary policy are shown for a standard Keynesian model in Diagram 2(a). The rightward shift of the DD schedule at price level P_0 discussed above is shown by an arrow. The excess demand prevailing at the price level P_0 is eliminated by a rise in the price level which will both stimulate extra production and also reduce aggregate demand. The new equilibrium is thus established at P_2, X_2, both price and output having increased.

Whereas the price level rises under the impact of expansionary fiscal and monetary policy, a cut in money wages which shifts the supply schedule to the right, as shown by the arrow in Diagram 2(b), lowers the equilibrium price level. The excess supply at the initial price level, P_0, is eliminated by a fall in the price level which stimulates an increase in aggregate demand and reduces the amount of output supplied.

We turn now to the special Keynesian cases of a 'liquidity trap' or of interest-inelastic investment. In these cases the DD schedule becomes vertical as discussed above and shown in Diagram 2(c), and 2(d). The DD curve does not, moreover, shift in response to changes in monetary policy — the vertical slope is itself evidence of the inability of changing real balances to affect aggregate demand. In response to changes in government spending, however, the DD schedule (and so equilibrium output) shifts by the full multiplier effect — see above for this result. The perfectly inelastic demand schedule also renders wage cuts ineffective as a means of increasing output and employment. As shown in Diagram 2(d) the excess supply at the price level P_0 is eliminated by a fall in

Standard Keynesian Model

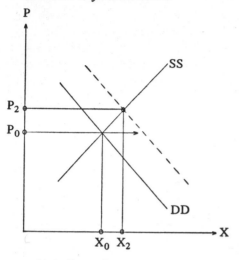

2(a) Espansionary Monetary
and Fiscal Policy

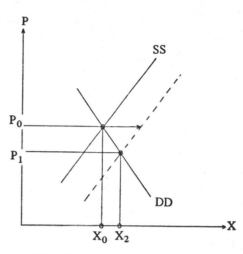

2(b) Wage Cut

Special Keynesian Cases

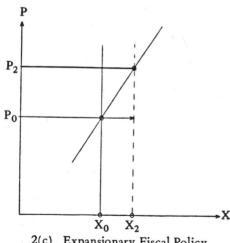

2(c) Expansionary Fiscal Policy

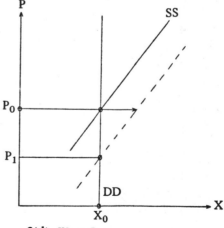

2(d) Wage Cut

Diagram 2. The effects on Output & the Price Level of Fiscal and Monetary
Policy and of Wage Cuts.

prices which has no effect in stimulating demand, but brings supply back to X_0 by raising real wages to the level prevailing before the wage cut.

Algebraic derivation of the effects of changes in policy and of wage cuts.

We wish to derive the effects of changes in G, M and W on X and P given the system of four equations (1), (2), (10), (11) in the four endogenous variables X, P, N, i. Since X is an increasing function of N alone, it is simpler to eliminate X by substitution and derive the effects of changes in G, M and W on N and P. The effect on X can easily be calculated later, given the effects on N.

The set of equations resulting from eliminating X from (1), (2), (10) and (11) is

(18) $F(N) - C[F(N)] - I(i) = G$

(19) $\qquad P L[F(N), i] = M$

(20) $\qquad P F_N(N) = W$

The differential equations are therefore

$$(21) \quad \begin{bmatrix} 0 & -I_i & (1-C_x)F_N \\ L & PL_i & PL_xF_N \\ F_N & 0 & PF_{NN} \end{bmatrix} \begin{bmatrix} dP \\ di \\ dN \end{bmatrix} = \begin{bmatrix} dG \\ dM \\ dW \end{bmatrix}$$

Using Cramer's Rule we can solve for dP

$$(22) \quad dP = \frac{\begin{vmatrix} dG & -I_i & (1-C_x)F_N \\ dM & PL_i & PL_xF_N \\ dW & 0 & PF_{NN} \end{vmatrix}}{\Delta_3}$$

where

$$(23) \quad \Delta_3 = LI_i\, PF_{NN} - F_N^2(I_iPL_x + PL_i(1-C_x))$$
$$= LI_i \Delta_2 - F_N^2 \Delta_1 > 0$$

Thus

$$(24) \quad \frac{\partial P}{\partial G} = \frac{P^2 L_i F_{NN}}{\Delta_3} > 0$$

$$\frac{\partial P}{\partial M} = \frac{I_i P F_{NN}}{\Delta_3} > 0$$

$$\frac{\partial P}{\partial W} = \frac{-F_N(I_iPL_x + PL_i(1-C_x))}{\Delta_3} = \frac{-F_N \Delta_1}{\Delta_3} > 0$$

Similarly for dN we have

$$(25) \quad dN = \frac{\begin{vmatrix} 0 & -I_i & dG \\ L & PL_i & dM \\ F_N & 0 & dW \end{vmatrix}}{\Delta_3}$$

Thus

$$(26) \quad \frac{\partial N}{\partial G} = \frac{-F_N PL_i}{\Delta_3} > 0$$

$$\frac{\partial N}{\partial M} = \frac{-F_N I_i}{\Delta_3} > 0$$

$$\frac{\partial N}{\partial W} = \frac{LI_i}{\Delta_3} < 0$$

and, since

$$(27) \quad \frac{\partial X}{\partial Z} = \frac{\partial X}{\partial N}\frac{\partial N}{\partial Z} = F_N \frac{\partial N}{\partial Z},$$

so

$$(28) \quad \frac{\partial X}{\partial G} = \frac{-F_N^2 PL_i}{\Delta_3} > 0$$

$$\frac{\partial X}{\partial M} = \frac{-F_N^2 I_i}{\Delta_3} > 0$$

$$\frac{\partial X}{\partial W} = \frac{F_N LI_i}{\Delta_3} < 0$$

It can easily be confirmed that in the special Keynesian cases (where $I_i=0$ and/or $L_i \to -\infty$), $\frac{\partial P}{\partial M}$, $\frac{\partial X}{\partial M}$ and $\frac{\partial X}{\partial W}$ are zero while $\frac{\partial X}{\partial G} = \frac{1}{1-C_X}$.

The Pigou Effect

The Pigou effect, discussed in Chapter 2, allows for prices to change aggregate demand via a wealth effect on consumption. A wealth variable should therefore be included as an argument in the consumption function. For present purposes the relevant wealth variable will take the form

$$(M+kB/i)/P, \qquad 0 \leqslant k \leqslant 1,$$

where k is a measure of the extent to which consumers treat as net private wealth the capitalised value of interest payments on government debt, B/i. In order to simplify the algebra, only the special case where $k = 0$ and bonds have no wealth effect is considered here. In this case the consumption function can be written as $C(X, M/P)$, where $\frac{d}{d(M/P)} C(X, M/P) \equiv C_m$, and C_m is assumed to be positive. This affects the aggregate demand relationship in two ways — the schedule shifts more in response to monetary policy and, for the same reason, it has a 'flatter' slope i.e. a higher price elasticity. This is because a rise in real balances, due either to expansionary monetary policy or to a reduction of prices, affects consumer demand via the Pigou effect as well as investment demand via interest rates. Indeed even in the special Keynesian cases mentioned above ($I_i=0$ and $L_i \to -\infty$) where real balances are powerless to affect investment, monetary policy and wage cuts will still affect aggregate demand through consumption.

The Pigou effect therefore eliminates the peculiar features of the special Keynesian cases noted in connection with Diagrams 2(c) and 2(d) and these cases can then be analysed in the manner of the standard Keynesian model treated in Diagrams 2(a) and 2(b).

Algebraically, we find that the slope of the demand relationship, measured with reference to the P axis, for given values of G and M, now becomes

$$(29) \quad \frac{\partial X}{\partial P} = -C_m \frac{M}{P} \frac{L_i}{\Delta_1} - \frac{I_i L}{\Delta_1} < 0$$

where the inclusion of the first (negative) term has the effect of 'flattening' the slope of curve as drawn in Diagram 1, cf. equation (7) above.

Whereas the effects of fiscal policy on the demand relationship are as before, cf. equation (8) above, the shift due to monetary policy becomes

$$(30) \quad \frac{\partial X}{\partial M} = \frac{C_m L_i}{\Delta_1} + \frac{I_i}{\Delta_1} > 0$$

where the extra first (positive) term measures the added impact of monetary policy through the consumption function.

Turning to the effects of policy on N taking account of both demand and supply relationships we have, in place of (25) and (23) above,

$$(31) \quad dN = \frac{\begin{vmatrix} C_m M/P^2 & -I_i & dG+C_m dM/P \\ L & PL_i & dM \\ F_N & 0 & dW \end{vmatrix}}{\Delta_4}$$

where

$$(32) \quad \Delta_4 = C_m M L_i F_{NN} + L I_i \Delta_2 - F_N^2 \Delta_1 > 0$$

and so for example

$$(33) \quad \frac{\partial N}{\partial M} = \frac{-C_m F_N L_i - F_N I_i}{\Delta_4} > 0$$

$$\frac{\partial N}{\partial W} = \frac{C_m M L_i}{P \Delta_4} + \frac{L I_i}{\Delta_4} < 0$$

and therefore

$$(34) \quad \frac{\partial X}{\partial M} = \frac{-F_N^2 (C_m L_i + I_i)}{\Delta_4} > 0$$

$$\frac{\partial X}{\partial W} = \frac{F_N C_m M L_i}{P \Delta_4} + \frac{F_N L I_i}{\Delta_4} < 0$$

So long as $C_m > 0$, then the partial derivatives in (29), (30) and (34) are not zero even in the special Keynesian cases.

Exercise.

The following numerical example is offered as an exercise. It can be solved fairly easily by first deriving the aggregate demand and supply relationships by substitution from the appropriate market equilibrium conditions. The resulting solution values (for P, N, X, i) are such that it is easy to use the formulae derived above to calculate the effects of changes in the various parameters.

Exogenous variables   :   G = 25, M = 100, W = 1

Behaviour relationships   :

     Consumption function (1) : $C = 50 + \frac{1}{2}X$

     Investment function   : $I = 125 - 25i$

     Demand for money   : $L = 100 + \frac{1}{2}X - 25i$

     Production function   : $X = 20\sqrt{N}$

     A similarly tractable example which includes the Pigou effect is given by modifying the consumption function to include real balances, thus:

     Consumption function (2) : $C = 25 + \frac{1}{2}X + \frac{1}{4}M/P$

but keeping all else the same.

Sources & further reading.

The diagrammatic treatment presented here has drawn heavily on

J. Tobin *Economics 111: Aggregative Models,* (mimeographed notes) Yale University, 1963.

An approach similar in some respects can be found in

D. C. Rowan, *Output Inflation & Growth*, London: Macmillan, 1968.

For the algebra the reader is referred to the Mathematical Appendices of

T. F. Dernburg and D. M. McDougall, *Macro-Economics*, London, McGraw-Hill, 1963,

also to Chapter 7 of

R. G. D. Allen, *Macro-Economic Theory*, London, Macmillan, 1967.

and lastly to

E. A. Kuska, *Maxima, Minima and Comparative Statics*, London, Weidenfeld and Nicholson, forthcoming.

READING LIST

Michaelmas and Lent Term, 1971-1972

GENERAL REFERENCES

Keynes, J.M. *The General Theory of Employment, Interest and Money*, London, Macmillan & Co., Ltd., 1961.

Patinkin, Don. *Money, Interest and Prices* (2nd edition), London, William Clowes & Sons Ltd, 1957.

The first section, entitled "Micro-economics" is particularly relevant to the course.

Gurley, J.G. and E.S. Shaw. *Money in a Theory of Finance*. Washington, Brookings Institution, 1960.

The general approach rather than the detailed analysis of this book is relevant.

Leijonhufvud, Axel. *On Keynesian Economics and the Economics of Keynes*. London, Oxford University Press, 1968.

This book is rather prolix; students might find it useful to start with the author's lectures on *Keynes and the Classics* London, Institute of Economic Affairs, Occasional Paper No. 30, 1969.

General References

Ackley, Gardner. *Macro-Economics Theory*. New York, Macmillan, 1961.

Newlyn, W.T. *Theory of Money* (2nd edition). Oxford, Clarendon Press, 1971.

Bailey, M.J. *National Income and the Price Level*. London, McGraw-Hill, 1962.

Mundell, R.A. *Monetary Theory*. Palisades, California, Goodyear Publishing Co., 1971.

Brunner, Karl. "A Survey of Selected Issues in Monetary Theory", *Schweitzerische Zeitschrift Fur Volkswirtschaft Und/* No. 1. (1971). Especially Chapters II, IV, VI, and VII. STATISTIK.

Collections of Relevant Articles

Croome, D.R. and Harry G. Johnson, (eds.). *Money in Britain: 1959-1969*, London, Oxford University Press, 1970. Especially articles by Walters (Chapter II, pp. 39-68) and Johnson (Chapter III, pp. 83-114).

Friedman, M. *The Optimum Quantity of Money*. Chicago. Aldine Publishing Company, 1969.

Gibson, W.E. and G.G. Kaufman. *Monetary Economics: Readings on Current Issues*. London, McGraw-Hill Book Company, 1971.

Johnson, Harry G. *Essays in Monetary Economics* (2nd edition). London, Allen & Unwin Ltd, 1969.

Mueller, M. *Readings in Macro-Economics*. New York, Holt, Rinehart & Winston, 1967.

Smith, W. and R. Teigen. *Readings in Money, National Income and Stabilization Policy* (revised edition). Homewood, Ill., Richard D. Irwin, Inc., 1970.
Thorn, Richard S. *Monetary Theory and Policy.* New York, Random House, 1966.

A controversial book

Pesek, B. and T. Saving. *Money, Wealth and Economic Theory.* London, Collier-Macmillan Co. Ltd., 1967.

Note on specific references

Students are definitely *not* required to read everything in the following Reading List. Some items will be presented fairly fully in the lectures; some are alternative sources for essentially the same analysis; some are intended as additional readings for those specially interested in one aspect of the subject. Required readings are indicated by an asterisk.

Part I

MACROECONOMICS

The Keynesian Model

*Hicks, J.R. "Mr. Keynes and the Classics", *Econometrica,* Vol. V (April 1937), pp. 147-59. Reprinted in *AEA Readings in the Theory of Income Distribution.* Homewood, Illinois, Richard D. Irwin, 1951, pp. 461-76.
Bailey, M.J. *National Income and the Price Level.* London, McGraw-Hill, 1962, Chapters 1, 2 and 3.
Johnson, Harry G. "Monetary Theory and Keynesian Economics" and "The General Theory after Twenty-five Years", *Money, Trade and Economic Growth.* London, George Allen & Unwin, Ltd, 1962, pp. 107-25 and pp. 126-47.
Leijonhufvud, Axel. *On Keynesian Economics and the Economics of Keynes.* London, Oxford University Press, 1968. Chapters 1,5 and 6.

The Theory of Economic Policy

Tobin, James. "Liquidity Preference and Monetary Policy", *Review of Economics and Statistics,* Vol. 29 (May 1947), pp. 124-31. Also "Comment" by Warburton and "Rejoinder" by Robin, *Review of Economics and Statistics,* Vol. 30 (November 1948), pp. 304-14.
Johnson, Harry G. "Theoretical Problems of the International Monetary System", *Pakistan Development Review,* Vol. VII (Spring 1967), pp. 1-28 Part I only.

The Consumption Function

*Friedman, M. *A Theory of the Consumption Function.* Princeton, NBER and
*Eisner, R. and R.H. Strotz. "Determinants of Business Investment" in Commission on Money

*Ando, A. and F. Modigliani. "The 'Life Cycle' Hypothesis of Saving: Aggregate Implications and Tests", *American Economic Review*, Vol 53 (March 1963), pp. 55-84. Reprinted in R.A. Gordon and L.R. Klein (eds.), *Readings in Business Cycles*, Homewood, Illinois, Richard D. Irwin, 1965, pp. 398-426.

Farrell, M.J. "The New Theories of the Consumption Function", *The Economic Journal*, Vol. LXIX (December 1959), pp. 678-96. Reprinted in R.A. Gordon and L.R. Klein (eds.), *Readings in Business Cycles*, Homewood, Illinois: Richard D. Irwin, 1965, pp. 379-97.

Suits, D.B. "The Determinants of Consumer Expenditure: A Review of Present Knowledge", *Impacts on Monetary Policy*, London, Prentice-Hall International, Inc., 1963, Commission on Money and Credit, pp. 1-57.

Ferber, R. "Research on Household Behaviour", *American Economic Review*, Vol. 52 (March 1962), pp. 19-63.

The Theory of Investment

*Eisner, R. and R.H. Strotz. "Determinants of Business Investment" in Commission on Money and Credit, *Impacts of Monetary Policy*, London, Prentice-Inc., 1963, pp. 59-337. Especially Part II and V.

*Witte, J.G. "The Micro-Foundations of the Social Investment Function", *Journal of Political Economy* (October 1963), pp. 441-56.

Business Cycles and Stabilization Policy

*Matthews, R.C.O. *The Trade Cycle.*, Cambridge: Cambridge University Press, 1959, Chapters 1 and 2.

*Hicks, J.R. "Mr. Harrod's Dynamic Theory", *Economica*, Vol. 16 (May 1949), pp.106-21. Reprinted in R.A. Gordon and L.R.Klein (eds.), *Readings in Business Cycles*, Homewood, Illinois: Richard D. Irwin, 1965, pp. 23-38.

*Phillips, A.W. "Stabilization Policy in a Closed Economy", *Economic Journal*, Vol. 64, (June 1954), pp. 290-323. For Summary see A.C.L. Day, "The Strength of Stabilizing Action", *Outline of Monetary Economics*, Oxford, Clarendon Press, 1957, pp. 339-51.

Phillips, A.W. "Stabilization Policy and the Time-Form of Lagged Responses", *Economic Journal*, Vol. 67 (June 1957), pp. 265-77. Reprinted in R.A. Gordon and L.R. Klein (eds.), *Readings in Business Cycles*, Homewood, Illinois: Richard D. Irwin, 1965, pp. 666-79.

Baumol, W.J. "Pitfalls in Contra-cyclical Policies: Some Tools and Results", *Review of Economics and Statistics*, vol. 43 (February 1961), pp. 21-26.

Econometric Applications of Macro-Economic Models

Suits, D.B. "Forecasting and Analysis with an Econometric Model", *American Economic Review*, Vol. 52 (March 1962), pp. 104-32. Reprinted in R.A. Gordon and L.R. Klein (eds.), *Readings in Business Cycles*, Homewood, Illinois: Richard D. Irwin, 1965, pp. 597-625.

Duesenberry, J.S., O. Eckstein and G. Fromm. "A Simulation of the US Economy in Recession", *Econometrica*, Vol. 28 (October 1960), pp. 749-809.

Duesenberry, J.S., G. Fromm, L.R. Klein and E. Kuh. *The Brookings Quarterly Econometric Model of the US,* Amsterdam, North-Holland Publishing Co., 1965

Part II

THEORY OF DEMAND FOR MONEY

Issues in Monetary Economics: Survey of the Field

*Johnson, Harry G. *Essays in Monetary Economics*, London, George Allen & Unwin, 1967, Chapter I.

Fundamentals of Monetary Theory: Role of Money in the Economy

*Hicks, J.R. *Critical Essays in Monetary Theory*, Oxford, Clarendon Press, 1967, Chapters 1, 2 and 3.

Pesek, B. and T. Saving. *Money, Wealth and Economic Theory*, London, Collier-Macmillan Ltd, 1967, Chapters 3, 4, 8 and 9.

Harris, L. "Professor Hicks and the Foundations of Monetary Economics", *Economica*, Vol. XXXVI (May 1969), pp. 196-208.

*Gilbert, J.C. "The Demand for Money: The Development of an Economic Concept", *Journal of Political Economy*, Vol. 61 (April 1953), pp. 144-59.

Kuenne, R.E. *The Theory of General Economic Equilibrium*, Princeton, Princeton University Press, 1963, Chapter 5.

Clower, R.W. "A Reconsideration of the Microfoundations of Monetary Theory", *Western Economic Journal*, Vol. (December 1967).

Classical Quantity Theory of Money

*Fisher, Irving, *The Purchasing Power of Money* (2nd edition), New York, Macmillan, 1920, (revised edition), New York, Kelley, 1963.

Pigou, A.C. "The Value of Money", *Quarterly Journal of Economics*, Vol. 32 (1917-18), pp. 38-65. Reprinted in *AEA Readings in Monetary Theory*, Homewood, Illinois: Richard D. Irwin, 1951, pp. 162-83.

Keynes, J.M. *Tract on Monetary Reform* London, Macmillan, 1923, Chapter II and Chapter II, Section i.

*Wicksell, K. *Lectures on Political Economy*, Vol II, *MONEY*, London, George Routledge & Sons Ltd, 1946.

Robertson, D.H. *Essays in Monetary Theory*, London, Staples Press Ltd, 1946.

Friedman, M. "The Quantity Theory of Money: A Restatement", *Studies in the Quantity Theory of Money* Chicago, University of Chicago Press, 1958.

Friedman, M. "The Quantity Theory of Money", *Encyclopedia of the Social Sciences,* 1968

The Keynesian Theory of Money: Role of Money in the Economy and the Fundamentals of the Portfolio Approach

Keynes, J.M. *The General Theory of Employment, Interest and Money*, London, Macmillan & Co., Ltd., 1961, Chapters 13-15, and 17.

*Modigliani, F. "Liquidity Preference and the Theory of Interest and Money", *Econometrica*, Vol. 12 (January 1948), pp. 543-64. Reprinted in *AEA Readings in Monetary Theory*, Homewood, Illimois: Richard D. Irwin, 1951, pp. 186-240.

Patinkin, D. "Price Flexibility and Full Employment", *American Economic Review*, Vol. 38 (September 1948), pp. 543-64. Reprinted in *AEA Readings in Monetary Theory*, Homewood, Illinois: Richard D. Irwin, 1951, pp.252-83.

Patinkin, D. "Keynesian Economics and the Quantity Theory", in *Post-Keynesian Economics,* K.K. Kurihara (ed), London, George Allen & Unwin, 1955, pp. 123-52.

Smith, W.L. "Graphical Exposition of Complete Keynesian System", *Southern Economic Journal,* Vol. 23 (September 1956), pp. 115-25. Reprinted in W.L. Smith and R.L. Teigen, *Readings in Money, National Income and Stabilization Policy* (reviewed edition), Homewood, Illinois: Richard D. Irwin, 1970, pp. 66-73.

Turvey, R. *Interest Rates and Asset Prices,* London, George Allen & Unwin, 1960.

*Hicks, J.R. "A Suggestion for Simplifying the Theory of Money", *Economica,* Vol. 2 (February 1935), pp. 1-19. Reprinted in *AEA Readings in Monetary Theory,* Homewood, Illinois: Richard D. Irwin, 1951, and J.R. Hicks, *Critical Essays in Monetary Theory,* Chapter 4, Oxford, Clarendon Press, 1967.

The Transactions Demand for Money: The Portfolio Approach

Johnson, Harry G. *Essays in Monetary Economics* London, George Allen & Unwin, 1967, Chapter 5.

*Baumol, W.J. "The Transactions Demand for Cash: An Inventory Theoretic Approach", *Quarterly Journal of Economics,* Vol. 66 (November 1952), pp. 545-56.

Tobin, James. "The Interest Elasticity of Transactions Demand for Cash", *Review of Economics and Statistics,* Vol. 38 (August 1956), pp. 241-47.

Demand for Money and Risk Aversion

*Tobin, J. "Liquidity Preference as Behaviour Towards Risk", *Review of Economic Studies,* Vol. 25 (February 1958), pp. 65-86.

*Hicks, J.R. *Critical Essays in Monetary Theory,* Oxford, Clarendon Press, 1967, Chapters 2 and 6.

Matthews, R.C.O. "Expenditure Plans and the Uncertainty Motive for Holding Money", *Journal of Political Economy,* Vol. 71 (June 1963), pp. 201-18.

Tobin, James. "The Theory of Portfolio Selection" in F. Hahn and F. Brechling, (eds.), *Theory of Interest Rates,* London, Macmillan & Co., 1965.

Baumol, W.J. *Economic Theory and Operations Analysis,* (2nd edition), London, Prentice-Hall International, Series in Management, 1965.

Hirschleifer, J. "Investment Decision under Uncertainty", *Quarterly Journal of Economics,* Vol. 79 (November 1965), pp. 509-36.

Portfolio Approach to Demand for Money. Market Clearing and Interest Rate Determination

*Sharpe, W.F. "Capital Asset Prices: A Theory of Market Equilibrium under Conditions of Risk", *Journal of Finance,* Vol. 19 (September 1964), pp. 425-42.

Hirschleifer, J. "Investment Decisions under Uncertainty", *Quarterly Journal of Economics,* Vol. 79 (November 1965), pp. 509-36.

Moore, Basil. *Introduction to hte Theory of Finance,* London, Collier-Macmillan Ltd, 1968.

Financial Intermediaries and the Portfolio Approach to the Demand for Money

*Hicks, J.R. "A Suggestion for Simplifying the Theory of Money", *Economica*, Vol. 2 (February 1935), pp. 1-19. Reprinted in *AEA Readings in Monetary Theory* and J.R. Hicks, *Critical Essays in Monetary Theory*, Chapter 4.

*Gurley, J. and E.S. Shaw. *Money in a Theory of Finance*, Washington, Brookings Institution, 1960, Chapters 4, 5 and 6.

*Patinkin, D. "Financial Intermediaries and the Logical Structure of Monetary Theory", *American Economic Review*, Vol. 51, (March 1961), pp. 95-116.

Marty, A.L. "Gurley and Shaw on Money in a Theory of Finance", *Journal of Political Economy*, Vol. 69 (February 1961), pp. 56-62.

*Tobin, James and W. Brainard. "Financial Intermediaries and the Effectiveness of Monetary Controls", *American Economic Review*, Vol. 53 (May 1963), pp. 383-400.

Tobin, James. "Commercial Banks as Creators of Money", *Banking and Monetary Studies*, D. Carson (ed.), Homewood, Illinois: Richard D. Irwin, 1963, pp. 408-19.

Part III

INTEGRATION OF MONETARY THEORY AND VALUE THEORY: REAL BALANCE EFFECT

Real Balance Effect: Pigou Effect, Macro Relationship between the Money and Goods Markets, Inside and Outside Assets

Johnson, Harry G. *Essays in Monetary Economics,*, London, George Allen & Unwin, 1967, Chapter 1,

*Patinkin, D. "Price Flexibility and Full Employment", *American Economic Review*, Vol. 38 (September 1948), pp. 543-64. Reprinted in *AEA Readings in Monetary Theory*, Homewood, Illinois: Richard D. Irwin, 1951, pp. 252-83.

*Pesek, B. and T. Saving. *Money, Wealth and Economic Theory*. London, Collier-Macmillan Co. Ltd, 1967, Chapters 1 and 2.

Johnson, Harry C. "Inside Money, Outside Money, Income, Wealth and Welfare in Contemporary Monetary Theory", *Journal of Money, Credit and Banking*, Vol. 1, No. 1 (February 1969), pp. 30-45.

Tobin, james. "Asset Holdings and Spending Decisions", *American Economic Review*, Vol. 42 (May 1952), pp. 109-23.

Micro-Economic Foundations of real Balance Effect

*Patinkin, D. *Money, Interest and Prices* (2nd edition), London, Harper & Rowe, 1965, Chapters 1, 2 and Appendix 2.

Lloyd, C. "Real Balance Effect, *Sine Qua* What?", *Oxford Economic Papers*, Vol. 14 (October 1962), pp. 267-74.

Lloyd, C. "The Real Balance Effect and the Slutsky Equation", *Journal of Political Economy*, Vol. 72 (June 1964), pp. 295-99.

Lloyd, C. "Two Calssical Monetary Models", *Value, Capital and Growth,* J.N. Wolfe (ed.), London, Aberdeen University Press, 1968, pp. 305-17.
Meinich, P. "Money Illusion and the Real Balance Effect", *Statskonomisk Tidsekrift,* Vol. 78 (March 1964), pp. 8-33.

Real Balance Effect and Integration of Monetary Theory and Value Theory

*Patinkin, D. *Money, Interest and Prices* (2nd edition), London, Harper & Rowe, 1965, Chapter 3 and 8.
Lloyd, C. "Real Balance Effect, *Sine Qua* What?", *Oxford Economic Papers,* Vol. 14 (October 1962), pp. 267-74.

Real Balance Effect: Long-Run Equilibrium and the Micro-Economic Foundations of Real Balance Effect

*Archibald, G.C. and R.G. Lipsey, "Monetary and Value Theory: A Critique of Lange and Patankin", *Review of Economic Studies,* Vol. 26 (October 1958), pp.1-22. Reprinted in *Monetary Theory and Policy*, R.S. Thorn (ed.), New York, Random House, 1966, pp. 297-323.
Marty, A.L. "The Real Balance Effect: An Exercise in Capital Theory", *Canadian Journal of Economics and Political Science,* Vol. 30 (August 1964), pp. 360-67.
Liviatan, N. "The Long Run Theory of Consumption and Real Balances", *Oxford Economic Papers,* Vol. 17 (July 1965), pp. 205-18.
Patinkin, D. *Money, Interest and Prices* (2nd edition), London, Harper & Rowe, 1965, Chapter 3 and Appendix 3.

Part IV

EMPIRICAL WORK IN MONETARY ECONOMICS

Empirical Studies of Demand for Money: Structural Equations

Bronfenbrenner,M. and T. Mayer. "Liquidity Functions in the American Economy", *Econometrica,* Vol. 28 (October 1960), pp. 810-34. Reprinted in *Readings in Macro-Economics,* M.G. Mueller (ed.), New York, Holt, Rinehart & Winston, 1967, pp.

*Friedman, M. "The Demand for Money: Some Theoretical and Empirical Results", *Journal of Political Economy,* Vol. 67 (August 1959), pp. 327-51. Reprinted in *Monetary Theory and Policy,* (ed.) R.S. Thorn, New York, Random House, 1966, pp. 86-117; and in *Readings in Business Cycles,* R.A. Gordon and L.R. Klein (eds.), Homewood, Illinois: Richard D. Irwin, 1965, pp. 427-55.
Harris, L. "Regularities and Irregularities in Monetary Economics", *Essays in Money and Banking,* D.R. Whittlesey and J.S.G. Wilson (eds.), Oxford, Clarendon Press, 1968, pp. 85-112.
Kavanagh, N.J. and A.A. Walters. "Demand for Money in the UK — 1877-1961: Some Preliminary Findings", *Bulletin of the Oxford University Institute of Statistics,* Vol.   (May 1966).

Khusro, A.M. "An Investigation of Liquidity Preference", *Yorkshire Bulletin of Economic and Social Research,* Vol. 4 (January 1952), pp. 1-20.

Laidler, David. *The Demand for Money,.* Scranton, Pa., International Textbook Company, 1969.

Laidler, David. "The Rate of Interest and the Demand for Money: Some Empirical Evidence", *Journal of Political Economy,* Vol. 74 (December 1966), pp. 543-55.

*Meltzer, A.H. "The Demand for Money: The Evidence from the Time Series", *Journal of Political Economy,* Vol. 71 (June 1963), pp. 219-46. Reprinted in *Monetary Theory and Policy,* R.S. Thorn (Ed.), New York, Random House, 1966, pp. 128-64.

Tobin, James. "The Monetary Interpretation of History", *American Economic Review,* Vol. 55 (June 1965), pp. 464-64.

Teigen, R.L. "Demand and Supply Functions for Money in the United States: Some Structural Estimates", *Econometrica,* Vol. 32 (October 1964), pp. 476-509.

Empirical Studies of Reduced Forms

*Friedman, M. and D. Meiselman. "The Relative Stability of Monetary Velocity and the Investment Multiplier", in Commission on Money and Credit, *Stabilization Policies,* Englewood Cliffs, Prentice Hall, 1963, pp. 165-268 [Note: especially pp. 166-80, 186-88, 213-216.]

*Ando, A. and Modigliani, F. "The Relative Stability of Monetary Velocity and the Investment Multiplier", pp. 693-728; "Rejoinder", pp. 786-90, *American Economic Review,* Vol. 55 (September 1965).

*DePrano and Mayer. "Autonomous Expenditures and Money", pp. 729-52; and "Rejoinder", pp. 791-92, *American Economic Review,* Vol. 55 (September 1965).

Friedman, M. and D. Meiselman. "Reply to Ando and Modigliani and DePrano and Mayer", *American Economic Review,* Vol. 55 (September 1965), pp. 753-85.

Tobin, James. "The Monetary Interpretation of History", *American Economic Review,* Vol. 53 (June 1965) pp. 464-85.

Ritter, L. "The Role of Money in Keynesian Theory", *Banking and Monetary Studies,* D. Carson (ed.), Homewood, Illinois: Richard D. Irwin, 1963, pp. 134-50. Reprinted in *Readings in Macro-Economics,* M.G. Mueller (ed.), New York, Holt, Rinehart & Winston, 1967, pp.

Friedman, M. and A. Schwartz. *A Monetary History of the US,* Princeton, NBER, Princeton University Press, 1963, Chapter 12.

Culbertson, J. "Friedman on the Lag in Effect of Monetary Policy", *Journal of Political Economy,* Vol. 68 (December 1960), pp. 617-21; also discussion "Reply", *Journal of Political Economy,* Vol. 69 (December 1961), pp. 467-77.

Friedman, M. and A. Schwartz. "Money and Business Cycles", pp. 32-65; and Okun, A. "Comment", *Review of Economics and Statistics,* Vol. 45, No. 1 Pt. 2 (February 1963), pp. 72-77.

Empirical Studies of Real Balance Effect and Role of Money in Inflation

*Patinkin, D. Money, Interest and Prices, (2nd edition), London, Harper & Rowe, 1965, Note M.

Cagan, P. "Monetary Dynamics of Hyper-Inflation", Studies in Quantity Theory of Money, M. Friedman (ed.), Chicago, University of Chicago Press, 1958, pp. 25-117.

Harberger, A.C. "Dynamics of Inflation in Chile", Measurement in Economics, C.F. Christ et al, Stanford, Stanford Univeristy Press, 1963, pp. 219-50

Spiro, A. "Wealth and the Consumption Function", Journal of Political Economy, Vol. 70 (August 1962), pp. 339-54.

THEORY OF INTEREST

Rate of Interest and Neutrality of Money

*Johnson, Harry G. Essays in Monetary Economics. London, George Allen & Unwin, 1967, Chapter 1, Part 1.B.

Metzler, L.A. "Wealth, Saving and the Rate of Interest", Journal of Political Economy, Vol. 59 (April 1951),, pp. 93-116. Reprinted in R.S. Thorn, Monetary Theory and Policy. New York, Random House, 1966, pp. 324-57.

*Gurley, J. and E.S. Shaw. Money in a Theory of Finance. Washington, Brookings Institution, 1960, Chapters II, III, and V.

Patinkin, D. "Keynesian Economics and the Quantity Theory", Post-Keynesian Economcs, (ed.) K.K. Kurihara, London, George Allen & Unwin, 1955, pp. 123-52.

Patinkin, D. Money, Interest and Prices. (2nd edition). London, Harper & Rowe, 1965, Part 2.

Theory of Term Structure of Interest Rates

*Conard, J. Introduction to the Theory of Interest. Berkley, University of California Press, 1959.

Meiselman, D. "Expectations, Errors, and the Term Structure of Interest Rates", Journal of Political Economy, Vol 71 (April 1963), pp. 160-71. Reprinted in R.S. Thorn, Monetary Theory and Policy. New York, Random House, 1966, pp. 482-99.

Grant, J.A.G. "Meiselman on the Structure of Interest Rates: A British Test", Economica, Vol. 31 (February 1964), pp. 51-71.

Malkiel, B. "Expectations, Bond Prices, and the Term Structure of Interest Rates", *Quarterly Journal of Economics,* Vol. 76 (May 1962), pp. 197-218.
*Telser, L.G. "A Critique of some Recent Empirical Research on the Explanation of the Term Structure of Interest Rates", *Journal of Political Economy,* Vol. 75, No. 4, Pt. II (August 1967), pp. 546-60.

Part V

SOME MAJOR POLICY ISSUES

The Supply of Money

Meade, J.E. "The Amount of Money and the Banking System", *AEA Readings in Monetary Theory.* Homewood, Illinois: Richard D. Irwin, 19 1, pp. 54-62.
*Sayers, R.S. *Modern Banking* (3rd edition). Oxford, Clarendon Press, 1951, Chapter 10.
Crouch, R.L. "The Inadequacy of 'New-Orthodox' Methods of Monetary Control", *Economic Journal,* Vol. 74 (December 1964), pp. 916-34
Crouch, R.L. "The Genesis of Bank Deposits: New English Version", *Bulletin of the Oxford University Institute of Statistics,* Vol. 27 (August 1965), pp. 185-99.
*Coppock, D. and N. Gibson. "The Volume of Deposits and the Cash and Liquid Assets Ratios", *The Manchester School,* Vol. 31 (September 1963), pp. 203-22.
Friedman, M. and A.J. Schwartz. *A Monetary History of the United States: 1969-1960.* Princeton, NBER, Princeton Univeristy Press, 1963, Appendix B, "Proximate Determinants of the Nominal Stock of Money", pp. 776-808.
Teigen, R.L. "Demand and Supply Functions for Money in the United States: Some Structural Estimates", *Econometrica,* Vol. 32 (October 1964), pp. 476-509.
*Cagan, P. *Determinants and Effects of Changes in the Stock of Money,* 1875-1960, New York, Columbia University Press, 1965.
Meigs, A.J. *Free Reserves and the Money Supply.* Chicago, University of Chicago, Studies in Economics, 1962.

Theory of Monetary Policy

Tobin, James. "An Essay on the Principles of Public Debt Management", in Commission of Money and Credit, *Fiscal and Debt Management Policies,* London, Prentice-Hall International, 1963.
*Tobin, James. "Money, Capital nd Other Stores of Value", *American Economic Review,* Vol. 51 (May 1961), pp. 26-37.
Cagan, P. "Why Do We Use Money in Open Market Operations?", *Journal of Political Economy,* Vol. 66 (February 1958), pp. 34-46.
*Rowan, D.C. "Radcliffe Monetary Theory", *Economic Record,* Vol. 37 (December 1961), pp. 420-41.
*Brunner, K. and A. Meltzer. "Some Further Investigations of Demand and Supply Functions for Money", *Journal of Finance,* Vol 19 (May 1964), pp. 240-83.

Monetarism versus Fiscalism

*Friedman, M. "The Role of Monetary Policy", *American Economic Review*, Vol. 58, (March 1968), pp. 1-17.

Anderson, L. and Jordan, G. "Monetary and Fiscal Actions: A Test of their Relative Importance in Economic Stabilization", *Federal Reserve Bank of St. Louis Review*, Vol.   (November 1968), pp.

Anderson, L. and K.M. Carlson. "A Monetarist Model for Economic Stabilization", *Federal Reserve Bank of St. Louis Review*, (April 1970).

Tobin, James. "Money and Income: Post Hoc Ergo Propter Hoc?", and "Rejoinder", Friedman, M. "Comment on Tobin", *The Quarterly Journal of Economics*, Vol. 84, No. 2 (May 1970), pp. 301-17; pp. 328-29; and pp. 318-27.

*Friedman, M. "A Theoretical Framework for Monetary Analysis", *Journal of Political Economy*, Vol. 78, No. 2 (March-April 1970), pp. 193-238. [NOTE: A symposium on this will be appearing later in the JPE.]

*Johnson, Harry G. "The Keynesian Revolution and the Monetarist Counter-Revolution", *American Economic Review*, Papers and Proceedings, Vol 61 (May 1971), pp. 1-14.

Kaldor, N. "The New Monetarism", *Lloyds Bank Review*, No. 97 (July 1970), pp. 1-18;

Friedman, M. "The New Monetarism: Comment", ibid., No. 98 (October 1970), pp. 52-3;

Kaldor, N. "The New Monetarism' Reply", ibid., No. 98 (October 1970), pp. 54-55.

Inflation Theory

Lipsey, R.G. "Appendix — Cost Push vs. Demand Pull: A Case Study", *An Introduction to Positive Economics*, London, Weidenfeld & Nicolson, 1963, pp. 431-43.

*Bronfenbrenner, M. and F.D. Holtzman. "A Survey of Inflation Theory", *American Economic Review*, Vol. 53 (September 1963), pp. 593-661.

Ball, R.J. *Inflation and the Theory of Money*. Chicago, Aldine Publishing Co., 1964.

Cagan, P. "The Monetary Dynamics of Hyper-Inflation", in M. Friedman (ed.), *Studies in the Quantity Theory of Money*. Chicago, University of Chicago Press, 1958, pp. 25-117.

*Bailey, M.J. "The Welfare Cost of Inflationary Finance", *Journal of Political Economy*, Vol. 64 (April 1956), pp. 93-110.

Mundell, R.A. "Inflation and the Real Rate of Interest", *Journal of Political Economy*, Vol. 71 (June 1963), pp. 280-83.

Phelps, E.S. "Anticipated Inflation and Economic Welfare", *Journal of Political Economy*, Vol. 73 (February 1965), pp. 1-17.

Kessel, R.A. and A.A. Alchian. "Effects of Inflation", *Journal of Political Economy*, Vol. 70 (December 1962), pp. 521-37.

Tullock, J. "Effects of Stabilization", *Journal of Political Economy*, Vol. 71 (August 1963), pp. 413-15.

Harberger, A.C. "The Dynamics of Inflation in Chile", in C.F. Christ, *et al Measurement in Economics*. Stanford, Stanford University Press, 1963, pp.

219-50.

Johnson, Harry G. "A Survey of Theories of Inflation", *Essays in Monetary Econiomics*, London, George Allen & Unwin, 1967, Chapter 3, pp. 104-142.

Friedman, M. "Government Revenue from Inflation", *Journal of Political Economy*, Vol. 79 (July-August 1971), pp. 846-56.

Money and Economic Growth

Tobin, James. "A Dynamic Aggregative Model", *Journal of Political Economy* , Vol. 63 (April 1955), pp. 103-15.

Enthoven, A. "Appendix", in J.G. Gurley nd E.S. Shaw, *Money in a Theory of Finance*, Washington, D.C., Brookings Institution, 1960, pp. 303-59.

*Tobin, James. "Money and Economic Growth", *Econometrica*, Vol. 33 (October 1965), pp. 671-84.

Harrod, R.F. *Towards a Dynamic Economics*. London, Macmillan, 1948, Lecture 3, pp. 63-100.

*Hahn, F. and R.C.O. Matthews. "The Theory of Economic Growth: a Survey", *Economic Journal*, Vol. 74 (December 1964), pp. 779-902. Reprinted in *AEA & RES Surveys of Economic Theory*, Vol. II, New York, Macmillan, 1965, pp. 1-124.

Mundell, R.A. "Growth, Stability and Inflationary Finance", *Journal of Political Economy*, Vol. 73 (April 1965), pp. 97-109.

Friedman, M. and A.J. Schwartz. "Money and Business Cycles", *Review of Economics and Statistics*, Vol. 45, No. 1, Pt. 2 (February 1963), pp. 32-65.

*Johnson, Harry G. "Money in a Neo-Classical One-Sector Growth Model", *Essays in Monetary Economics*, London, George Allen & Unwin, 1967, Chapter IV, pp. 143-78.

Sidrauski, M. "Rational Choice and Patterns of Growth in a Monetary Economy", *American Economic Review*, Proceedings and Papers, Vol. 57 (May 1967), pp. 534-44.

Tobin, James. "Notes on Optimal Monetary Growth", and Marty, A.L. "The Optimal Rate of Growth of Money", *Journal of Political Economy*, Vol. 76 (July-August 1968), pp. 833-59 and 860-73.

Patinkin, D. and D. Levhari. "The Role of Money in a Simple Growth Model", *American Economic Review*, Vol. 58 (September 1968), pp. 713-53.

Friedman, M. *The Optimum Quantity of Money*. Chicago, Aldine, 1969.

Johnson, Harry G. "Is there an Optimal Money Supply?", *Journal of Finance*, Vol. XXV, No. 2 (May 1970), pp. 435-42. See also companion paper by R.W. Clower.

Stein, J.L. "Monetary Growth Theory in Perspective", *American Economic Review*, Vol. 60 (March 1970), pp. 85-106.

The Monetary Standard and International Monetary Arrangements

Friedman, M. "Commodity Reserve Currency", pp. 204-50; and "The Case for Flexible Exchange Rates", *Essays in Positive Economics*, Chicago, University of Chicago Press, 1935, pp. 157-203.

Johnson, Harry G. *International Trade and Economic Growth*, London, George Allen & Unwin, 1958, Chapters 6 and 7.

Sohmen, E. *Flexible Exchange Rates,* Chicago, University of Chicago Press, 1968, (2nd edition).
Johnson, Harry G. "Equilibrium under Fixed Exchanges", pp. 112-19;
Caves, R.E. "Flexible Exchange Rates", pp. 120-29;
Kenen, P.B. "International Liquidity: The Next Steps", pp. 130-38;
Fleming, J.M., H.C. Eastman, and J.H. Furth. "Discussion", pp. 139-46; *American Economic Review,* Papers and Proceedings, Vol. 53 (May 1963).
Mundell, R.A. "The Monetary Dynamics of International Adjustment Under Fixed and Flexible Exchange Rages", *Quarterly Journal of Economics,* Vol. 74 (May 1960), pp. 227-57.
Mundell, R.A. "Capital Mobility and Stabilization Policy under Fixed and Flexible Exchange Rates", *Canadian Journal of Economics and Political Science,* Vol. 29 (November 1963), pp. 475-85.
Mundell, R.A. "A Theory of Optimum Currency Areas", *American Economic Review,* Vol. 51 (September 1961), pp. 657-65.

Machlup, F. and Malkiel. *International Monetary Arrangements: The Problem of Choice,* Princeton, International Finance Section, 1964.
Prais, S.J. "Some Mathematical Notes on the Quantity Theory of Money in an Open Economy", *IMF Staff Papers,* Vol. 8 (May 1961), pp. 212-26.
"Money Supply and Domestic Credit", *Economic Trends,* No. 187 (May 1969), pp. xxi-xxv.
Johnson, Harry G. "The Case for Flexible Exchange Rates, 1969", in H.G. Johnson and J.E. Nash, *UK and Floating Exchange Rates,* London, Institute of Economic Affairs, Hobart Paper No. 46, May 1969, pp. 9-37; *Federal Reserve Bank of St. Louis Bulletin,* Vol. 51 No. 6 (June 1969), pp. 12-24; Reprinted in George N. Halm (ed.), *Approaches to Greater Flexibility of Exchange Rates: The Burgenstock Papers,* Princeton, Princeton University Press, 1970, Chapter 8, pp. 91-111.

REVIEW PROBLEMS

1. The following propositions are either true, false or uncertain. The problem is to determine which, and to provide reasons for your answers.

(i) A tax increase cannot reduce inflationary pressures unless there is a "liquidity trap" in the demand for money.

(ii) If the demand for goods were a function of real income only, and the demand for money were a function of interest rates only, then the demand for bonds must be a function of both real income and interest rates.

(iii) The higher the rate of interest, the lower will be the Keynesian multiplier.

(iv) The "permanent income" hypothesis is refuted by the fact that big winners on the pools frequently use part of the money to buy themselves a better house.

(v) The "permanent income" hypothesis is refuted by the fact that people who have played the pools for years and eventually win a large sum frequently treat themselves to an expensive vacation.

(vi) If the capital stock is growing, the marginal efficiency of investment must be greater than the marginal product of capital.

(vii) If a country has a balance-of-payments deficit, the proper policy is to cut its overseas military expenditures.

(viii) The life-cycle savings hypothesis is in contradiction with the Marxist hypothesis that capitalists save and workers don't.

(ix) Controls on imports are a better method of coping with a balance-of-payments deficit than devaluation, because they avoid the inflationary effect of a rise in domestic prices of imported goods;

(x) Keynes' "marginal efficiency of capital schedule" enables one to determine how much investment would be undertaken at a given rate of interest. (Note: this one raises two separate theoretical points.)

2. Develop a theory of economic policy for an open economy. In the light of your theory, examine the contentions that a country with full employment and a balance of payments deficit should:

(i) devalue its currency;
(ii) reduce overseas government expenditure by the amount of
(iii) the deficit;
(iv) impose restrictions on imports of "luxury" goods;
(v) subsidise investment in order to increase productivity.

3. Analyse the conditions under which (i) fiscal policy alone, (ii) monetary policy alone, will be effective in remedying mass unemployment. What differences would be made to your answer by the assumptions (i) that some money is "outside" money, (ii) that people capitalize their tax liabilities into the value of their wealth.

4. 'In *The General Theory* Keynes postulates a supply function for labour, a demand funcion for money and a consumption function, none of which is derived from the principles of neoclassical micro theory'. Explain this statement and discuss whether the conclusions of the model would be altered if these functions were replaced by functions which were derived from those principles.

5. Compare and contrast the "permanent income" and "life-cycle saving" hypotheses about the consumption function. In what sense if any can either be said to involve a capital-stock-adjustment theory similar to that commonly employed in the theory of investment. Can you suggest an application of capital theory to the explanation of the downward rigidity of money wages that is the basic assumption of the Keynesian theory of employment?

6. "The crucial problem in introducing money into growth models is to provide a motivation for the holding of money". Discuss this proposition and develop its implications for theory. Compare the "utility" and "transactions" approaches to the demand for money in this connection.

7. Discuss the view that the modern theories of the demand for money and the supply of money are based on the same principles as the theory of investment. Is it possible to test empirically the validity of such an approach?

8. What are the social gains attributable to the invention of money, as contrasted with dependence on barter?

9. Consider two general equilibrium systems, one in which money is entirely "outside" money printed by the government and one in which money is entirely "inside" money created by the purchase of private "bonds". Contrast these systems with respect to the following matters:

    a.   the validity of the "classical dichotomy";
    b.   the nature and function of the "real balance effect";
    c.   the application of the concept of "the inflation tax";
    d.   the influence of the long-run rate of increase of the money supply on the characteristics of the equilibrium growth path.

10. "The supply of bank deposits and the demand for the liabilities of non-bank financial intermediaries are determined by the same principles of portfolio management as apply to the demand for money". Consider the validity of this view and discuss its implications for the effectiveness of monetary policy.

11. Explain the theory of the Phillips curve. In what sense, if any, do (or can) empirical measurements of the Phillips curve provide relevant evidence in the

controversy between the Keynesian and Quantity theory approaches to inflation.

12. Discuss the contention that inflation is an efficient instrument for promoting economic growth. Include in your answer a description of other policies that a government using inflation as a growth policy should avoid.

LECTURES IN ECONOMICS 2

INTRODUCTORY ECONOMETRICS

Kenneth F. Wallis
London School of Economics

Dr. Wallis's lectures on introductory econometrics have been given to students of the M.Sc. (Economics) course at the London School of Economics for several years. The course begins with a discussion of economic models and the presentation of economic theories in a form suitable for estimation and testing, an orientation that distinguishes his approach from the majority of econometric textbooks which concentrate on estimation from the outset.

A simple national income determination system is used as an example, initially in static form, but subsequently extended to illustrate a discussion of dynamic behaviour. The identification problem is presented in terms of familiar demand and supply models, and several estimation methods are described in the last (and longest) chapter.

Each chapter is supplemented by carefully selected exercises, and review problems are provided at the end of the book. Outline solutions are given for half of the exercises and problems. Students and teachers will especially appreciate Dr. Wallis's clear, systematic exposition, his attention to detail and his talent for compressing the essentials of his subject into a readable and comparatively short text.